I've DIBEL'd, *Now What?*

Next Edition

Designing Targeted Interventions
With **DIBELS** *Next* Data

Susan L. Hall

Cambium
LEARNING® | Sopris
Group

Printed in the United States of America

Published and Distributed by

4093 Specialty Place • Longmont, Colorado 80504
(303) 651-2829 • www.soprislearning.com

CREDITS:
Cover, title page: boy. © Getty Images. girl, Zoe Houseman. © Adam & Imthiaz Photography.

v: © iStockphoto.com/Christopher Futcher. 1: © Getty Images. 5: © Getty Images. 19: © iStockphoto.com. 45: © Getty Images. 79: © Getty Images. 113: © Getty Images. 139: © Getty Images. 167: © Getty Images. 177: © Getty Images. 193: © Getty Images. 195: © Getty Images. 207: © Getty Images. 208: cat. © iStockphoto.com/Erik Isselée. 211: cat. © iStockphoto.com/Erik Isselée. dog. © iStockphoto.com/bubaone. 212: bee. © 123rf.com/Melinda Fawver. bird. © iStockphoto.com/Andrew Howe. 213: cat. © iStockphoto.com/ Erik Isselée. 214: car. © iStockphoto.com/pagadesign. 217: bee. © 123rf.com/Melinda Fawver. 223: © iStockphoto.com/Nancy Louie. 241: © iStockphoto.com/Carmen Martinez Banús. 244: bee. © 123rf.com/Melinda Fawver. 249: © iStockphoto.com/Parker Deen. 262: people. iStockphoto.com. 263: iStockphoto.com/Christopher Futcher. 277: iStockphoto.com/Viorika Prikhodko. 279: iStockphoto.com/Viorika Prikhodko.

Dedication

To my husband, David, who is a constant support in my life's work. He makes it possible for me to follow my passion that 95% or more of students will read at grade level.

To all the teachers I've worked with across the country who have taught me so much.

Acknowledgments

Thanks to Stephanie Stollar from Dynamic Measurement Group for reviewing Chapters 1–3 and Jenny McGuire for reviewing some chapters.

Many educators have contributed to this book. The following educators are quoted within this book:

- Donna Bush, Louisiana
- Mary Kay Murphy, Michigan
- Karen Sabados, Illinois
- Carolyn Shipley, Pennsylvania
- Carol Massey, Arkansas

About the Author

Susan Hall, Ed.D., is a reading consultant specializing in teacher training in early reading. Dr. Hall is president and founder of 95 Percent Group Inc., an educational consulting and professional development company. The company provides consulting and teacher training to districts and schools in how to use early literacy assessment data to inform data-driven small-group tiers of intervention to address specific skill deficits. Susan is a *DIBELS Next®* mentor and a national trainer for *LETRS®* (*Language Essentials for Teachers of Reading and Spelling*). Susan is author of two other books: *Jumpstart Response to Intervention: Using RTI in Your Elementary School Right Now* and *Implementing Response to Intervention: A Principal's Guide*. She is coauthor with Dr. Louisa Moats of three books, *Straight Talk About Reading, Parenting a Struggling Reader*, and *Language Essentials for Teachers of Reading and Spelling* (*LETRS*): *Module 7, Second Edition*. Susan can be reached at shall@95percentgroup.com or through her Web site www.95percentgroup.com.

Contents

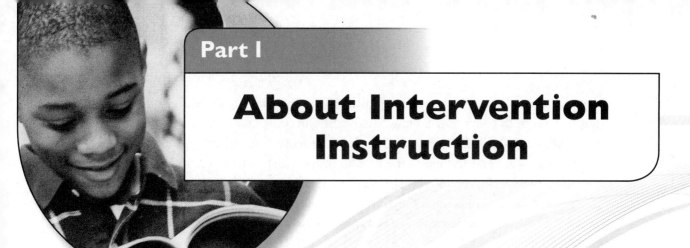

Part I

About Intervention Instruction

This is an exciting time to be involved in the field of early reading. We know more than ever about how students learn to read, and what happens when reading doesn't come easily. We also know about effective procedures to determine which students are at risk of experiencing reading difficulties and how to intervene early to help avert later trouble. Early literacy assessment instruments have played a significant role in preventing problems because they enable schools to screen all students for signs of delay as part of a preventive approach. By providing good core reading instruction, along with differentiated intervention instruction to small groups of struggling readers, we can help many students avoid the major problems they would have faced if the reading difficulty had been dealt with much later.

Prevention of reading problems is based on several important premises about early reading. First, all but a few students can be taught to read proficiently. Second, prevention of reading difficulties in kindergarten through third grade is far more cost effective and efficient than remediation in later grades. Third, relying on research findings about assessment tools and the components of effective instruction can prevent reading failure. There is no question that reading research has brought to light important insights about the process of learning to read.

Yet in order to put research into practice, a school will need to implement three things:

1. A systematic process for periodically screening all students in kindergarten through third grade to determine which students are not meeting critical milestones in early literacy.

2. Procedures to provide data-informed, differentiated intervention instruction in small groups when a student's scores on the screening assessment indicate that he[1] is at risk for later reading difficulty or already experiencing difficulty.

3. Continued monitoring to ensure that the struggling student is making progress and that he stays on track once benchmark has been reached.

---

1 Author's note: Throughout the book, the pronouns *he* and *she* (*his* and *her*) are used when referring to a teacher or student to avoid the awkward language of *he or she* (*his or her*) each time a student is mentioned.

Increasing numbers of schools have initiated the first part by screening all students, but the use of the data may be less consistent. Success is more than simply having the tool or even administering it. Too often the scores are sitting on the shelf. Merely assessing and not using the data to inform instruction is a waste of time. Teachers need to know how to use the data, including making decisions about how to diagnose deficit skills once they have been flagged by an early literacy screener and determining what instruction is appropriate to address the students' deficits.

The research findings about the effectiveness of early identification and intervention to prevent reading difficulties are extensive. The challenge continues to be in the area of how to achieve sustained implementation of this research into practice. The purpose of this book is to help teachers learn how to interpret and use data from one early literacy screening instrument called the *Dynamic Indicators of Basic Early Literacy Skills Next* (*DIBELS Next*®). Although many of the procedures included in this book may apply to other screening instruments, explaining how to make that translation is beyond the focus of this book.

The title of this book reflects the topic. This book is for teachers who are wondering what to do after they have completed administering and scoring the *DIBELS Next* assessment. There are three main topics covered in this book. First, a detailed, step-by-step process for analyzing a single student scoring booklet to look for error patterns is provided. Second, a process is included for how to identify which students need further diagnostic assessment after *DIBELS Next* in order to pinpoint mastered and missing skills. Third, a description of how to plan the type of instruction that each group needs is discussed.

One of the unique features in this book, a step-by-step approach to analyzing an individual *DIBELS Next* student scoring booklet, is included because of the author's belief that the data available to inform instruction far surpasses the score alone. By analyzing the error patterns and reviewing the scoring page on each indicator, it's possible to gain clues about whether the student has specific gaps in his knowledge or if his deficits are minimal or pervasive. On each measure, it's possible to see whether fluency or accuracy is the issue, or both. There are many other specific observations for each measure. For example, on Phoneme Segmentation Fluency (PSF), it's possible to observe whether the student understands the concept of segmentation and whether he is partially or completely segmenting the sounds in words. What percentage of the time did the student earn 2 points for isolating solely the first sound versus a cluster of sounds in First Sound Fluency (FSF)? On the *DIBELS* Oral Reading Fluency (DORF), did the student accurately read phonetically regular words, multisyllable words, and nonphonetic sight words?

It's critical that groups are not formed simply from randomly assigning students with others who are recommended for the same level of strategic or intensive intervention. There are better ways to group students than placing those in the intensive category together and those in the strategic category together. While it may work in some cases, this approach ignores some of the information available. Better placements are possible by analyzing the data for each indicator in a more systematic way in order to determine where there is adequate information for grouping and when diagnostic screener data will be needed as a second step after *DIBELS Next*.

After using the *DIBELS®* data along with other information to place a student in a group with others whose deficits are similar, the last step is to select the appropriate programs or strategies for instruction. There are more than 200 published intervention programs available today. Many of these programs are excellent, and schools often select several different ones so that they have a portfolio of materials for use in small intervention groups. My recommendation to schools is that some groups should be placed in programs and other groups would best be served by lesson plans that enable teaching specific missing skills rather than teaching an entire program from beginning to end. Part II of this book contains sample activities and strategies that teachers can use for practice after explicit instruction.

Regardless of whether teachers design intervention lessons or use purchased programs, professional development is the key to success. Even when teachers are using program materials, instruction must be differentiated in response to the errors each student makes. Intervention instruction should be focused and provide immediate feedback and error correction, along with opportunities for appropriate and extensive practice. A key piece of implementing intervention instruction is learning how to use progress monitoring data to guide decisions about increasing the intensity of instruction as necessary to ensure that the student will achieve benchmark.

A reasonable goal is that 95% of all students will reach *DIBELS* benchmarks with the instruction they receive in the core program during the language arts block plus small-group intervention instruction as needed. To achieve these results, schools need to implement systematic procedures to screen at least all elementary students and intervene intensively with instruction that is data informed. This goal is achievable when teachers receive sustained professional development and coaching to learn to interpret *DIBELS Next* data to inform decisions about which students need intervention instruction. We must set our goals high and be relentless in our determination that all students *will* read.

Susan Hall, Ed.D.

Chapter 1

The Importance of Prevention

These resources facilitate a continuous cycle of assessment and instruction. This combination provides a much-needed road map for teachers to use to intervene and support students before concerns become major roadblocks to literacy.

Curriculum Specialist, Regional Education Association

Continuing a Model to Avert Reading Difficulties

One of the most important changes in education during the past two decades is the realization that early identification and intervention can prevent reading problems for many students. Compared to even five years ago, now it's rarely necessary to make the case for early intervention; there is widespread acceptance of its benefits. Teachers don't need to be convinced that early intervention works, but instead what they need is more information, coaching, and time to make it happen. Widely available screening instruments make early intervention possible because they help identify those students in kindergarten through second grade who are at risk for, or are already beginning to experience, reading difficulties. Schools can provide intervention instruction immediately after a student is identified as at risk, sometimes before a student has even begun formal reading instruction. With early intervention, many students will avoid the major problems they would have faced if the reading difficulty had been dealt with much later. That is why the early identification and intervention approach is called the "Preventive Model," as opposed to the model that schools are increasingly abandoning, which is sometimes referred to as the "Wait-to-Fail Model."

The Preventive Model (American Federation of Teachers 2004) is based on three important premises about early reading. First, all but a very few students can be taught to read proficiently. Second, prevention of reading difficulties in kindergarten through third grade is far more cost effective and efficient than remediation in later grades. Third, relying on research findings about assessment tools and the components of effective instruction can prevent reading failure. These premises convey high expectations for all students in reading and a sense of urgency for them to have a strong start in early reading.

In contrast to the Preventive Model, the Wait-to-Fail Model refers to a lack of institutional processes designed to look for, and respond to, early signs of delay in reading progress. The Wait-to-Fail Model is based on the premise that students who experience reading difficulties in the early grades are experiencing developmental delays and will catch up. Schools using this model generally keep struggling readers in regular reading instruction without providing special help, and they do not test for reading deficiencies until students are in third or fourth grade or later. The Wait-to-Fail Model is a thing of the past in most schools. Let's think about why it's outdated. There are many research findings that influenced us to use prevention. Some of the most important findings show that students who start out behind in reading almost always stay behind.

- The probability of remaining a poor reader at the end of fourth grade, given a student was a poor reader at the end of first grade was .88 (Juel 1988).

- Seventy-four percent of students who are poor readers in third grade remain poor readers in ninth grade (Francis et al. 1996).

The Wait-to-Fail Model has failed too many students, and that's why schools aren't using it any longer.

Prevention Within a Response to Intervention Framework

Before 2005, reading identification and intervention was sometimes called "early reading intervention"; since then, it's generally embedded within the Response to Intervention (RTI) framework. Prevention of reading difficulties requires the school to have three essential practices in place:

- A systematic process for periodically screening all students in kindergarten through third grade to determine which students are not meeting critical milestones in early literacy skills.

- Procedures to provide data-informed, differentiated intervention instruction in small groups when a student's scores on the assessment indicate that he is at risk for later reading difficulty or already experiencing difficulty.

- Continued monitoring to ensure that the struggling student is making progress, and that she stays on track once benchmark has been reached.

The role of assessment instruments cannot be overestimated in implementing early intervention practices. One key reason that prevention is even possible is because of the development of efficient and brief screening measures over the past 15 years. Without these effective assessments, this approach might not be possible. Implementation of RTI in mathematics has been slower to emerge, partially because there's been a delay in having the same kind of assessments as those available for reading. The assessments most critical to success are called curriculum-based measures (CBMs), and they have several important characteristics:

- They assess indicators of reading rather than all skills and use performance on critical and predictive indicators to represent overall reading ability.

- They track changes in performance repeatedly with alternate forms.

- They are sensitive to small changes in performance, thereby enabling measurement of improvement over time.

Examples of CBMs include *DIBELS®* and *AIMSweb®*. There are many other types of assessment that provide other information and are useful to teachers, but they are not CBMs. For example, there are several very popular assessments that provide teachers with information about the levels of text that are most appropriate for instruction. While necessary to identify a level in order to select appropriate books for students, these assessments do not serve the same purpose as CBMs that are used as universal screeners within the RTI framework.

Screening all elementary students in at least kindergarten through third grade multiple times each year with a research-based early literacy screening instrument makes it possible to determine which students are not meeting critical milestones in early literacy skills. Some of these milestones must be met before most students begin formal reading instruction. Skills assessed include letter naming, letter-sound relationships, and phoneme identification. Screening for students in late first grade through third grade includes observing students read grade-level passages and indicate their comprehension of the material just read. The best screening instruments are very accurate at predicting which students are at risk for later difficulty based on missing critical milestones in earlier developing literacy skills. Prevention of reading difficulties is possible only because the screening assessments are brief; screening all students is impossible if this could not be done in less than 10 minutes per student.

Routine screening of all students two or three times a year for essential early reading skills ensures that no student compensates for a weak skill by using a strong one. An example of this would be the student who memorizes many words in kindergarten and first and second grades, but who cannot sound out longer words introduced in third grade. Without early screening, this student would not be "discovered" to have a reading difficulty until third grade, when the words in reading material are more numerous and longer, preventing the student from being able to rely on memorization skills.

Accurate identification of at-risk students is merely the first step in preventing reading difficulties. Screening is meaningless without targeted intervention that changes reading outcomes for students. Therefore, schools need an organized approach to providing all students who miss milestones with effective and immediate intervention instruction. Early intervention within an RTI model assures that each student who lacks any critical reading skill is immediately placed in a small group and given instruction targeted toward developing the weak or missing skill. Intervention instruction is most effective when delivered in small groups of three to five students who are working together because of the similarity of their instructional needs. The teacher or aide working with the small group targets specific skills, provides extensive opportunities for practice, and gives immediate corrective feedback to the students.

Using an assessment tool designed for repeated administrations is essential in an RTI framework. Progress monitoring data show within weeks of placement in an intervention group whether the student is making enough progress to be on the trajectory toward achieving benchmark in a particular skill by the end of the year. This means that intervention groups need to be flexible. A student moves out of one group as soon as he reaches benchmark. Conversely, a student whose skills are not improving fast enough can be moved to another group or the intensity of intervention can be increased immediately, with continued monitoring to ensure that the student will reach grade-level benchmarks. If the student's rate of progress isn't adequate for her to reach benchmark on time, changes can be made immediately, within a few weeks of initiating intervention. Teachers need to be relentless in their determination to help the student catch up, and data play a critical role in helping with this effort.

What's Different in Early Reading Intervention in 2011 Versus 2005?

Compared to 2005, there are dramatic changes regarding prevention through early intervention in 2011. Now, nearly all schools give early literacy assessments. On June 24, 2011, the University of Oregon's Web site reported that *DIBELS*, 6th Edition, has been used by more than 22,000 schools and 11 million students (e-mail from support@dibels.uoregon.edu). How extensively are the data used? Many schools are doing an excellent job of this; however, other schools are not using the data enough or are analyzing the data at merely a surface level. One red flag signaling that the data are not used at a deep enough level is when there is an overreliance on the three colors: green, yellow, and red. There is so much more to analyzing the data than it's possible to see when looking solely at the Composite Scores in *DIBELS Next®*, or the three instructional recommendation levels (as labeled in 6th Edition). Another issue is that many administrators are using the data reports at a surface level because they haven't been provided training in interpreting the data.

Since 2005, there has been a noticeable increase in teachers' knowledge about reading. Several reasons for this are:

- the professional development provided to teachers in schools that received Reading First training;

- an increase in learning from peers on the job through Professional Learning Communities (PLCs), reading coaches, and team collaboration meetings; and

- professional development models that have moved away from the "drive-by," one-time workshops to those based on more sustained approaches to learning over time with experiences, reflection, etc.

Other traits can be observed in schools. Within many districts, it's possible to identify schools where early literacy interventions have worked. These models of success, sometimes called "demonstration sites," are used as places where teams from other buildings can observe effective practices. Additionally, attention to language development and its interwoven relationship to reading has increased. And there is increased sensitivity to the needs of the English language learners in our schools.

During the past six years, many schools have transitioned from one-on-one programs in which a teacher or reading specialist served only 16 to 20 first-grade students across the year to establishing programs that provide early intervention to small groups, beginning with kindergarten students. Each interventionist can work daily with about 30–45 students, assuming that she sees nine small groups of three to five students each for 30-minute time blocks. Additionally, more students are served when they are moved in and out of groups across the year. Other schools are restructuring their Title I programs around the Prevention Model or supporting classroom teachers in establishing small-group intervention instruction within the day.

Since the first edition of this book, much has changed in the area of qualification for special education. Because of the *Individuals with Disabilities Education Act of 2004* (IDEA), states are encouraging districts to implement RTI and to use data from a student's time in a Tier 2 or Tier 3 intervention group as a part of the dialogue in determining whether a student qualifies to receive special education services. Response to Intervention is a dynamic problem-solving process in which data is integral in making decisions about what skills struggling readers lack and whether intervention instruction provided to date has been effective (Hall 2008). (See the Appendix, page 277, for a list of resources on RTI.) These new procedures avoid the time it takes for a student to show a large discrepancy between potential and achievement. In most states, the discrepancy used to be measured by the difference between a student's score on an IQ test, which represents a measure of potential, and a standardized achievement test. Because students are generally not taught to read passages until first grade, failure to read is not visible until second or third grade. Even if a problem surfaces early, the procedures for testing and evaluation for special education often take months to establish qualification and for educators to decide on remediation services before help is provided.

> *When the Preventive Model is well implemented, referrals for special education evaluations decline.*

The Preventive Model avoids relying on special education services and expensive and time-consuming diagnostic testing for many students. Help is not tied to a legal qualification process, as with special education. Prevention and special education are, in fact, inversely related. When the Preventive Model is well implemented, referrals for special education evaluations decline. No special education label is necessary before students are eligible to receive early intensive intervention instruction. Formal, standardized diagnostic testing and referrals for special education are given only to those few students who show persistent weaknesses in skills after receiving small-group intervention instruction.

The Preventive Model is also distinct from special education in that it is primarily a general education initiative administered and controlled by the classroom teacher. The classroom teacher, not a psychologist, generally administers or participates in the screening of students. School psychologists may participate on assessment teams with classroom teachers, reading specialists, specially trained aides, speech and language pathologists, and others, but the assessments used for screening do not require a psychologist's training to administer. After assessment occurs, the classroom teacher, not a special education teacher, is intimately involved in providing the intervention or supervising others who provide this special instruction. Additionally, intervention instruction does not replace the core classroom instruction in reading as it often does for students on an Individualized Education Plan (IEP), but rather it is in addition to the core program.

In the Preventive Model, students targeted for early intervention are served outside of the special education venue. Teachers and aides generally provide intervention instruction in groups of three to five students in a classroom or similar setting rather than in a resource room setting. Intervention groups are formed to combine students with similar needs so instruction can be targeted to address particular early reading skills. Students move in and out of flexible intervention groups on a fluid basis without any need for staffing meetings, IEP meetings, or parental permission. Students are referred for special education testing only when their skills don't respond well to the increasingly intensive instruction they have received in Tier 2 and Tier 3 groups, there is evidence of a possible learning disability, and they will benefit from instruction delivered with the resources provided through special education services.

Research Basis for Prevention

Over the past two decades, scientific research has led to major revelations about how expert readers read, how students learn to read, and what goes wrong when students fail to read easily. One of the most significant findings is how important early intervention is to averting later problems for students at risk of reading difficulties (Torgesen 2004). It is considerably more efficient and effective to deliver intervention earlier rather than later in the elementary school years. According to the National Institute of Student Health and Human Development (NICHD) branch of the National Institutes of Health (NIH), it takes four times as long to remediate a student with poor reading skills in fourth grade as in late kindergarten or early first grade (Lyon and Fletcher 2001). That means that the earlier we can provide reading help to a student, the less time that student will need to catch up.

Researchers also have informed the educational community of the importance of assuring that students get off to the right start in reading. What has been learned repeatedly in multiple studies is that students who get a slow start in learning to read aren't simply experiencing a developmental lag but lack critical early reading skills that they will not learn without targeted intervention instruction. If students don't learn these critical early reading skills, they may never catch up. As mentioned above, the longer we wait to provide intervention, the more time the intervention takes to be successful. This finding, replicated numerous times, helps teachers confirm that it is critical not to allow a student to get behind in reading.

Schools need practices that ensure students get off to a strong start and stay on track. In an article titled "Early Warning System," reading research experts Dr. G. Reid Lyon and Dr. Jack Fletcher (2001) advocated for schools to adopt early identification and intervention systems. They questioned why so many more students today are being identified with learning disabilities (LD), particularly older students, and why the gap isn't closed by special education instruction.

"Early intervention can greatly reduce the number of older students who are identified as LD. Without early identification, students typically require intensive, long-term special-education programs, which have meager results. Early intervention allows ineffective remedial programs to be replaced with effective prevention while providing older students who continue to need services with enhanced instruction so they can return to the educational mainstream." (Lyon and Fletcher 2001, 24)

In this 2001 article, the authors explained the rise in the incidence of LD as the result of three factors:

1. Current measurement practices worked against identifying struggling readers before second grade.

2. It is more difficult to get results when remediation is started after second grade.

3. Federal and school policies allowed ineffective assessment and teaching practices to continue.

They described problems related to the definition and diagnosis of learning difficulties and argued for discontinuation of the discrepancy formula for justifying that a student is eligible for special services. At that time, they suggested "it makes no sense to wait for a discrepancy to reveal itself" (Lyon and Fletcher 2001). These observations encouraged adoption of practices that are widely referred to now as Response to Intervention.

Students identified as reading disabled after second grade rarely catch up to their peers. One of the most cited longitudinal studies is the Connecticut Longitudinal Study directed by Dr. Sally Shaywitz of Yale University (Shaywitz 1996). Students were studied from kindergarten through twelfth grade. The students in the study who were determined to have a reading disability made some progress in reading from ages 6 to 12. Yet they never closed the gap, and, furthermore, they reached a plateau near age 12, after which their rate of growth leveled off and they fell further behind. These meager outcomes were found even though more than half of the students in this group were receiving special education services (Lyon and Fletcher 2001).

While researchers find that students who get behind generally stay behind, what evidence is there that it's possible to identify those who will struggle and thus avert failure? Researchers have confirmed that it is possible to predict which students will struggle and then actually change the trajectory for these students. A longitudinal study followed 201 students randomly selected from five schools that served students from mixed socioeconomic status and ethnic backgrounds, where

28% received free and reduced lunch. These students were followed from the beginning of first grade through the end of fourth grade.

In this study, the researchers followed the students to validate whether their prediction of which students were at risk was accurate. Based on measures of phonemic awareness and letter knowledge at the beginning of first grade, students were divided into two groups: those at risk and those thought to be at low risk of difficulty. Both groups of students had roughly equivalent levels of overall ability, as measured by their IQ. The at-risk group was in the bottom 15% in phonemic awareness and letter knowledge. By the end of fourth grade, the at-risk students had achieved only a mid-second-grade level in reading, as measured with a combination of reading accuracy and comprehension. The group considered at low risk finished fourth-grade reading at the beginning of the fifth-grade level. This research project is known as a "passive observation study," which means that the researchers didn't provide any intervention once they determined which students might be at risk. The purpose was to validate that the screening instruments could effectively predict which students were at risk.

The researchers who conducted this study then received funding to go back to the same five schools (see *Figure 1.1*, next page). The mission of their second study was to see whether they could act on their predictions to prevent a new group of at-risk students from following this trajectory of failure. Two changes were implemented: The schools adopted a new research-based comprehensive core reading program, and students from the bottom 15% in phonemic awareness and letter recognition were randomly assigned to two groups. One group served as the control group, and they received only the new core reading program. The second group received the new core reading program plus intervention instruction delivered in small groups during first and second grade. The new core reading program produced slightly better outcomes, with a 3.2 reading level. The group that received the new core program plus intervention reached a 4.9 reading level by the end of fourth grade, nearly closing the gap and reaching their not-at-risk peers at 5.2 (U.S. Department of Education 2002).

A series of research studies validates the effectiveness of early identification and intervention. In a series of five studies, students were identified through screening assessments and received intervention instruction, varying from one-on-one tutoring to intervention instruction in groups as large as eight students (Denton and Mathes 2003). In these five studies, between 0.7% and 4.5% of the total students in the schools did not achieve benchmark levels in early reading indicators (see *Table 1.1*). Most researchers now assert that effective early intervention practices can bring the percent of struggling readers down to the 2%–5% range.

Figure 1.1

Comparison of Core Reading Program Alone Versus Core Plus Intervention Instruction (U.S. Department of Education, 2002)

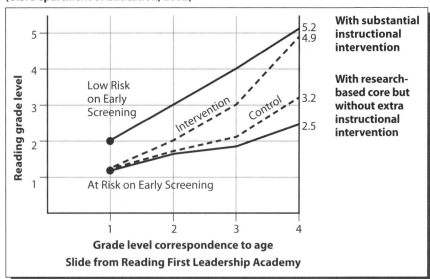

Slide from Reading First Leadership Academy

Table 1.1

Summary of Studies About Preventing Reading Problems (from Denton & Mathes 2003)
Percent of Children Scoring Below the 30th Percentile After Intervention

Study	Hrs. of Instruction	Student/ Teacher Ratio	Reading %ile for Initial Identification of Risk Status	% of Lowest Readers Reading Below 30th %ile After Intervention	% of Students Reading Below 30th %ile After Intervention Extrapolated to the Total Population
Felton 1993	340 hrs.	1:8	16	24%	3.4%
Vellutino et al. 1996	35–65 hrs.	1:1	15	30%	4.5%
Torgesen et al. 1999	88 hrs.	1:1	12	23%	4.0%
Torgesen et al. (Manuscript in preparation)	92 hrs.	1:3	18	8%	1.0%
Torgesen et al. 2002	80	1:3	18	4%	.7%

How to Implement the Preventive Model

Many times when teachers and administrators hear about the effectiveness of early identification and intervention, they want to establish this practice in their school. Often their question is, "How do we get started?" Schools that succeed with the Preventive Model have strong leaders in both administration and among the teachers. These leaders help to bring about the cultural change that leads to better reading performance for almost all students.

> *Without the use of* DIBELS *to screen our students, we would not be able to effectively service the students' needs as consciously as we do now. All students deserve a literacy journey that will bring them to not only reading for information, but the enjoyment of reading.*
>
> Reading Coach

Cultural Change May Be Necessary

In most schools, a cultural change occurs when RTI is implemented. Teachers must view early identification and intervention as so important that they are willing to change practices in a number of ways. First, teachers have to invest the time and energy to learn to administer and score an early literacy assessment instrument. Once data are available that shows the percentage of students at each grade level below benchmark, the staff needs to engage in honest dialogue about needed improvements to the core instruction if more than 20% of students are below benchmark. Next, they need to learn to analyze the student scoring booklets to discover error patterns and determine which below-benchmark students are ready for placement in groups and which students need a diagnostic screener after *DIBELS.* After grouping students with similar deficits, staff members need to determine the appropriate materials and instructional strategies that will best assist them in delivering intervention instruction. One of the greatest challenges for some teachers is determining a way to deliver intervention groups and setting up the structures. Will they organize small groups all within their classroom, or will they work with their grade-level colleagues to group across classes? Are other teaching staff members available to work with intervention groups so that it's possible to have those students furthest behind working in small groups of three to five students or less?

It's interesting to observe how readily teachers learn to love the data and look forward to receiving the next set of progress monitoring data because they know there will be celebration. In the past, teachers have not had such clear evidence that their struggling students were making progress. One teacher who had just started using this approach wrote in her journal:

> *This has given me more things to celebrate through repeated progress monitoring and testing. I have a chance to celebrate even the little gains. It also gives me direction and focus for my teaching and for grouping.*
>
> Classroom Teacher

A principal in a school that implemented early literacy assessment and intervention spoke in a focus group setting about how her teachers know their students better by using this type of data. Teachers also reported feeling more credible in speaking with parents about delays they observe when they have assessment data to share. At the end of the first year of implementing early intervention, a group of 50 classroom teachers and aides strongly agreed (4.8 on a 5-point Likert scale) with a statement that they would recommend their school continue providing small-group interventions next year (Hall 2004).

What Does It Take to Implement Early Intervention Procedures in a School?

Success involves more than simply having the tool or being required to administer it. Success requires professional development for teachers that is sustained and job embedded, including coaching and discussions at grade-level meetings, if at all possible.

Teachers need to learn how to use a data-informed approach to evaluate the effectiveness of the core instruction as well as to plan and evaluate small-group intervention instruction. They need professional development to learn how to decide which data are most critical in forming groups, how to analyze whether a student is struggling with accuracy or fluency in a skill area, and how to use the student scoring booklets to determine what a student already knows and what skills he lacks.

Some of the most effective approaches to professional development combine workshop days with follow-up coaching and discussions at grade-level meetings.

Some of the most effective approaches to professional development combine workshop days with follow-up coaching and discussions at grade-level meetings. Case studies of sample students are analyzed during the workshop, followed by teachers analyzing a scoring booklet for a student in their class. Learning becomes grounded for a teacher when his own students' data are involved. An expert facilitator can engage teachers in discussions about observations that are not only factual but that also require inference and interpretation. A trained reading coach can help teachers engage in dialogue about their students' data.

In addition to helping teachers learn to use data to inform instruction, two additional factors help ensure success in implementation of the Preventive Model approach. Effective administrative leadership from the principal allows teachers to focus on reading and provides time in the schedule for intervention instruction. Principals need to organize the building and the schedule of the day so teachers have help through additional staffing and prioritized blocks of time for reading. Scheduling grade-level planning time is critical for teachers to learn to implement these new practices. Teacher leadership is also important in modeling for others effective small-group instruction in the classroom.

Conclusion

The research findings about the effectiveness of early identification and intervention to prevent reading difficulties are extensive. The challenge now is not in implementing in single school sites. We are beyond that. It's to implement large-scale and to sustain the practices even when district and school administrative teams change. The only way that students will receive early intervention in reading is if schools routinely provide screening on early literacy skills and then have a process in place to intervene immediately if any student is below benchmark. The research is clear about which practices will benefit students. Schools need a process to help teachers learn how to use a screening instrument and to plan intervention, and that process will most likely include some form of professional development. Teachers need workshops with planned follow-up that includes support, modeling, and opportunities to learn how to use the data collaboratively with their colleagues. This cultural change in the way a school uses assessment data may not be easy, but it's well worth it given the hundreds of students per school each year whose reading difficulties will be averted by implementing procedures for early literacy screening and intervention instruction.

Chapter 2

Overview of DIBELS Next®

The use of DIBELS Next® *data empowers teachers by helping them to understand where their students' literacy needs are. This prescriptive teaching approach has motivated many staff members and re-ignited their passion for teaching all students.*

Reading Coach

Selecting an Effective Assessment Instrument

Selecting an effective assessment instrument for routine screening of elementary students is a critical step in implementing RTI to avert reading difficulties. The most effective screening instruments have four critical characteristics:

1. They have met minimum research criteria as valid and reliable in identifying at-risk students.

2. They are teacher-friendly.

3. They provide valuable information.

4. They take the shortest time possible to administer.

If the screening assessment isn't efficient as well as effective, it's very difficult to gain teacher buy-in and maximize the time devoted to instruction because assessment time is minimized.

Efficiency of the assessment instrument is critical so that teachers aren't spending any more time than necessary screening their students. Teachers today have many demands and are pressed for valuable instruction time. Most screening assessments for elementary students are administered one-on-one with students two or three times a year. Unfortunately, some popular screening assessments take between 20 and 45 minutes per student to administer. Some of the instruments that take 45 minutes have two levels where an interim scoring determines whether a more in-depth section is necessary. Unfortunately, schools with high percentages of students who enter kindergarten at risk for language deficits have to deliver the entire thing for nearly all students. Therefore, the very teachers who need to be dedicating every possible moment to teaching intervention groups are spending the longest time simply completing the initial benchmark screening at the beginning of the school year. Adopting an instrument that takes so long to administer and score can be a recipe for teacher reluctance and misuse of the screening process.

DIBELS Next is one of the best early literacy assessment instruments available today. It is efficient to deliver, taking an average of 3 to 8 minutes per student for kindergarten through second grade and longer for third grade through sixth grade (time depends on whether Daze is group or individually administered). *Table 2.1* includes information that is contained in the *DIBELS Next Assessment Manual*.

Table 2.1

Time Required for Benchmark Assessments

Periods	Kindergarten	Grade 1	Grade 2	Grades 3–6 (each period)
Beginning of Year	3 minutes (FSF, LNF)	5 minutes (LNF, PSF, NWF)	8 minutes (NWF, DORF including Retell)	6 minutes per student (DORF including Retell) **plus** 5 minutes to assess Daze individually or in a group **plus** 1–2 minutes per student to score worksheet
Middle of Year	6.5 minutes (FSF, PSF, LNF, NWF)	8 minutes (NWF, DORF including Retell)	6 minutes (DORF including Retell)	
End of Year	5 minutes (LNF, PSF, NWF)	8 minutes (NWF, DORF including Retell)	6 minutes (DORF including Retell)	

Table 2.1 is adapted from Table 4.2: Time Required for Benchmark Assessments, from *DIBELS® Next Assessment Manual*, copyright © 2011, Dynamic Measurement Group.

The *DIBELS Next* assessment is administered one-on-one, typically by a teacher or aide. For schools that are not using one of the data-management systems, there is additional time to compute the DORF Accuracy Score and the Daze Adjusted Score, as well as to complete the Composite Score calculations on the worksheets that are available in Appendix 6 of the *DIBELS Next Assessment Manual* and also as a free download from the following Web sites:

- Cambium Learning® Sopris (www.soprislearning.com/dibels)

- Dynamic Measurement Group (www.dibels.org)

Why Is It Called *DIBELS* Next?

Let's start with the acronym, "DIBELS." It stands for *Dynamic Indicators of Basic Early Literacy Skills*. Each word is significant.

- **D**ynamic—The instrument is dynamic because the measures change over time to match the evolving developmental progression in early reading. Different skills are assessed at each grade, based on which skills are most highly predictive of reading success and failure at that particular grade level. There are six indicators, some of which are administered only in kindergarten, others are administered primarily in kindergarten/first grade, and Daze is added for third grade through sixth grade.

- **I**ndicators—The subtests in *DIBELS Next* are referred to as *indicators* because they quickly and efficiently provide an indication of a student's performance and/or progress in acquiring a larger literacy skill. For example, the number of segments a student produces per minute on Phoneme Segmentation Fluency (PSF) is an indicator of a student's development of the larger construct of phonemic awareness.

- **B**asic—The skills that are assessed are basic in that they are early to develop and critical to accurate and fluent reading and to comprehension.

- **E**arly—*DIBELS Next* assesses only those skills critical to early reading.

- **L**iteracy—*DIBELS Next* doesn't address skills in math or other academic domains.

- **S**kills—The indicators in this assessment are targeted at key underlying skills that are important in learning to read.

- **Next**—This version of *DIBELS* follows the 6th Edition but is not a revision of it. The word *Next* was added to the name to distinguish it as a new assessment, where all measures were newly created. Some measures look similar to the previous version, but there were new instructions added and changes made; therefore, the measures were researched with a new pool of students.

The authors prefer that the assessment is called *DIBELS Next* instead of the 7th Edition. The change of the assessment name coincided with another significant change. *DIBELS Next* is copyrighted by Dynamic Measurement Group (DMG), the private for-profit company of authors Dr. Roland Good III and Dr. Ruth Kaminski. Versions published prior to the 6th Edition of *DIBELS* were available at the University of Oregon's Web site for free; the 6th Edition and *DIBELS Next* are copyrighted by DMG.

Schools administer the *DIBELS Next* assessment three times a year—typically fall, winter, and spring—to all students. A student's scores are compared to empirically derived benchmarks based on a large national sample of students. Additionally, *DIBELS Next* provides 20 alternate forms for five of the six critical indicators (all but Letter Naming Fluency), which can be used to frequently measure the progress of students who are receiving intervention instruction.

What Is the Purpose of *DIBELS Next?*

Understanding the purpose of an assessment instrument helps protect against confusion over what conclusions can be drawn from the data and how to use that information in decisions about the curriculum to teach students.

Assessment instruments meet one or more of four purposes (Reading First Academy Assessment Committee 2002).

- **Outcome**—Assessments that provide a bottom-line evaluation of the effectiveness of the reading program.

- **Screening**—Assessments that identify which students are at risk for reading difficulty and need additional intervention.

- **Diagnosis**—Assessments that help teachers plan instruction by providing in-depth information about students' skills and instructional needs; may also help determine the presence of a developmental disorder that requires specialized treatments and interventions.

- **Progress Monitoring**—Assessments that determine if students are making adequate progress or need more intervention to achieve grade-level reading outcomes.

In 2002, eight researchers were appointed by the U.S. Department of Education to serve on the Reading First Assessment Committee. The task of this peer review committee was to evaluate early literacy assessment instruments for Reading First. For each instrument submitted for review, the committee determined whether there was an adequate body of research to meet minimum criteria for validity and reliability for use for one or more of the four purposes. At that time, *DIBELS Next* didn't exist, but *DIBELS* was submitted for review and the committee found it to be valid and reliable as a screening, progress monitoring, and outcome measure but not as a diagnostic measure.

To see a complete list of the assessment instruments that were validated by the Reading First Assessment Committee, visit www2.ed.gov. Instruments may not be on the list for reasons other than their failure to meet the criteria; one of the most common reasons is simply that they were not submitted for review. The committee's analysis and subsequent report provide excellent information for schools evaluating assessment tools, whether or not the school is eligible for Reading First funding. Although this list can help you select from among the best early literacy instruments available, keep in mind that much has changed in the ten years since it was compiled.

Many research reviews demonstrate that *DIBELS Next* is reliable in predicting whether a student is on track to becoming a reader by the end of third grade (Good, Gruba, and Kaminski 2001). *DIBELS Next* does this by assessing whether students are achieving critical milestones along the way to proficient reading. For more information on the research supporting *DIBELS Next*, visit www.dibels.org.

DIBELS Next as a Screening Instrument

The assessments administered in the fall, winter, and spring are called *Benchmark Assessment Screenings*. The Benchmark Screening is given to all students to determine whether they are on track or at risk for reading difficulty. Benchmark Screening assesses whether students are achieving certain critical milestones that good readers achieve. It's important to keep in mind that *DIBELS Next* measures indicators and then estimates the likelihood of later reading success based on performance levels on these specific indicators. Students who do not achieve these Benchmark Goals may be placed in intervention groups after confirming the need for intervention through teacher observation and other data.

Many times teachers ask how to describe a screening instrument to parents. Here's an analogy that may be helpful. When someone goes to the emergency room of the hospital, what does the triage nurse do (after asking for a health insurance card)? The triage nurse takes the patient's temperature, listens to heart rate, and measures blood pressure. Why does the nurse do this? These vital signs are indicators of the patient's overall state of health. The triage nurse is responsible for determining who needs immediate service and who can wait a bit longer before seeing a doctor. Skyrocketing blood pressure or an accelerated heart rate may be an indication that the patient is experiencing a serious immediate health risk, such as a heart attack or internal bleeding. The nurse uses these data, along with information from the patient and her own observations of the patient's behavior and speech, to decide the severity of the patient's injuries.

The vital signs don't tell the doctors everything they need to know, but they help. Just as with vital signs, *DIBELS Next* doesn't tell you everything there is to know about the student's reading development and skills, but it does give you vital information about the overall progress the student is making toward becoming a proficient reader.

DIBELS Next as a Progress Monitoring Instrument

The progress monitoring capability of *DIBELS Next* is one of the more important characteristics of this assessment instrument. With *DIBELS Next*, educators can conduct frequent, repeated administrations of the same indicators by using 1 of 20 alternate forms. This is possible because *DIBELS Next* indicators are sensitive to change over a short period of time. Repeated administration helps in monitoring the progress of students receiving intervention instruction.

DIBELS Next progress monitoring assessments are administered primarily to students whose benchmark screening indicated that they were at some level of risk and, therefore, are receiving intervention instruction. *DIBELS Next* is good for measuring students who are receiving intervention for fluency or phoneme segmentation. Depending on the deficit skill area, sometimes an alternate form of a diagnostic screener gives more specific progress monitoring data than can be measured with the *DIBELS Next* indicators. Progress monitoring can be repeated as often as weekly, although most teachers assess their intervention students

> *Depending on the deficit skill area, sometimes an alternate form of a diagnostic screener gives more specific progress monitoring data than can be measured with the* **DIBELS Next** *indicators.*

every two to three weeks. Some teachers choose to strategically monitor students who fell in the *At or Above Benchmark* range once in between benchmark periods, especially those who have missed a lot of days of school. It's also useful to progress monitor students whose scores were just above the benchmark goal; these students are sometimes referred to as *fence sitters*.

One of the reasons that having a range of alternate forms is critical is that it's very difficult to know exactly which instructional strategies will lead to success with each student. Matching the right materials with the right student at the right time for the appropriate duration of time is a complex task. If the research enabled teachers to prescribe exactly the right instruction for every individual, then reading difficulties might not exist. Teachers need knowledge of the development of reading skills and effective research-based practices. They also need to match that knowledge with their insights about the needs of the particular student. One of the advantages of progress monitoring data is that teachers can know in a timely manner whether the instruction selected is effective for the student.

DIBELS Next progress monitoring data help teachers make professional judgments about whether the intervention instruction should be continued or changed. Teachers feel relieved that they have progress monitoring data to help them determine, within weeks of beginning special instruction, whether the strategies and materials they have selected are helping the student succeed. If intervention is not working, then the teacher can make adjustments right away, without waiting until the end of the school year to measure the level of success. Being able to adjust the intervention instruction is critical because time counts—the clock is ticking for that student. There are a limited number of school days during the first several years of a student's life in which she needs to learn to read. By charting progress and comparing interim movements in a student's scores, it's possible to estimate whether the current rate of progress is likely to result in the student reaching benchmark by the end of the year.

When a student's scores on a progress monitoring assessment show that he is failing to make progress or is making progress at a rate that is inadequate to close the gap, then the teacher can change the intervention instruction in several ways:

1. Increase the time allowed for intervention.

2. Decrease the size of the group so that each student receives more feedback.

3. Change the materials or strategies used.

4. Move the student to a different group that more effectively targets the skills the student needs.

For students in kindergarten through second grade, teachers see progress generally within six to nine weeks of when a student starts in an intervention group of three or fewer students meeting for 30 minutes daily. Sometimes lack of progress is most evident when two students in a group are making gains and the scores of the third student are level, even though he has been receiving exactly the same instruction. By examining intervention logs that contain records of what instructional practices were followed for this group, teachers and reading coaches can make decisions about what to change for the student who is not making adequate progress. This is where those record-keeping practices really pay off for students.

Intervention groups need to be flexible. They are not the reading groups of the past when a student stayed in the "blue birds" group for the entire year. Flexible means that students are regrouped (or considered for regrouping) at least every nine weeks, based on the data and teacher observation. If students' progress is monitored every three weeks, then teachers will have three sets of data at the nine-week point. Progress monitoring data make regrouping decisions far easier. A third-grade teacher reflects on her fellow teacher's acceptance of the regrouping process:

> *At first, some staff members were hesitant about "ability grouping." But after they saw that the groups can change frequently and more importantly, the positive results, they were "on board"!*
>
> Third-Grade Teacher

DIBELS Next as an Outcome Measure

DIBELS Next data can be consolidated for the school or district. At the school level, the data can help inform administrators about the level of resources needed for intervention instruction. It's possible to note how well the preschools and community are preparing students for kindergarten based on the fall kindergarten benchmark scores. Some schools that have identified weaknesses have initiated meetings with their feeder preschools. Examples of the types of questions that can be answered with the data follow:

- For the students who enter kindergarten with benchmark level skills, are the core curriculum and instruction enabling them to continue at or above benchmark by the middle and end of the year?

- For the students who enter kindergarten at risk, how effective is the core and intervention instruction at helping them catch up to benchmark?

- How do the results of school x compare to those of the other schools in their own district?

What Does *DIBELS* Next Measure?

DIBELS Next uses several indicators to measure early reading skills. The indicators are similar to subtests in other assessment instruments. The six indicators measure the following skills:

- **First Sound Fluency** (FSF)—Ability to recognize and produce initial sounds in words.

- **Letter Naming Fluency** (LNF)—Ability to recognize and name a random mixture of uppercase and lowercase letters on a page, in an early reader font called Report School.

- **Phoneme Segmentation Fluency** (PSF)—Ability to segment a spoken word of two to five phonemes into the individual sounds.

- **Nonsense Word Fluency** (NWF)—Ability to read two-letter and three-letter pseudowords, primarily consonant-vowel-consonant patterns.

- *DIBELS* **Oral Reading Fluency** (DORF)—Ability to accurately and fluently read grade-level passages aloud as measured by words read correctly per minute.
    - **Retell** (included with DORF)—Ability to read for meaning; measured immediately following the passage reading.

- **Daze**—Ability to use reasoning processes that are necessary to comprehend.

Word Use Fluency (WUF), a measure of vocabulary that appeared in previous editions of *DIBELS*, is still under research at the time of this printing and was not included in the first release of *DIBELS Next*. As of the date of publication of this book, schools can continue using the 6th Edition WUF or participate as a research partner using a revised version of WUF called WUF-R.

Although there are six indicators, at any given time for an individual student, only one to four are administered. Administering the maximum number of four indicators occurs only once: in the winter of kindergarten. At two of the administration times, only two indicators are given. *Table 2.2* shows when each indicator is administered.

Table 2.2

Administration of *DIBELS Next* Indicators by Grade Level and Time Period

Indicator	Kindergarten			Grade 1			Grade 2			Grades 3–6
	Beginning of Year	Middle of Year	End of Year	Beginning of Year	Middle of Year	End of Year	Beginning of Year	Middle of Year	End of Year	Each Period
First Sound Fluency (FSF)	X	X								
Letter Naming Fluency (LNF)	X	X	X	X						
Phoneme Segmentation Fluency (PSF)		X	X	X						
Nonsense Word Fluency (NWF) –CLS* –WWR**		X X	X X	X X	X X	X X	X X			
DIBELS Oral Reading Fluency (DORF) including Retell				X	X	X	X	X	X	X
Daze										X

*CLS = Correct Letter Sounds
**WWR = Whole Words Read

When *DIBELS* was first developed, it included more measures; but, fortunately, the research team was sensitive to feedback from teachers. The more skills assessed in an early literacy screening instrument, the longer it takes to administer with each student. Teachers said that the instrument had to be short to be practical to implement in schools. Over time and with much work, the researchers were able to tell which measures were important and which could be eliminated without jeopardizing the ability to predict accurately who was on track and who was at risk.

After the initial development period, *DIBELS* included five indicators for many years. With the National Reading Panel's articulation of the five essential components of reading instruction, there was increasing focus on the need to assess all five of these areas:

- Phonemic Awareness

- Phonics and Word Attack Skills

- Accurate and Fluent Reading of Connected Text

- Reading Comprehension

- Vocabulary and Language Skills

Around that same time period, *DIBELS* was expanded to include Retell Fluency (an indicator of comprehension), and Word Use Fluency (an indicator of vocabulary). There is also a Spanish version of *DIBELS* called *IDEL*. As of the release date of this book, *DIBELS Next* was available only through grade 6; the research team advises that grades 7–9 are under development.

What *DIBELS Next* Doesn't Include

As mentioned above, *DIBELS Next* is not intended to be an exhaustive measure of all skills involved in acquiring early literacy abilities—just the skills that are the most highly predictive of later passage reading ability. If you examine different early literacy assessment instruments, you will notice that some instruments contain measures of skills not included in *DIBELS Next*. Examples include:

- Concept of word

- Print and book awareness

- Reading lists of real words, as opposed to pseudowords

- Assessing for letter sounds using lists of letters

- Spelling inventory

Why aren't these skills measured in *DIBELS Next*? The *DIBELS Next* research team determined that these other indicators were either unnecessary for the purpose of predicting which students will have difficulty or they measured substantially the same skills as the existing measures. For example, concept of word and book and print awareness, while interesting and potentially necessary for reading, are not as powerful in their predictive ability as the skills measured by *DIBELS Next*.

Reading single words out of context accurately and rapidly is decidedly important in learning to read and is an excellent predictor after mid-first grade, but the problem with using real words in an assessment instrument is that it is impossible to know whether students can use their phonics skills to decode new words or whether they have simply memorized the words that appear on any given list.

DIBELS Next does not assess sound-symbol associations by showing the student a list of letters and asking for the sound of each one as is done in some other measures. Instead, this skill is assessed within the pseudoword format (CLS, or Correct Letter Sounds), along with the student's ability to apply these letter-sound correspondences to blend words (WWR, or Whole Words Read).

DIBELS Next does not assess advanced phonics concepts separately from the appearance of words with these patterns in DORF passages. NWF assesses the VC and CVC patterns only. Many diagnostic screeners use pseudowords to assess later phonics patterns beyond the consonant-vowel-consonant pattern assessed in *DIBELS Next*.

> *Assessing with nonsense words is essential in first grade. Many students know and memorize words but do not understand the syllable patterns. This becomes extremely problematic when they try to decode multisyllabic words, especially in the content areas. When students read nonsense words, it helps us to determine which students need additional interventions in certain syllables.*
>
> **First-Grade Teacher**

Spelling inventories provide rich information, yet they are time-consuming to score. They can still be administered to selected students as needed, rather than to all students in the initial benchmark screening.

The composition of a screening instrument, as well as the weighting of measured reading skills, determines how well the instrument predicts reading outcomes. For example, in some screeners, concept of word, book and print awareness, and rhyming skill are heavily weighted in a student's total score and phoneme segmentation is barely weighted at all; this type of assessment may not be as powerful in identifying at-risk students. Therefore, the selection of the assessment instrument your district or school uses is one of the most critical decisions affecting the ultimate success of your RTI implementation.

How Are the Six *DIBELS Next* Indicators Linked to the Five Essential Components?

The six *DIBELS Next* indicators are closely tied to the five essential components of reading articulated in the National Reading Panel Report (National Reading Panel 2000). Although there are two measures of phonemic awareness and comprehension, and letter naming does not relate as clearly to the components, the relationship is quite straightforward for the others, as shown in *Table 2.3*.

Table 2.3

Relationship of *DIBELS Next* Indicators to Five Essential Components

DIBELS Next Indicators	Five Essential Components of Reading Instruction
First Sound Fluency (FSF)	Phonemic Awareness
Phoneme Segmentation Fluency (PSF)	
Letter Naming Fluency (LNF)	
Nonsense Word Fluency (NWF)	Basic Phonics (CLS tied to letter-sound correspondence; WWR tied to blending)
DIBELS Oral Reading Fluency (DORF) including Retell	Accuracy and Rate of Reading Text, Reading Comprehension
Daze	Reading Comprehension (Retell tied to oral reading; Daze tied to silent reading)
No current measure; Word Use Fluency-R in the future	Vocabulary

Importance of Different Skills at Different Grade Levels

The ultimate goal of reading instruction is to teach students to comprehend what they read. Comprehension depends on accurate and fluent decoding and on understanding the words and concepts that are included in the reading passages. In fact, many studies have shown that oral reading fluency measures are valid at measuring not only fluency, but at predicting a student's overall reading comprehension, as well. One study found that the validity of an oral reading fluency measure in predicting comprehension was .91 (Davidson and Towner 2001). In this same study, only 2% of first-grade students not identified as at risk on an oral reading fluency measure were later found to be poor readers on a grade 2 end-of-year general test.

Yet research has also shown that waiting until a student can read an oral reading fluency passage, generally during the second half of first grade, is not early enough to permit optimum intervention. Throughout kindergarten and early first grade, it's critical to measure the precursor skills that predict a student's ability to successfully read connected text later. Although fluent reading of connected text is the best indicator of reading abilities, a kindergarten student would not be expected to read connected text fluently, if at all. However, a kindergarten student would be expected to identify letters by name, to identify sounds in spoken words, and to match some letters and sounds. Therefore, those are the skills that *DIBELS Next* assesses in kindergarten and at the beginning of first grade.

By the middle of the year, a first-grader would be expected to read connected text but not nearly as fluently or accurately as a second-grader; even an excellent first-grade reader is still mastering basic skills. For that reason, *DIBELS Next* measures not only connected text reading in first grade but also phonemic awareness (PSF), letter-sound correspondence (CLS in NWF), and blending of VC and CVC patterns (WWR in NWF). At the beginning of second grade, *DIBELS Next* measures basic phonics (NWF) in addition to connected text reading because some beginning second-graders are still struggling with the concepts of matching sounds and letters and blending letter sounds.

By focusing on the skills that we teach and expect students to master at various stages during kindergarten through third grade, *DIBELS Next* gives teachers the information they need to design intervention for the basic skills immediately when it has been determined that a student is missing those skills. As Dr. Roland Good says, "These are remarkably powerful one-minute measures."

Are the Six Indicators Linked to Each Other?

Three of the indicators link to skills that are typically acquired in a progression of reading development. In fact, the research team refers to these as *Stepping Stones* from one important early reading skill to the next, through the developmental progression. These Stepping Stone indicators that precede oral reading fluency are First Sound Fluency (FSF), Phoneme Segmentation Fluency (PSF), and Nonsense Word Fluency (NWF). Letter Naming Fluency (LNF) is a risk indicator that is measured to help predict which students may struggle later.

Reading books fluently with comprehension is the ultimate goal, a feat that is not accomplished until second, third, or a later grade for some students. Yet if schools wait until third grade to determine whether the student reads well, critical time has been lost when early intervention may well have averted the reading difficulty. Because of the importance of intervening early, it's imperative to look for indications of risk long before the student is beginning to read text. Even waiting until the middle of first grade, when students are expected to begin reading simple text, to explore the possibility of difficulties and begin intervention is too late. The solution is to look in kindergarten and at the beginning

> **DIBELS Next** *uses the early developing skills of letter naming, phoneme identification, and phoneme segmentation to predict how likely it is that the later skills that ultimately lead to proficient reading will also develop.*

of first grade for pre-reading skills that link to the ultimate skill of reading passages. *DIBELS Next* uses the early developing skills of letter naming, phoneme identification, and phoneme segmentation to predict how likely it is that the later skills that ultimately lead to proficient reading will also develop.

DMG publishes a table of expected levels of performance for students who are likely to achieve later reading success. They have established a level that is considered the *Benchmark Goal* for the three benchmark assessment periods. There are very useful summary tables in the *DIBELS Next Assessment Manual* and as free downloads from www.soprislearning.com/dibels and www.dibels.org. Benchmark Goals can be interpreted as the level where the odds are 80%–90% in favor that the student will achieve later important reading outcomes.

DIBELS Next incorporates an approach of predicting the likelihood that a student will reach a later Benchmark Goal based on performance on current indicators. A student who reads a minimum of 47 words correct per minute (wpm) at the end of first grade is more likely to read on grade level in second and third grade than a student who doesn't reach this important goal. What earlier indications predict whether a student will read 47 wpm at the end of first grade? The strongest predictor in *DIBELS Next* of whether a student will read 47 wpm at the end of first grade is his adeptness at decoding pseudowords in the middle of first grade. If a student in the middle of the first grade reaches the established level of reading 43 correct letter sounds (CLS) per minute, where the vowels represent the short sound in pseudowords, the probability that he will read passages at benchmark level at the end of first grade is extremely high. Similarly, if a student reaches the Benchmark Goal of 40 on Phoneme Segmentation Fluency (PSF) by the end of kindergarten, there is a high probability that he will also reach the next benchmark, which is for Nonsense Word Fluency (NWF), by the winter of first grade. As you can see, reaching benchmark on any one step along the progression increases the chance that the student will stay on benchmark and continue along until he reads well at the end of third grade.

There are many terms used in *DIBELS Next* to describe a student's level of performance. Some terms are new. The following is a description of the terms, along with some terms previously used in the 6th Edition that will no longer be used.

DIBELS Next *Terms*

- **Benchmark Goal:** This revised term in the *DIBELS Next* framework indicates the score that is the minimum number a student must reach in order for the odds to be in favor (80%–90%) of reaching later reading goals.

- **Cut Point for Risk:** This new term in *DIBELS Next* indicates the score below which a student is unlikely (10%–20%) to reach later reading outcomes unless instruction changes.

- **At or Above Benchmark:** This term now describes the score that indicates that the benchmark goal level has been met or the score is above it. These students are likely to continue to make progress with Tier 1 core reading instruction alone and, at this time, probably are not in need of extra support.

- **Below Benchmark:** This is the term that *DIBELS Next* uses to indicate scores between the Benchmark Goal and the Cut Point for Risk. Strategic Support may be recommended for these students.

- **Well Below Benchmark:** This term, which is new in *DIBELS Next*, is defined as the category of scores that fall below the Cut Point for Risk. These students are likely to need Intensive Support to reach future Benchmark Goals and other important reading outcomes. These three terms (at or above, below, or well below) are the main performance levels.

- **Core, Strategic, or Intensive:** Based on the benchmark categories above, a student is assigned a "Likely Need for Support." These include "Likely to Need Core Support," "Likely to Need Strategic Support," and "Likely to Need Intensive Support." *Core* means "the instruction that students receive typically delivered in the reading block." *Strategic* and *Intensive* refer to "additional support," often called *Tier 2* or *Tier 3* within the RTI framework.

6th Edition Terms No Longer Used in DIBELS Next

- **Low Risk**, **Some Risk**, and **At Risk**: These terms, from 6th Edition, were used when a skill was measured before it was supposed to be at the mastery level. They referred to whether a student's scores fell in the range above benchmark, between the benchmark and the at-risk level, or below the at-risk level. For example, PSF was expected to be mastered by the end of kindergarten at which time the benchmark level was 35 phoneme segments per minute. When PSF was measured in the middle of kindergarten, a student whose scores fell above the interim mid-year benchmark of 18 was considered at low risk of not being able to achieve the ultimate goal of 35 by the end of the year.

- **Established**, **Emerging**, and **Deficit**: These terms were used as categories of a student's status once the indicator was supposed to have reached its mastery level, and were used again for each measurement period after that. Continuing with the PSF example, when PSF was measured at the end of kindergarten and again at the beginning of first grade, these three categories replaced the risk categories above. The *DIBELS Next* research team has replaced these two sets of terms for performance with the *At and Above*, *Below*, and *Well Below* terms.

- **Instructional Recommendation Level**: This term was used to represent the consolidated score that was calculated by a data-management system to combine a student's performance levels on all the measures given at that time period. This calculation is replaced by the Composite Score in *DIBELS Next*.

- **Benchmark**, **Strategic**, and **Intensive**: These terms still appear in *DIBELS Next*, but their use has changed somewhat. Instead of appearing within the column for Instructional Recommendation Level, they now are used only within the description of what level of support is suggested for students falling within At or Above Benchmark, Below Benchmark, and Well Below Benchmark. Instead of serving as category names, they are used as likely levels of support.

Benchmark Goals

Benchmark Goals provide teachers with an indication of whether a student seems to be on track for later success in reading. In the 6th Edition, there was discussion about the importance of reaching particular Stepping Stones by a grade and time of year. The discussion was that it was important for students to reach mastery of Initial Sound Fluency (ISF) of 25 by the middle of kindergarten, PSF of 35 by the end of kindergarten, and NWF of 50 by the middle of first grade. In *DIBELS Next*, these time periods for mastery are not emphasized in the same manner. Based on a benchmark goal study, it is now known that students need to be at or above the benchmark on each measure every time it is assessed in order to be on track (see *Table 2.4*).

Table 2.4

Benchmark Goals for PSF and NWF in Selected Periods

Indicator	Time Period	Benchmark Goal at That Time
Phoneme Segmentation Fluency (PSF)	Kindergarten—End of Year	40 phoneme segments per minute
Nonsense Word Fluency (NWF) • Correct Letter Sounds (CLS) • Whole Words Read (WWR)	Grade 1—Middle of Year Grade 1—End of Year	43 sounds per minute 13 words per minute

There are a couple of surprises for me in the Benchmark Goals for *DIBELS Next*. It's interesting to note that the PSF Benchmark Goal had been 35 in the 6th Edition and is now 40 in *DIBELS Next*. On the other hand, the research team had provided guidance to use 15 for recoded words in NWF (NWF-WRC); now the NWF-WWR goal is 13. It is also intriguing to me that students need to read only 8 CVC words recoded by the middle of first grade; this seems low for two reasons. First, the benchmark goal for CLS of NWF is 28 at the end of kindergarten. This means that by the end of kindergarten, students would be able to correctly give the letter-sound correspondences for 28 letters within a minute when presented with VC and CVC pseudowords. If students are able to do that by the end of kindergarten, it seems that they are making significant progress toward being ready to learn to blend those letter sounds into recoded CVC words. It's hard to imagine that with good solid core instruction during the first half of first grade, those students wouldn't be able to read more than eight words blended by the middle of the year. I realize that this goal is based on the data from the research pool, and it is the minimal acceptable level that will hopefully be exceeded by many students.

Second, when advising schools, we consistently advocate that the goal for the beginning of first grade is to help students read simple 3-sound words, such as *cat*, *pet*, *mom*, and *man*, blended by the middle of the year. This is necessary because there are other word patterns that must be mastered in first grade to be on track. Most first-graders are expected to read all the closed-syllable word patterns including CVC words plus short-vowel words with consonant digraphs and consonant blends. Long vowel silent-*e* is typically mastered by the end of first grade, as well. It takes some time and lots of exposure for students to keep short and long vowels straight between CVC and CVCe words. Most first grade curricula also provide exposure to vowel teams and vowel-*r* words, even though they are taught more in second grade.

The goals for oral reading fluency are especially important starting in first grade. *Table 2.5* provides the end of the year Benchmark Goals for grades 1 through 6.

Table 2.5

DIBELS Oral Reading Fluency (DORF) Benchmark Goals for Grades 1–6

Grade	DIBELS Next Benchmark Goal—Year-End Words Read Correctly per Minute	DIBELS Next Benchmark Goal Accuracy Percentage	DIBELS, 6th Edition, Benchmark Goal—Year-End* Words Read Correctly per Minute
1	47	90%	40
2	87	97%	90
3	100	97%	110
4	115	98%	118
5	130	99%	128
6	120	98%	135

*DIBELS Next and 6th Edition goals were empirically derived using different passages, so they are not comparable.

One of the most notable things in *Table 2.5* is the high level of the accuracy scores that are considered Benchmark Goals. In second through sixth grade, students need to be able to read the *DIBELS Next* passages at accuracy rates of 97%–99%, which is considerably higher than the 95% goal that is generally used to determine a student's independent reading level. Later in this book, there will be more discussion about the importance of accurate reading for success. Too little attention has been paid to accuracy in the past, and one thing that is likely to happen with the release of *DIBELS Next* is an increased focus on the student's accuracy level. In all our workshops on how to use *DIBELS* data, we have emphasized the importance of calculating the accuracy rate for each of the three passages because it helps determine whether there may be decoding issues that would merit further examination with a phonics diagnostic screener. It's exciting that the accuracy calculation is now part of the *DIBELS Next* student scoring booklet. Additionally, later in this book I'll discuss how significantly the accuracy rate is weighted into the student's Composite Score along with the impact of the Retell score.

As discussed earlier in this chapter, *DIBELS* employs an approach of using performance on indicators at one period to predict the likelihood that a student will reach later goals. The Composite Score is a new feature of *DIBELS Next*; it's a score that represents a student's overall performance by incorporating scores on important indicators measured at a specific time period. *Table 2.6* summarizes the probabilities of a student reaching the *DIBELS* Composite Score in the next benchmark period after she has achieved intermediary goals at several different times.

Table 2.6

Probabilities of Achieving Composite Score Benchmark at Next Period

Indicator At or Above Benchmark	Percentage of Students Who Reach This Goal Also Reach *DIBELS* Composite Score Benchmark Goal at Next Benchmark Period
FSF at beginning of Kindergarten	81% achieve MOY benchmark DIBELS Composite Score.
FSF at middle of Kindergarten	76% achieve EOY benchmark DIBELS Composite Score.
PSF at middle of Kindergarten	75% achieve EOY benchmark DIBELS Composite Score.
NWF–CLS at middle of Kindergarten	82% achieve EOY benchmark DIBELS Composite Score.
NWF–CLS at beginning of grade 1	83% achieve MOY benchmark DIBELS Composite Score.
NWF–CLS at middle of grade 1	**85%** achieve EOY benchmark DIBELS Composite Score.
NWF–WWR at beginning of grade 1	81% achieve MOY benchmark DIBELS Composite Score.
NWF-WWR at middle of grade 1	**85%** achieve EOY benchmark DIBELS Composite Score.
DORF Words Correct at middle of grade 1	**88%** achieve EOY benchmark DIBELS Composite Score.
DORF Accuracy at middle of grade 1	**87%** achieve EOY benchmark DIBELS Composite Score.
DORF Words Correct BOY at grades 3–6	**89%–93%** accurate in predicting next period's Composite Score.
DORF Accuracy BOY at grades 3–6	83%–**89%** accurate in predicting next period's Composite Score.
Daze BOY at grades 3–6	82%–**90%** accurate in predicting next period's Composite Score.

DIBELS Next Benchmark Goals Composite Score, DMG, December 1, 2010.

In *Table 2.6*, all scores at or above 85% are shown in bold to highlight the highest predictive values. From this table, it's clear to see that once a student is assessed with DORF, words correct is the best predictor of the next period's Composite Score. Daze is quite predictive all by itself. It's also evident that designing measures of Stepping Stone precursor skills that successfully predict later reading outcomes is challenging because many of these measures aren't as strong individually in predicting the next period's Composite Score. However, it's important to note that there are more indicators that contribute to the Composite in earlier years, so when they are taken together as a group rather than each one individually, their predictive value increases.

The safest course is to advise teachers that their goal is to assure that each student achieves all the goals—and achieves them on time—to be on track for successful reading. It is not sufficient to meet only one early literacy goal; a student must meet each of these goals to stay on track and be a successful reader. *DIBELS Next* not only provides information about the minimum benchmark a student must achieve, but also the range of scores that should be considered at risk.

How Was *DIBELS* Next Created?

DIBELS were initially developed to extend Curriculum-Based Measurement (CBM) procedures to early literacy. The assessment procedures known as CBM were created by Deno and colleagues at the Institute for Research and Learning Disabilities at the University of Minnesota (e.g., Deno and Mirkin 1977; Deno 1985; Deno and Fuchs 1987; Shinn 1989). *DIBELS* is the culmination of a program of research and development that began in the late 1980's with a research team at the University of Oregon.

At Dynamic Measurement Group, the authors of *DIBELS* led the research and development of *DIBELS* 6th Edition and now *DIBELS Next*. Many research studies guided the development of *DIBELS Next*, including a benchmark goals study, a passage readability study, and a pilot and beta testing. For more information, visit www.dibels.org.

Some users have asked whether *DIBELS* in the early grades is a strong predictor of whether a student will pass a state's high stakes test. The *DIBELS Next* Composite Score at the end of the year correlates .73–.80 with the *Group Reading Achievement and Diagnostic Evaluation (GRADE)*, a nationally norm-referenced reading assessment. The *DIBELS Next* DORF Words Correct correlates .83–.97 with the Standard 4th Grade Reading Passage used in the National Assessment of Educational Progress (NAEP) 2002 Special Study of Oral Reading. Similar correlations have been found for *DIBELS* 6th Edition with state assessments, including, Arizona, Colorado, Illinois, and Oregon.

Additional Information About *DIBELS Next*

There are several other topics that are important to understanding *DIBELS Next*, including a discussion about why the measures are timed and the importance of standardized and unrehearsed assessment.

The Importance of Fluency

For reading success it is important that a student can perform certain skills automatically and without conscious thought, so she can devote total attention to making meaning. Therefore, we need to know not just whether a student knows letters, sounds, and letter-sound associations, but also whether she can process this information quickly and without a great deal of conscious analysis. *DIBELS* relies on the speed with which a student can perform a task accurately to predict whether the student is at risk for reading failure or on track for reading success.

All of the *DIBELS Next* measures are fluency measures, and the student's responses are timed to measure her ability to rapidly process information while performing a task. Although teachers are accustomed to thinking of fluency as a term associated with reading connected text, in *DIBELS Next*, the term *fluency* is used to indicate whether a student can perform a task associated with early reading quickly enough for it to be automatic and useful in skilled reading.

Predictive Test

DIBELS Next is different from standardized, norm-referenced tests such as the Woodcock-Johnson III assessments that yield percentile ranks and standard scores. Although the designers of *DIBELS Next* have gathered a very large set of data from about 3,800 students in grades K–6, the purpose is to establish predictive benchmarks or indicators of later reading success. *DIBELS Next* indicators are not norm referenced but are empirically derived, criterion-referenced benchmark goals. Once the assessment is given to a student in your school, you will immediately know if the student is at risk by comparing his score to the published benchmark table. You will need to use other types of tests, however, to compare the student to a national normative sample.

Standardized Administration

There are many benefits of using *DIBELS Next*, including the immediate feedback of comparing a student's scores to the published benchmarks. On the other hand, the assessment requires standardized administration in order to yield reliable and valid results: It must be given the same way every time in order for the results to be valid. Students are timed, directions and practice items are given in a standardized way, and corrective feedback is given in a prescribed manner. The purpose of the corrective feedback is to teach the procedure, not to teach the skill. If the student doesn't seem to understand the directions, you can teach him at a later time how to do the task, using materials other than *DIBELS Next*, and then reassess.

It is an administrative challenge to ensure that all teachers and instructional assistants who will be administering *DIBELS Next* have been properly trained and are consistently and accurately using the standardized directions and scoring procedures. In order to assure that *DIBELS Next* is administered and scored correctly, someone in your school should be an expert in scoring and administration, and this "DIBELS Next expert" should oversee the fidelity of the assessment process. Some teachers are not accustomed to administering this type of one-on-one test and find it very difficult not to give students a little extra coaching or time. Deviation from the directions, scoring, or timing prescribed may jeopardize the validity of the data as an accurate predictor of which students are at risk.

Administration Is Timed and Must Be "Cold"

All of the measures are timed and intended to be administered "cold"; that is, the student is not to practice reading or answering using the *DIBELS Next* words or passages before the screening takes place. The reason practice is not permitted is that the assessment is intended to see if students have the skills to perform the tasks without having seen the materials before. All students have the same disadvantage, and the benchmarks have been created using data from students who were seeing the materials for the first time.

DIBELS Next Can Inform Instruction but Is Not Diagnostic

DIBELS Next was not designed to be a diagnostic assessment instrument. In fact, when the authors submitted an earlier version of *DIBELS* for review by the Reading First Assessment Committee, they did not submit it for review as a diagnostic instrument. The score on a *DIBELS Next* indicator, when compared to benchmark scores, simply tells whether the student is on track or requires intervention. The score alone will not make the reason for the deficit clear, but it is possible to gain information from studying the student scoring booklets. Teachers are finding that by carefully analyzing the errors in a student's scoring booklet, they can find patterns in the response errors, which give them specific information useful to planning next steps regarding further diagnostic assessment for intervention instruction.

For example, a kindergarten student who is above benchmark in letter naming probably does not need any additional help in that area. If he is behind in knowing the initial sounds in words, his score will indicate lack of a critical early emerging skill in phonemic awareness.

There is a great deal of confusion about whether analyzing the student scoring booklet for error patterns is using the data diagnostically. It is not. Teachers analyze student writing samples and make decisions about what students may not know based on listening to them read aloud. Every day, we use student work to make decisions about what a student seems to understand and where he might need clarification or additional instruction. Analyzing a *DIBELS Next* student scoring booklet is no different.

Informal Versus Formal Diagnostic Data

The type of information derived from analyzing a *DIBELS Next* student scoring booklet is informal and not equivalent to the thorough exploration of a student's background, history, knowledge, and abilities that is included in a formal diagnostic evaluation. The purposes are completely different.

The purpose of a formal diagnostic evaluation is to determine the underlying processing issues that cause a student to struggle in learning. The types of instruments used to make these determinations are extensive and require a highly trained and skilled evaluator, usually someone with training in psychological testing, to administer an extensive battery of tests and to observe with a careful and experienced eye how a student performs on each test.

The *DIBELS Next* assessment is far too brief to be able to tell why a student is struggling with learning. Its purpose is to see if the student can perform a quick task and then to compare his scores to those of other students who were studied to see their ultimate success at reading. The approach to analyzing the student error patterns recommended in this book would not be appropriate for diagnosing whether a student has dyslexia or a related learning disability. Yet once a student is identified for intervention instruction, teachers need to make judgments about where to begin intervention and which students to place together in a group. Based on a careful analysis of the student's error patterns, teachers can make some observations about:

- Whether he is stable on beginning, ending, and medial sounds (PSF).

- How well he is able to attack CVC words using sound-symbol correspondences with an unknown word (NWF).

- How fluently he is pulling all the skills together in reading a passage (DORF).

The data also tell you which skills are established, and this helps in determining how to avoid wasting time reteaching what a student already knows. Any decisions made based on analyzing the student scoring booklets are best confirmed with additional assessment before placing a student in an intervention group. An effective intervention instructor can tell quite quickly whether a student has mastered a skill or needs instruction at a more basic level. Because intervention groups are typically between three and five students, instructors are better able to observe which students are responding to questions with correct or incorrect answers.

In addition to the intervention instructor's observations, frequent progress monitoring serves as a feedback loop about whether students are grouped appropriately and if the instruction is helping each student make progress. If the progress monitoring assessments show that the student is not responding to intervention, first the teacher may try changing the intervention by increasing time, moving the student to a different group, lowering the group size, or changing the type of instruction given. If these changes do not work, the teacher can decide whether to continue intervention or recommend the student for more extensive testing to diagnose the problem, including exploring the possibility of a learning disability.

What Research Has Validated the Effectiveness of *DIBELS Next*?

There is an expansive body of research that has informed the design, development, and revisions of *DIBELS* for more than 15 years. The best way to learn about this research base is to go to the *DIBELS* Web site (www.dibels.org) and click "Publications and Presentations."

Benefits of Using *DIBELS Next*

DIBELS Next is most effective when there is a sense of urgency about improving reading in a school and screening is embedded in a setting where early identification leads to intervention instruction to prevent reading problems. One of the most important benefits of adopting *DIBELS Next* in a school is that it focuses teachers on very important practices in early reading. Some additional benefits include focusing teachers' and administrators' attention on the following key points:

- The importance of early identification and intervention.

- The benefits of using data to inform instruction.

- The importance of implementing small-group instruction to meet the needs of struggling readers.

- The necessity for the teaching team to monitor the effectiveness of the core reading program in instructing all students.

- The vital nature of the five essential components of reading instruction.

- The key stages of skills development in early reading development: from phonemic awareness to alphabetic principle, phonics, vocabulary, and oral language; the fluent and accurate reading of connected text; and comprehension.

- The philosophy of establishing goals for all students reaching grade level and then being held accountable for constant improvement toward this goal.

Potential Areas of Confusion

Sometimes there are questions about whether using *DIBELS Next* encourages teachers to teach only the skills that are assessed. Clearly, teachers do need to teach a broader range of skills than just the skills measured by *DIBELS Next*. For example, students who show deficiency in Letter Naming Fluency should work not only on letter matching, formation, and naming, but on alphabetizing skills if those are also lacking. If students show a deficit in Phoneme Segmentation Fluency, teachers must ensure that students can both blend and segment phonemes in words, even though *DIBELS Next* measures only segmenting. In fact, it's beneficial for students to be able to auditorily manipulate syllables and onset-rime units in addition to phonemic units. If students show a deficit in Nonsense Word Fluency, teachers need to ensure that students can read both real and pseudowords, and they must include instruction for accurate and fluent reading of words in their intervention groups. They also need to teach many phonic patterns beyond the ones that are assessed in NWF. Some reading of connected text should also be included, and, in some cases, students will need help with spelling, a skill not measured by *DIBELS Next*.

It must also be kept in mind that small-group intervention instruction is always in addition to the core, comprehensive reading program instruction. Instruction during intervention time does focus only on one or two skills at a time. Because of this, it's essential that students are still present for instruction in the remaining five essential components of reading instruction during the core reading program time. For example, while a kindergarten student is receiving extra help in phonemic awareness in an intervention group, it's critical that he also participates in instruction on reading comprehension during a read-aloud story. Although *DIBELS Next* does not measure some skills that are essential to fluent reading, it does measure the most important early reading skills that have been shown to be necessary for students to read at grade level by the end of third grade. The reading skills of verbal reasoning, prediction, inference, and so on, tend to be higher-level skills that are covered in the core reading curriculum. Spelling and writing skills are important adjuncts to reading comprehension but are not assessed during screening.

The intent of *DIBELS Next* is to sample only the critical early reading skills that predict successful reading, including comprehension, by the end of third grade. It does not attempt to access all the skills that constitute a complete reading program. That is why a core, comprehensive reading program is an essential tool for the classroom and why teachers need a strong professional development experience to keep the "big picture" in mind.

Uses of *DIBELS Next* Data

DIBELS Next is an assessment instrument that measures how successfully a student is progressing in achieving critical milestones along the way to proficient reading. This tool assesses several early reading skills and uses the student's status in these areas to predict how likely it is that he will read fluently. A student's score in each skill falls into one of three levels—benchmark, at risk of reading difficulty, or somewhere in between. These three levels indicate whether the student's skill is developing on track at a given time, compared to the scores of a large pool of students in the same grade. Yet identifying whether a single student is at benchmark is not the only use for data from this assessment instrument.

DIBELS Next has three primary uses:

1. It is a screening instrument that determines whether all the major skills are in place for a student to read on grade level.

2. It offers progress monitoring assessments that measure whether a student is moving toward critical goals with the core—and in some cases also intervention—instruction being provided.

3. It is used as an outcome assessment that measures the effectiveness of a school's reading instructional program.

In practice, the data are used for many more purposes. For example, principals use *DIBELS Next* data for these reasons:

- To examine reading progress of their school over time.

- To observe whether the lowest readers are improving at the same pace as the highest readers.

- To follow progress of the school's intervention program in closing the gap for struggling readers.

- To question the effectiveness of the core reading curriculum in helping all students achieve reading goals.

> *As a school and as a district, we use* DIBELS Next *data to look at growth or lack thereof. Where we see growth, we know that what we are doing is working and should be continued. Where there is a lack of growth, we analyze factors that we can control: curriculum, instruction, materials, time, group size, and sometimes attendance. We then create a plan of action for improvement.*
>
> Reading Coach

District administrators use *DIBELS Next* data to evaluate district needs for professional development and district staffing needs for reading coaches and specialists. Having an assessment tool and this type of data helps administrators drive reading reform at the building level and can be invaluable in establishing district and school goals for yearly progress in early reading outcomes for students. The data can become a centerpiece of district conversations with principals about their building goals, interim successes in implementing early intervention programs, and identifying additional needs to continue improvements. When administrators have data that indicate success in getting students off to a strong start in reading, they are better able to hold schools accountable for this all-important goal of the early elementary years.

While data from *DIBELS Next* are important for principals and administrators, this book focuses on how teachers can use the data to make informed decisions about students. Teachers are increasingly finding the information in the benchmark and progress monitoring student scoring booklets useful for determining students' error patterns and planning intervention instruction.

Cautions About Inappropriate Uses of *DIBELS* Next Data

Two inappropriate uses of the data are to decide to retain a student based on his *DIBELS Next* scores or to use the data to determine grades on report cards. Retention generally does not solve a reading problem. For too long, there has been a misperception that retaining a struggling reader will give him the "gift of time." The better alternative is to use the data to intervene aggressively and to keep changing the intensity of the instruction until it is right and the student is on track to reach those critical reading milestones. For more information on retention, see the position statement published by the National Association of School Psychologists (www.nasponline.org/about_nasp/pospaper_graderetent.aspx).

Chapter 3

Understanding the DIBELS Next® Indicators

> DIBELS Next® *provides educators with a reliable and efficient tool through which to identify student needs in basic early literacy skills.*
>
> Curriculum Specialist, Regional Office of Education

The purpose of this chapter is to provide information on each indicator so that readers are prepared to interpret the data in later chapters. The purpose is not to teach how to administer and score the assessment; the best print resource on administration and scoring is the *DIBELS Next Assessment Manual*, which is available from Cambium Learning® Sopris (www.soprislearning.com). This chapter is organized into the following sections:

- List of top ten changes from 6th Edition to *DIBELS Next*.

- Changes in *DIBELS Next* that affect more than one indicator.

- Information on each of the *DIBELS Next* indicators.

- Background information on the *DIBELS Next* Composite Score.

- Overview of the more consistent readability of *DIBELS Next* passages.

Top Ten Changes From the 6th Edition to *DIBELS Next*

While working with schools that have used *DIBELS®* previously and are transitioning to *DIBELS Next*, the changes that I believe are the most notable appear in the list below in **order of significance**.

1. All new oral reading fluency passages that have more consistent readability levels.

2. Creation of a Composite Score where the weighting of the indicators is apparent and assessors can calculate the score manually. The Composite Score replaces the instructional recommendation levels, which were calculated by a data management system or could also be calculated based on look-up tables that were publicly available for download.

3. Consolidation of Oral Reading Fluency (ORF) score and Retell into one measure called *DIBELS* Oral Reading Fluency (DORF), which also incorporates an accuracy score.

4. Change in instructions for Nonsense Word Fluency (NWF) to encourage reading whole words.

5. Replacement of the kindergarten measure Initial Sound Fluency (ISF) with another early phonemic awareness measure called First Sound Fluency (FSF).

6. Stratification of items on the probes so that easy, medium, and hard items occur in the same places on every probe.

7. Phoneme Segmentation Fluency (PSF) dropped after the beginning of first grade (previously it continued to be assessed at the middle and end of first grade).

8. Scoring of First Sound Fluency (FSF) awards students 2 points for producing a single individual phoneme at the beginning of a word and 1 point for an initial combination of sounds.

9. Narrative and Expository passages tailored by grade level (two-thirds narrative in grades 1 through 3, and two-thirds expository in grades 4 through 6) and carefully distributed triads for difficulty as well as text type.

10. Student-friendly fonts for Letter Naming Fluency (LNF), NWF, and DORF passages through grade 2.

Changes From the 6th Edition That Affect More Than One Indicator

New Probes and Directions: All of the student probes for every measure are new in *DIBELS Next*. Additionally, the directions that the administrator reads to the student, along with the practice items, are completely new.

Easier-to-Follow Format of Student Materials: The formatting of items in the student materials has changed through several means. In the downloadable version, there are now lines under the rows in LNF and NWF or alternating color blocks for rows in the printed version. There is a cursor, or arrowhead, to the left of the first item directing the student where to start on the page and the direction in which to proceed.

More Student-Friendly Font: In LNF, NWF, and DORF Levels 1 and 2, the Times font has been replaced with a font that looks more like what students are accustomed to seeing in text. Additionally an "early reader font" is used in NWF and in passages for grades 1 and 2.

More Emphasis on Analysis of Patterns of Errors: At the bottom of each scoring sheet, except FSF, there are check boxes for the assessor to note whether the student made any of the typical response patterns for that indicator.

Overview of Terms and Concepts That Are New in *DIBELS Next*

Several terms and concepts that are new in *DIBELS Next* are listed here, along with a brief explanation of each.

- **Stratification**. Stratification is a term used to explain an approach the research team employed for arranging items on a page so that the student sees a mixture of easier and harder items within a row, or short number of items. While under development the items were first placed in categories by the level of difficulty. Then, they were randomly selected from a category and arranged in a pattern on the assessment probe. For example, in NWF, the nonsense words were divided into difficulty categories based on the specific pattern of vowels and consonants, and also on the relative difficulty of categories. This ensures that each probe is of approximately equivalent difficulty.

- **Composite Score** (discussed in more detail later). In brief, the Composite Score is a number that compiles the important measures assessed at that time into a single score. It is used to compare one consolidated number with a goal in order to see if a student is overall where they need to be when taking all the measures together. The Composite Score helps us answer the question, "Is this student on track to become a successful reader?"

- **Refined Benchmark Goals**. The Benchmark Goal is the number that is the bare minimum acceptable score to be considered "passing." The *DIBELS* authors define them as "empirically derived, criterion-referenced target scores that represent adequate reading progress" (Dynamic Measurement Group 2010b). The Benchmark Goal defines the skill level a student should achieve at each assessment period so that she is likely to reach the Benchmark Goal on the next indicators up the Learning to Read progression (see *Figure 3.1*). The Benchmark Goal in *DIBELS Next* is established so that students will achieve the 40th percentile or above on the *Group Reading Assessment and Diagnostic Evaluation* (*GRADE*) and will be at or above benchmark on subsequent *DIBELS* assessments. The *DIBELS* goals were based on research using scores for 3,816 kindergarten through sixth-grade students administered the *DIBELS Next* assessment during the 2009–2010 school year. About one-third of those participants were also given the *GRADE* outcome measure as a comparison. The pool included students who were normally progressing as well as some who were struggling.

Figure 3.1

Learning to Read Progression

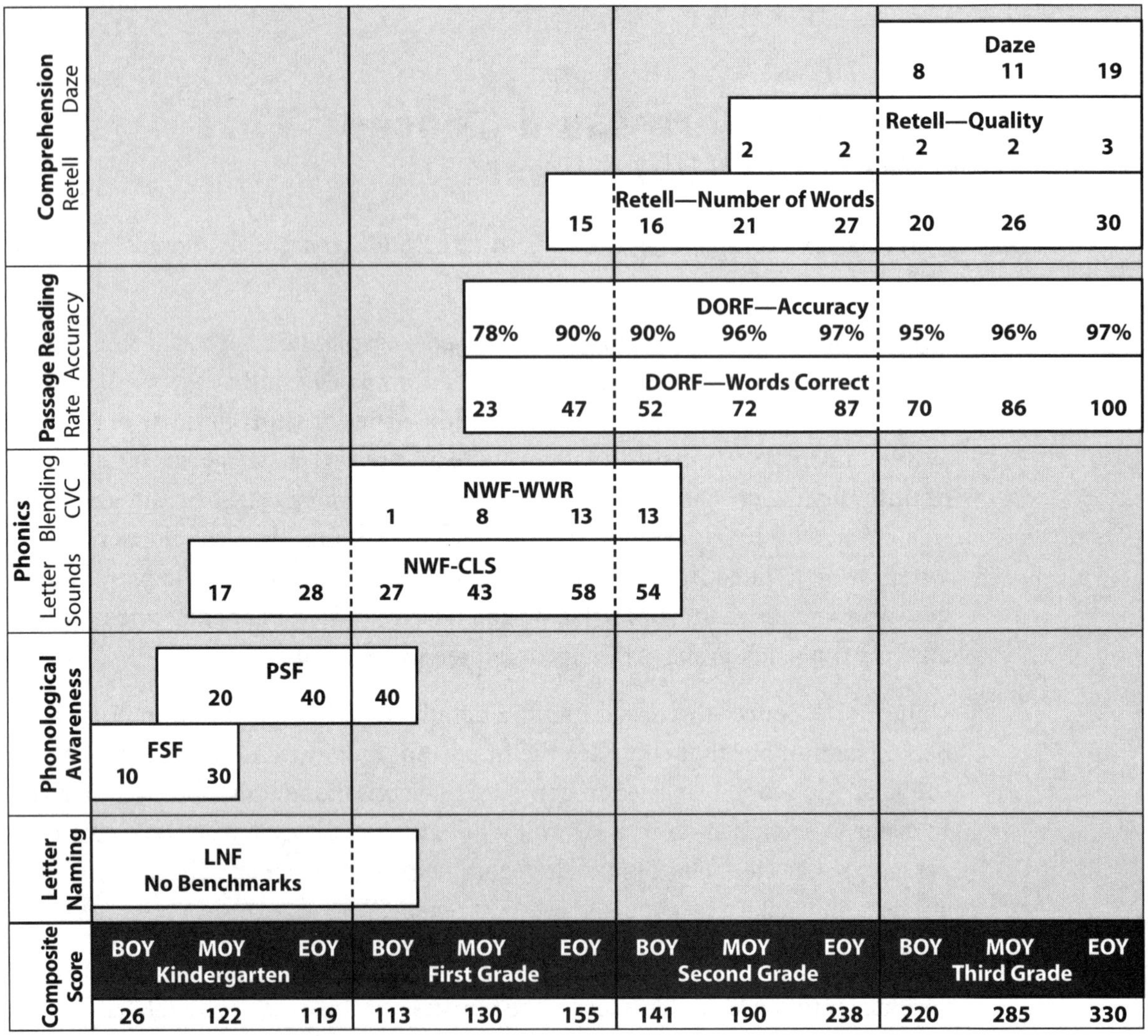

		Kindergarten		First Grade			Second Grade			Third Grade		
		BOY	MOY	EOY	BOY	MOY	EOY	BOY	MOY	EOY	BOY	MOY	EOY
Comprehension — Daze											8	11	19
Retell—Quality									2	2	2	2	3
Retell—Number of Words							15	16	21	27	20	26	30
Passage Reading — DORF—Accuracy						78%	90%	90%	96%	97%	95%	96%	97%
DORF—Words Correct						23	47	52	72	87	70	86	100
Phonics — NWF-WWR (Blending CVC)					1	8	13	13					
NWF-CLS (Letter Sounds)			17	28	27	43	58	54					
Phonological Awareness — PSF			20	40	40								
FSF		10	30										
Letter Naming — LNF	No Benchmarks												
Composite Score		26	122	119	113	130	155	141	190	238	220	285	330

Numbers equal Benchmark Goals as of this printing.

- **Cut Points for Risk**. The Cut Point for Risk is the score below which the student is unlikely to be successful in reaching the next Benchmark Goal. The student may need intensive instruction if his score falls below the Cut Point level where the odds are only 10%–20% that he will score at the Benchmark Goal level on the next benchmark assessment. All scores between the Benchmark Goal and the Cut Point for Risk are considered in need of strategic support. All of the *DIBELS* indicators, as well as the Composite Scores, "represent a conditional probability of a student meeting a later reading outcome" (Dynamic Measurement Group 2010e). Students at or above benchmark level enjoy odds in their favor of making the next goal up the learning to read progression. Students below a Cut Point for Risk are unlikely to make the next Benchmark Goal without intervention. Students whose scores fall in between the Cut Point for Risk and the Benchmark Goals are harder to predict—this group of students may need strategic instruction.

Information on Each *DIBELS* Next Indicator

In this section, each indicator is discussed in more detail. This discussion is divided into the following sections:

- What Has Changed From the 6th Edition

- Skill Measured by Indicator

- Measurement Approach

- Scoring Procedures

- Notes or Observations About This Indicator

First Sound Fluency (FSF)

What Has Changed From the 6th Edition?

First Sound Fluency (FSF) is a new measure in *DIBELS Next*, and it replaces the Initial Sound Fluency (ISF) indicator in previous editions. FSF is easier to administer than ISF because it is no longer necessary to start and stop a stopwatch and there are no pictures. In the 6th Edition the student had to remember the names of four pictures on a page and could point to, or say, the word that began with the target sound. Many educators believed that this format was difficult for some young students because they had to remember the names of the pictures, which sometimes were called something other than the name that was familiar to them (e.g., couch versus sofa). The authors share data to show that FSF may be more predictive than ISF, as follows:

- FSF is more strongly correlated (.502) with PSF than was ISF (.401).

- FSF is more strongly correlated (.544) with NWF than was ISF (.492).

- FSF is more strongly correlated (.45) with CTOPP than was ISF (.33).

(Sources: *DIBELS Next® Technical Manual* for FSF and *6th Edition Technical Report #6* for ISF, DMG.)

One possible reason for this improvement in validity may be because the student has to produce an answer rather than just being able to point to a picture. Kindergarten teachers appreciate being able to use a timer rather than a stopwatch since the stop and start feature that was required to administer ISF is now replaced with continuous 1-minute timing in FSF. Additionally, this change should minimize the timing inconsistency from one assessor to another of turning a stopwatch on and off throughout the minute.

Skill Measured by FSF

FSF measures early phonemic awareness. Specifically, it measures a student's fluency in isolating and identifying the initial sound, or sounds, in words.

Measurement of FSF

The assessor orally provides one word at a time and the student is asked to say the first sound in that word. The format is similar to PSF in that the assessor says a word and the student gives a verbal response without any text or manipulatives, except the task is to give only the first sound rather than segment all the sounds in the word. A table is provided in the student scoring booklet with all possible answers and the assessor circles one of the options provided or slashes a zero if the student responds incorrectly or doesn't say anything. The assessor continues providing one word at a time until the end of 1 minute.

Scoring Procedures for FSF

The possible answers listed in the student scoring booklet are arranged in a table under two columns: a 1-point column and a 2-point column. The student receives full credit (2 points) if she says solely the initial sound correctly within 3 seconds. Partial credit (1 point) is earned if within 3 seconds she says the first sound plus adds the next sound or sounds. Depending on the word, there may be one to three options for earning 1 point:

- Initial consonant plus a vowel

- Consonant blend

- Consonant blend plus the vowel sound

There is no credit if the student does not correctly provide the first sound, adds an incorrect sound attached to a correct initial sound, repeats the whole word, or doesn't respond within 3 seconds. The assessor totals the points as:

$$\text{Total Score} = (\text{number of 2-point responses}) \times 2 + (\text{number of 1-point responses})$$

Notes or Observations About FSF

All three of the practice items are concrete three-sound nouns (*man, moon, sun*) that should be in the oral language of kindergarten students. Yet not all assessment items are concrete nouns. Some of the test words are verbs (*laughed, knock, rang, hide, blame, peek, thank, clang, plow, steal*) and inanimate concepts (*mild, peace, sad*). Including verbs and concepts may not be an issue for most students as long as the words are familiar to kindergarten students. However, it's possible that English language learners will be less likely to know some of the conceptual words than concrete nouns. A student would be able to segment the initial sound of an unfamiliar word, yet this task may be more difficult when holding an unknown word in working memory long enough to isolate and name the first sound.

Another observation is that teachers will need to consider the score carefully because the ability to segment merely the initial sound is a more complex skill than clustering other sounds with it. My recommendation to teachers is to study the student scoring booklet to note what portion of the score was earned from 1-point answers versus 2-point answers. It's possible that a student could go quickly enough to make the benchmark score yet be unable to isolate just the first sound, especially in the fall when the benchmark is 10 versus in the winter when it's 30. It is still possible to reach the winter benchmark score of 30 by giving all 1-point responses with an average pace of a response every 2 seconds. Especially for this measure, looking at the data and not simply the score will be important. Pulling the initial sound from the consonants or vowels that follow is an important skill for reading and spelling. A student who consistently provides just the initial sound and receives 2 points has mastered initial sound isolation. A student who provides more than just the beginning sound, even though they may have a benchmark score, still needs more instruction on this skill. Also, when students get to the PSF measure, they will need to be able to segment each sound.

When scoring the FSF measure, if the student adds a schwa sound (/ŭh/) to an initial consonant, it is not counted as an error. This may be confusing to teachers since many have been taught that it's important to teach students to isolate a sound without adding a schwa (e.g., /p/ instead of /pŭh/). Also, teachers may have been taught that blends stay together and find it confusing that there are 2 sounds in a consonant blend (e.g., /s/ and /t/ instead of /st/).

Letter Naming Fluency (LNF)

What Has Changed From the 6th Edition?

There are four major changes in LNF from the 6th Edition to *DIBELS Next*:

1. The font used may be easier for young students to recognize all the letters.

2. The letters are arranged intentionally so that easier, medium, and harder letters are strategically mixed in an approach the *DIBELS* team refers to as *stratification*.

3. All 26 upper- and lowercase letters appear before any are repeated.

4. Benchmark Goals and Cut Points for Risk are not provided by the research team (at time of this publication).

In response to teacher comments from previous editions, the font of the letters has been changed so that it is more student friendly. The assessment no longer has the Times font recognition difficulty for the letters *g*, *q*, or *a*, which were easy for adults to recognize, but some teachers felt were less familiar to young students. The probe still contains a mixture of upper- and lowercase letters.

Letters are categorized into three groups based on whether they are easier, medium, or harder to learn. Then one letter was randomly selected from each category to place as every third letter. This way, there cannot be any disproportionate number of easier or harder letters anyplace in the assessment. All letters are mixed throughout the probe so that no matter how far the students read during the minute, they are presented a mixture of letter difficulty.

Perhaps the most significant change is that, as of the date of publication of this book, the research team is not presenting Benchmark Goals for LNF. With the 6th Edition, teachers were provided benchmarks that were determined as the 40th and 20th percentiles for students in the data system at one point in time. No progress monitoring probes were provided because LNF was used as a risk indicator and not an instructional goal. In *DIBELS Next*, there are no LNF progress monitoring probes, Benchmark Goals, or Cut Points for Risk. The decision to not provide Benchmark Goals is going to be difficult for teachers to accept because they are accustomed to knowing an expected level of performance on a skill that is important enough to assess. However, in conversations with DMG, they have shared that they continue to examine the data on LNF, and it's important to check the DMG Web site to see if there are any changes since the publication of this book. Although DMG did not initially release a benchmark score, teachers will quickly realize that it's possible to assume a level of performance for letter naming by backing into it from the Composite Score. It will be tempting to consider a derived goal as the necessary benchmark for this skill and to work with kindergarten students to make sure they make this level.

There are some reasons that it's problematic to use a derived Benchmark Goal for LNF and dedicating instructional time to helping students reach this level so they will reach benchmark in the Composite Score. First, the mid-year letter-naming goal would be incredibly high. Column A in *Table 3.1* shows a derivation of the benchmark LNF score if all indicators other than LNF are exactly at the Benchmark Goal level. The derived benchmark level for LNF at the middle of kindergarten would be 55 letter names in a minute. This goal compares to the 6th Edition level of 27 letter names at midyear and 40 at year-end. This is unrealistically high, and teachers shouldn't be working toward this goal at the middle of the year. Second, considering 55 letter names as the goal can be misleading. LNF doesn't have to be that high if the phonemic awareness measures are stronger. In columns B and C of *Table 3.1*, examples are provided showing that when students score higher in other areas, the LNF score doesn't have to be at as high of a level.

Table 3.1

Analysis of LNF Benchmark Goals from Composite Scores

| | Kindergarten | | | | | | | | | Grade 1 | | |
| | Beginning | | | Middle | | | End | | | Beginning | | |
	A	B	C	A	B	C	A	B	C	A	B	C
FSF	**10**	14	18	**30**	35	40						
PSF				**20**	25	30	**40**	45	50	**40**	42	44
NWF CLS				**17**	22	27	**28**	30	32	**27**	30	32
Subtotal	**10**	14	18	**67**	82	97	**68**	75	82	**67**	72	76
Composite Score	**26**	26	26	**122**	122	122	**119**	119	119	**113**	113	113
LNF (calculated from scores above)	**16**	12	8	**55**	40	25	**51**	44	37	**46**	41	37

As demonstrated in columns B and C in *Table 3.1*, if a student's other scores are only a few points higher, the LNF score needed to reach exactly the benchmark level for the Composite Score declines quickly. This is why deriving a score for LNF and using it as a Benchmark Goal is not recommended by myself or by DMG.

Skill Measured by LNF

The interpretation of which skill is measured in the LNF indicator is very intriguing. On the surface, it's quite simple. The indicator measures the student's ability to accurately and fluently name letters, yet interpreting what it means is much more complex. The authors of *DIBELS* have consistently sent messages to teachers that LNF is a strong predictor of later reading risk. Many researchers have repeatedly shown that assessing letter naming fluency is a powerfully significant predictor of later reading ability. The reasons behind its predictability are harder to clarify. Some suggest that letter naming may actually be measuring important factors such as preschool preparation, the parent's involvement in the student's education, or other things. Because of its predictive capability, LNF is included in the composite calculation in all the time periods in which it is measured; that is, in all three periods of kindergarten plus the beginning of the year in first grade.

As previously mentioned, at the time of publication of this book DMG does not publish Benchmark Goals or Cut Points for Risk for LNF. Their rationale for not providing them is that letter naming is not a basic early literacy skill because it's possible to learn to read without naming letters. Dynamic Measurement Group (2011b) writes on their Web site under DIBELS FAQs, "LNF has always been used as an indicator of risk rather than an instructional target." DMG feels that teaching letter names is beneficial; however, teaching them will not guarantee reading. Teaching the other skills, such as phoneme segmentation and letter-sound correspondence, leads to better reading. It's a difference that affects decisions about priorities of instructional goals. DMG also is examining letter naming again and there may be some changes in the future. Please check their Web site to see if there are any changes on this measure.

Measurement of LNF

LNF is perhaps the simplest *DIBELS Next* indicator to administer. Students view a page with 11 rows containing 10 letters each. They are asked to name the letters going across the rows. At the end of 1 minute, the assessor draws a bracket to show where the student finished.

Scoring Procedures for LNF

Scoring LNF is also simple. The assessor calculates the total number of correct letters named in 1 minute. There is a checklist in the student scoring booklet to note error patterns.

Notes or Observations About LNF

Although the *DIBELS* authors suggest that it is not essential for students to know letter names to learn to read, they recognize that students may benefit from knowing letter names. While learning letter names may not be essential for learning to read, students benefit from knowing letter names because so many names incorporate the letter sound, thereby assisting in learning letter-sound correspondences. Additionally, students would find it nearly impossible to absorb instruction in a classroom without knowing letter names because they are used in many ways, including the oral dictation of how to spell a word. The extent to which students learned letters in preschool and kindergarten may indicate they are more prepared and perhaps more successful in learning other reading skills. I advocate that if a student is lacking letter naming, instruction should be provided. However, the derived mid-year benchmark of 55 letter names per minute at mid-kindergarten should not be viewed as an expected level of performance on this skill because it is unrealistically high.

Phoneme Segmentation Fluency (PSF)

What Has Changed From the 6th Edition?

The changes to PSF from the 6th Edition are less visible. All the probes are new and were constructed in a different way. One evident change is that, in *DIBELS Next*, PSF is not given in the middle and end of first grade. Assessment starts at the same time, which is the middle of kindergarten. PSF is administered only three time periods instead of five. The difference in assessment periods is shown in *Table 3.2*.

Table 3.2

Difference in Assessment Periods for the Administration of PSF

Administration of PSF	Kindergarten			Grade 1		
	Beginning	Middle	End	Beginning	Middle	End
DIBELS Next		X	X	X		
DIBELS, 6th Edition		X	X	X	X	X

The research team says that the reason for the change is that they want teachers to focus on teaching alphabetic principle rather than phonemic awareness after the beginning of first grade. Sometimes when students have mastered phonemic awareness and moved on to reading text, their PSF scores can dip at the middle and end of first grade. Although the authors decided to remove PSF from the benchmark screening for the middle and end of first grade, it is still necessary to assess phonemic awareness skills of students who are receiving intervention instruction in phonemic awareness. This can be done by using PSF progress monitoring probes.

Another change is that the assessment items are now stratified by level of difficulty, similar to other *DIBELS Next* indicators. Words with the consonant-vowel-consonant (CVC) pattern that start with continuant sounds (e.g., /s/, /m/, /n/) are easier than those that start with stop sounds (e.g., /p/, /t/). CVC words are easier than those that start or end with blends. The difficulty of the probes was also managed by careful placement of where the words with more phonemes (up to five phonemes) appear, as well as how many of each appear in a probe.

The directions have also been changed slightly, particularly in the feedback to the practice word. In the 6th Edition, the assessor told students that they would say a word and that the student was expected to tell all the sounds in the word. Then the assessor modeled by segmenting the name *Sam* into the three sounds: /s/ /ă/ /m/. In *DIBELS Next*, the assessor starts out telling the student that they are going to say all the sounds in words. The assessor then models with the word *fan*. When the student is given feedback, it is now more explicit. If the student gives the correct response for the first practice word, *soap*, the assessor says, "Very good saying all the sounds in *soap*." Additionally, the directions now include modeling a four-phoneme word (*jump*).

Skill Measured by PSF

PSF measures a student's accuracy and fluency in segmenting a spoken word into sounds. The best score will be obtained when the student segments each sound. For example, in the word *sand*, when all four sounds are pronounced correctly, the student receives 4 points. However, if the student says three sounds, /s/ /ă/ /nd/, he earns only 3 points because the final consonant blend wasn't broken into its two sounds. The goal is for the student to develop the ability to segment every sound. When a student can do this, he is better prepared to substitute sounds, such as in the following task: Say *sand*. Change /s/ to /h/. What's the new word? (*hand*)

Measurement of PSF

When administering the PSF indicator, the assessor says a word and asks the student to say all the sounds in the word. The assessor underlines each correct sound segment the student says in the word. A sound segment is defined as any different, correct part of the word. Incorrect answers are slashed. The scoring directions indicate to circle whole words that the student repeats without segmenting. Write "sc" above any errors that were marked wrong and then self-corrected within 3 seconds.

Scoring Procedures for PSF

The student earns 1 point for each different, correct part of the word. Upon completion of administering the measure, the assessor calculates the points across each row and then adds the points down the column to get a total score.

Notes or Observations About PSF

PSF is perhaps the indicator that has changed the least from the 6th Edition to *DIBELS Next*.

Nonsense Word Fluency (NWF)

What Has Changed From the 6th Edition?

The most significant change from the 6th Edition to *DIBELS Next* is that the directions have been changed so students know that reading pseudowords blended as whole words is preferable. The student is instructed to read the word. In the directions, the student is told if she can't read the whole word to say any sounds that she knows. The name of the measure for blended words was changed from Words Read Correctly (WRC) to Whole Words Read (WWR), and the score is calculated differently than before.

Skill Measured by NWF

There are actually two skills measured in the NWF indicator: letter-sound correspondence and basic phonics. Starting with the 6th Edition Revised, NWF included the calculation of two scores: Correct Letter Sounds (CLS) and Words Read Correctly (WRC). For quite some time, there wasn't a Benchmark Goal for the WRC and then, for a while, the "best guess target" of 15 was released. Now the Benchmark Goal is derived and increases from 1 to 8 to 13 across time periods. In *DIBELS Next*, WRC has become WWR, which stands for Whole Words Read. WWR is a measure of the number of words a student reads blended without sounding out the phonemes. CLS measures letter-sound correspondence, and WWR measures blending or recoding of sounds into words. WWR is an important skill and accounts for a variance in performance where a student knows letter sounds (CLS) but struggles with blending words. When a student's oral reading fluency is low at the end of grade 1 or beginning of grade 2, the WWR score will help pinpoint whether that student is proficient at blending two- and three-sound words with short vowels.

Measurement of NWF

The student views a page with vowel-consonant (VC) and consonant-vowel-consonant pseudowords (CVC). The assessor marks in the student scoring booklet how the student decodes these syllables. When the student reads the letters sound by sound, each correct letter is underlined separately. If the student blends sounds, a continuous line is drawn to connect the letters representing those sounds. Any letters read incorrectly are slashed. Any words read entirely correctly as a whole word are marked by an underline completely under the word. To get credit for a WWR, the student must read the word accurately and automatically the first time she attempts it without sounding out the phonemes (not even under her breath). Remember, for a response to count as a WWR, it must be the word, the whole word, and nothing but the word!

Scoring Procedures for NWF

The assessor presents the student with a page of pseudowords and marks what the student says using standardized scoring procedures. Then two scores are counted from the scored page. When counting the CLS score, the student receives 1 point for each letter-sound correspondence read correctly, whether it's underlined separately or within a longer line for two sounds or the entire word. When counting the WWR score, the student receives 1 point for each blended word read where all sounds in the word are correct and the whole word was read without first saying the sounds. If a student read the letters *v-o-b* as *vob*, the answer will add 3 points to his CLS calculation as well as 1 point for the WWR calculation.

Notes or Observations About NWF

NWF is like Cinderella. It is the most criticized and downtrodden indicator, yet it is perhaps the most useful one for the early grades. It is very revealing. When assessing students in kindergarten through second grade, it's very difficult to find VC and CVC words that students will not recognize instantly by sight. When students successfully read these simple closed syllables, it's impossible to know whether they are reading the word as a memorized word they instantly recognize or if they are applying their knowledge of letter-sound correspondences to read the word. NWF is measuring what students will be able to do when they come to syllables they don't already know and have to use their phonics knowledge to decode unfamiliar words. In multisyllable words, the root is a syllable that doesn't stand alone and is not recognizable to some students. Therefore, being able to decode it is a critical skill.

The major limitation is that only VC and CVC patterns are measured in NWF. In order for teachers to examine the developing phonics skills of students, it would be necessary to assess their skills in reading words with other patterns, such as long vowels, vowel teams, and vowel-*r* syllables. Many phonics diagnostic screeners use the pseudoword approach to assess which patterns a student has mastered and which ones are deficit and, therefore, merit intervention instruction, including the phonics screener available from the author's company, 95 Percent Group (see *Phonics Screener for Intervention*™ at www.95percentgroup.com).

DIBELS Oral Reading Fluency (DORF) (Including Retell)

The new passages were written by professional authors to be authentic text students will encounter. There was a set of design specifications for the text that the professional authors followed when writing the text. Following is the list of design specifications, as shown in the *DIBELS Next Technical Manual* (Dynamic Measurement Group 2011b).

Figure 3.2

General Passage Design Specifications for *DIBELS Next* Passages

1. Passages should have a beginning, middle, and end.
2. In narrative passages, proper names should be simple and decodable according to basic phonics rules. Names in first through third grade passages should be no more than two syllables. Names in fourth through sixth grade passages should generally not be more than three syllables. Names should represent diverse cultural, racial, and ethnic groups. In expository passages, avoid unnecessary proper names. Proper names in expository passages should generally appear in grades where those names match the criteria for narrative passages.
3. Passages should be engaging in the first paragraph.
4. Passages should be gentle, positive, and friendly, modeling positive pro-social behaviors (without being preachy). For example, if a passage is about bike-riding, the subject should wear a helmet. Characters should try to be friendly. Conflict should be minimized and reduced, not escalated, e.g., siblings should cooperate.
5. Passages should be sensitive and respectful to all groups and subgroups.
6. Diversity should frequently be incorporated incidentally into passages, including issues of diversity in terms of socio-economic status, disability, race, ethnicity, family structure, background, culture, urban and rural settings, etc.
7. Passages should be grammatically correct, with mature phrasing and conventional sentence structures.
8. Avoid extensive dialogue.
9. Passages should flow rather than being abrupt and staccato. They should follow an easy and engaging sequence. Avoid lists of things, e.g., "I like strawberry, chocolate, peach, and cherry."
10. Avoid repetitive sentence structures, e.g., "He would do this. He would do that. He would do something else."
11. Avoid sad or frightening topics such as natural disasters or third-degree burns.
12. The initial passage set should have a mix of about 40% expository and 60% narrative for first through third grades, and about 60% expository and 40% narrative for fourth through sixth grades.
13. Passages must be factually correct.
14. The first word of the title should not be the same as the first word of the passage.
15. All passages must meet readability criteria for the grade level as measured by the DIBELS Passage Revision Utility, which is software that identifies the target word length, rare words, and sentence length for a passage and provides guidance when a passage is outside of the target ranges specified by the DMG Passage Difficulty Index.

What Has Changed From the 6th Edition?

On my list of the most significant changes from the 6th Edition to *DIBELS Next*, the new passages with more consistent readability levels was listed as the number 1 most important change—this reason alone makes transition to *DIBELS Next* worth the effort. The passages in *DIBELS Next* are all completely new and were field-tested with students. In the research preceding the release of the *DIBELS Next* passages, those that had the largest range of variability in readability level were eliminated or rewritten. Then the best passages that remained were not only empirically leveled but carefully arranged. They were placed in triads of easier, medium, and harder categories and placed in benchmark assessments so that one from each category fell into each benchmark assessment period. This is called stratification.

> *The* DIBELS *seem to be more reliable than the screeners that only require students to read one passage. I have found that for the majority of students, the middle score is an accurate representation of their ability.*
>
> Third-Grade Teacher

Another significant change is that narrative and expository passages were placed more carefully into triads in *DIBELS Next*. In grades 1 through 3, two-thirds of the passages are narrative. The mix is reversed in grades 4 through 6, where two-thirds of the passages are expository. In the 6th Edition, the mixture of narrative and expository text was not specifically defined.

The font for younger grades (grades 1 and 2) was changed to an easier-to-read style.

Skill Measured by DORF

DORF measures a student's fluency at orally reading a passage for 1 minute. In addition to calculating a score for the number of correct words read in a minute, the accuracy of the reading is measured.

Measurement of DORF

The administration procedure for DORF is to listen to a student read a passage orally for 1 minute. It is critical that this reading is what we call a "cold read," meaning that the student does not practice reading it and has never seen the passage before. Words read correctly are left blank, and errors are marked with a slash. Substitutions, omissions, and hesitations of more than 3 seconds are considered errors.

The *DIBELS* team encourages assessors *not* to write in the student scoring booklet what the student says because they want to make sure that the assessor devotes full attention to scoring the passage correctly and is not distracted by trying to record errors. Because my focus is on helping teachers get the most information possible from administering assessments, I encourage teachers to make notes on what the student said if it doesn't interfere with accurate scoring. In my experience, the majority of students who read below benchmark are reading slowly enough that it's possible to record errors.

At the end of reading for 1 minute, the assessor marks a bracket to note the last word read before the end of the minute. Since the assessor is only marking errors, the bracket is necessary to know how far a student got before time was up.

Scoring Procedures for DORF

The scoring of DORF is calculated as follows:

$$\text{Words Correct} = \text{total words read minus errors}$$

$$\text{Accuracy Rate} = 100 \times \frac{\text{median words correct}}{\text{median words correct} + \text{median errors}}$$

Notes or Observations About DORF

The field testing of the passages will make a significant difference for *DIBELS Next* since there were many specific passages in the 6th Edition that were lightning rods for teacher criticism. The investment in writing new passages and field-testing them will quiet much of this criticism.

Retell

Retell is now a part of DORF. It is not a separate indicator and is now called Retell and not Retell Fluency (RTF).

What Has Changed From 6th Edition?

The most significant change in Retell is that it is required and is included as one of the scores in the DORF indicator. It is no longer a separate measure that can be skipped. If a student reads less than 40 words on a passage, it's up to the assessor to determine whether to ask the student to provide a retell. In *DIBELS Next*, there is a separate Benchmark Goal for Retell.

One of the other changes in Retell is that the assessor also determines a score for the quality of response on a rating scale of 1 to 4. This is new in this edition, and may give teachers a way to record even more information while listening to the student's retelling of the passage.

Skill Measured by Retell

Retell is one approach to measuring a student's reading comprehension. DORF and Retell combined measure the following skills:

- Advanced phonics and word attack skills

- Accurate and fluent reading of connected text

- Reading comprehension

In Retell, the student talks about what she has just read. She is not asked to summarize or identify the main idea. Those are different skills than retell. The retell approach to measuring comprehension is equally applicable to narrative and expository text. The student cannot guess the answer to a question based on vocabulary, background knowledge about a topic, or general reasoning skills as she might be able to do when presented with a specific set of questions.

The purpose of assessing comprehension after an oral reading fluency assessment is to identify any students who decode without understanding what they've read. An additional benefit is that it signals to students that they should be reading for meaning. A teacher once told me that a student asked, "Do you want me to read for speed or to be able to tell you what I have read?" By adding Retell as a required procedure, students should never again confuse oral reading fluency with speed reading. With the new quality rating scale in *DIBELS Next*, the assessor will also be noting the quality of a student's retell.

Measurement of Retell

While the student is talking about what she read, the assessor draws a line through numbers on a line to estimate the quantity of words in the retell. The assessor makes a judgment about whether what the student is saying relates to the text just read and will discontinue counting words if the student veers away from talking about what was in the passage.

Scoring Procedures for Retell

There will be two scores from Retell. The first score is an estimate of the number of words a student said in the retell about what was read. The second score is a number, 1 through 4, to indicate the quality of the retell. *Table 3.3* describes the scoring for retell quality.

Table 3.3

Quality of Retell Scoring Rubric

Score	Number of Details	Sequence of Ideas	Main Idea
1	2 or fewer		
2	3 or more		
3	3 or more	In meaningful sequence	
4	3 or more	In meaningful sequence	Captures main idea

Notes or Observations About Retell

There will be some teachers who may express concern about why Retell is now required. There are two common concerns I hear from teachers about the Retell indicator. The first concern is how this way of assessing really measures comprehension. A great deal of communication and explanation will be needed to address their concerns. The second concern is about whether they are measuring it accurately. It's hard to be sure that when you're drawing a line through numbers as a student is talking that the score is accurate. My response is that it's an estimate and not an exact science. Being off a few words will not usually make a difference in whether a student reaches the Benchmark Goal. For more information, this question is addressed on the DMG Web site under "Frequently Asked Questions" and in the *DIBELS Next Technical Manual*, which is also available as a free download at www.soprislearning.com/dibels.

Daze

What Has Changed From the 6th Edition?

The Daze, or *DIBELS* maze measure, is a new measure in *DIBELS Next* that was not part of *DIBELS* in previous editions. Daze is given for grades 3 through 6 based on the maze procedure for assessing comprehension, where the student selects one word from a choice of three words that would make sense in context.

Skill Measured by Daze

According to the *DIBELS Next Assessment Manual*, "The purpose of a maze procedure is to measure the reasoning processes that constitute comprehension" (Dynamic Measurement Group 2011a, p. 109). The *DIBELS* authors list the following processes that are used to construct meaning:

- Word recognition skills

- Background information and prior knowledge about the topic

- Syntax

- Morphology

- Cause and effect reasoning skills

Daze measures comprehension while reading silently and is different from Retell, which is measured after an oral reading rather than a silent reading. The passages included in Daze were written to match the DMG readability criteria, except Daze passages are longer (around 350 to 500 words in grades 3 through 5).

The first sentence in each Daze passage is always left complete. Starting with the second sentence, approximately every seventh word has been replaced with a box that contains the correct word and two distractor words. In composing the assessment, the authors skipped some words and the next word was selected; they skipped words such as proper names, prepositions, articles, and abbreviations.

A computer program developed by DMG selected the test item words (correct answer) and generated two distractor words that were randomly selected from a pool of other words that appeared in the passage. Distractors were checked and replaced if they made sense in the context of the sentence.

The addition of the Daze component is an excellent tool for getting a peek into the thinking process of our students. By analyzing the incorrect answers students choose, we are able to determine if the errors are caused by a decoding issue or a vocabulary issue.

Reading Coach

Measurement of Daze

Daze is the only *DIBELS* measure in which the student writes answers, and takes about 4 minutes to administer, including 1 minute to practice directions plus 3 minutes that students are given to work on the passage. It can be assessed individually or given to a group, including an entire classroom. Students silently read a passage and circle their answers on the paper. Every so often, in place of a word, there is a box with three words listed. The student has to select which of the three words makes the most sense in the context of the sentence and passage. These boxes occur about every seventh word.

Scoring Procedures for Daze

Assessors use an answer key to score this measure. Slash incorrect items, including any items left blank, if they occur before the last item the student reached. Items the student didn't reach are not counted as errors. The Daze score is the total number of circled words that are correct minus half the number of incorrect answers (marked with a slash). Subtracting half the value of the incorrect answers is a procedure to correct for the possibility that the student was correct simply by guessing.

Notes or Observations About Daze

AIMSweb® has used the maze procedure as their comprehension measure. It is interesting that the *DIBELS* team decided to include two measures of comprehension. While they explain that Retell measures comprehension of oral reading and Daze measures comprehension during silent reading, teachers will need to work with the data to be convinced of the value of having two measures, given the additional amount of assessment and scoring time that will be required. Dynamic Measurement Group (2011c) reports a strong correlation between Daze and DORF, as shown in *Table 3.4*.

Table 3.4

Correlation Between Daze and DORF

Grade	Predictive criterion-related validity of DORF (ORF and Retell) at middle of year predicting Daze at end of year
3	.78
4	.79
5	.79
6	.78

DMG has published data showing that the Daze score correlates well with the comprehension subtest of the *GRADE* outcome measure. In grades 3 through 6 at the beginning of the year, the predictive validity coefficients for Daze and *GRADE* are .56–.67. Also at the end of the year, the concurrent validity coefficients between Daze and the *GRADE* comprehension subtest is .64–.68 for grades 3 through 6 (Dynamic Measurement Group 2011c).

DIBELS Next Composite Score

The Composite Score, which is new in *DIBELS Next*, is a single number that compiles and weights the student's performance on the significant indicators measured at that time point. The purpose of the Composite Score is to provide the best estimate of the student's overall early literacy skill or reading proficiency. It is used to determine if, overall, a student appears to be on track or may need some intervention instruction. DMG has conducted extensive research on the Composite Score, including an analysis of how well the Composite Score predicted *GRADE* results versus prediction solely based on DORF Words Correct. What they found was that the Composite Score with Retell explains more variance in reading outcomes than ORF Words Correct alone does. As Dynamic Measurement Group (2011e) explains:

> Across first through sixth grade, the median additional variance explained is 9%, ranging from 3% to 17%, generally with greater additional variance explained in the upper grades. In other words, although DORF Words Correct alone is very good, the *DIBELS* Composite Score is even better in meaningful and important ways.

Composite Scores replace the Instructional Recommendation Levels from *DIBELS*, 6th Edition. Although the purpose of the Composite Score is similar to the Instructional Recommendation Levels, the calculation of the numbers is very different. In the 6th Edition, instructional recommendations were based on look-up tables. In *DIBELS Next*, the assessor can calculate the Composite Scores from materials provided and compare a student's score to the published Benchmark Goal. Most data-management systems will calculate the Composite Score. The Composite Score allows teachers to evaluate whether a student has reached the Benchmark Goal for each separate indicator as well as an overall level of performance represented by the Composite Score. For example, in the middle of the year, a first grade student whose score on DORF Words Correct fell somewhat below benchmark, but whose performance on all the other measures including the accuracy value was high enough, could allow his Composite Score to place him in the benchmark range. Although it's important to evaluate whether the student needs more help with fluency in connected text or sight words, this student may be at less risk overall at this moment than other students whose Composite Scores placed them in the below or well below benchmark range.

> *The Composite Score allows teachers to evaluate whether a student has reached the Benchmark Goal for each separate indicator as well as an overall level of performance represented by the Composite Score.*

At many assessment periods, the Composite Score is a simple addition of each of the scores included for that time of year; yet for some indicators, there are multipliers other than 1. From the beginning of kindergarten through the beginning of first grade, the scores are simply added together. From the middle of first grade onward, there are multipliers that range from 2 to 4 except in one case (passage accuracy), in which it's necessary to look up a value on a table. A discussion of the Composite Score calculation by grade level and time of year for the benchmark screenings is shown in *Tables 3.5* and *3.6* and *Table 3.7* (page 68).

Table 3.5

Composite Score Calculations by Grade and Time Period

Grade	Benchmark Period	Factors Included in Composite Score
Kindergarten	Beginning of year	Simple addition of FSF + LNF
	Middle of year	Simple addition of FSF + LNF + PSF + NWF-CLS
	End of year	Simple addition of LNF + PSF + NWF-CLS
1	Beginning of year	Simple addition of LNF + PSF + NWF-CLS
	Middle of year	(NWF-CLS) + (NWF-WWR) + (DORF Words Correct) + (DORF Accuracy Value)
	End of year	(NWF-WWR × 2) + (DORF Words Correct) + (DORF Accuracy Value)
2	Beginning of year	(NWF-WWR × 2) + (DORF Words Correct) + (DORF Accuracy Value)
	Middle of year	(DORF Words Correct) + (Retell × 2) + (DORF Accuracy Value)
	End of year	(DORF Words Correct) + (Retell × 2) + (DORF Accuracy Value)
3–6	All periods	(DORF Words Correct) + (Retell × 2) + (Daze × 4) + (DORF Accuracy Value)

Table 3.6

Grades K–1 Composite Score Chart

Grade	Time of Year	FSF	LNF	PSF	NWF-CLS	NWF-WWR	DORF Words Correct	DORF Accuracy Value
K	BOY	×1	×1					
	MOY	×1	×1	×1	×1			
	EOY		×1	×1	×1			
1	BOY		×1	×1	×1			
	MOY				×1	×1	×1	×1*
	EOY					×2	×1	×1*

*The DORF Accuracy Value can be found by taking the DORF Accuracy Percent and applying it to a conversion chart.

Table 3.7

Grades 2–6 Composite Score Chart

Grade	Time of Year	NWF-WWR	DORF Words Correct	Accuracy Value	Retell Score	Daze Adjusted Score
2	BOY	×2	×1	×1*		
	MOY		×1	×1*	×2	
	EOY		×1	×1*	×2	
3	BOY		×1	×1*	×2	×4
	MOY		×1	×1*	×2	×4
	EOY		×1	×1*	×2	×4
4	BOY		×1	×1*	×2	×4
	MOY		×1	×1*	×2	×4
	EOY		×1	×1*	×2	×4
5	BOY		×1	×1*	×2	×4
	MOY		×1	×1*	×2	×4
	EOY		×1	×1*	×2	×4
6	BOY		×1	×1*	×2	×4
	MOY		×1	×1*	×2	×4
	EOY		×1	×1*	×2	×4

* The DORF Accuracy Value can be found by taking the DORF Accuracy Percent and applying it to a conversion chart.

There are three interesting areas to discuss in the composite calculation. First is the change in how the two NWF scores are compiled into the Composite Score. Over time, different combinations of the two scores for NWF are factored into the Composite Score. *Table 3.8* shows the NWF scores included in the Composite Score.

Table 3.8

NWF Measures Included in Composite Score

NWF Scores	Kindergarten		Grade 1		Grade 2	
	MOY	EOY	BOY	MOY	EOY	BOY
CLS	×1	×1	×1	×1		
WWR				×1	×2	×2

During the two periods in kindergarten when NWF is given (MOY and EOY), only the CLS score is factored into the Composite Score. That seems appropriate because kindergarten students are not expected to be reading vowel-consonant and consonant-vowel-consonant words blended at that point in time. At the beginning of first grade, only the CLS score is added into the composite. Then in the middle of first grade, both NWF (CLS and WWR) scores are added. Because the CLS scores are larger numbers, they will outweigh the influence of the WWR score, which is why the WWR score is multiplied by 2. See the example in *Table 3.9*.

Table 3.9

Grade 1 Middle- and End-of-Year Composite Score at Benchmark Level

Composite Score	Grade 1	
	Indicator Goal—MOY	Indicator Goal—EOY
NWF-CLS	43	
NWF-WWR	8	(13 × 2) = 26
DORF Words Correct	23	47
Accuracy Value	56	75
TOTAL of Components	130	148
Benchmark Goal Composite Score	130	155
Note: Accuracy Percentage	78%	90%

The multipliers for WWR allow their scores to weight more heavily into the Composite Score.

In the middle of first grade, the Benchmark Goal for NWF-CLS is 43 and the Benchmark Goal for NWF-WWR is 8. The score for WWR is generally going to be only about a third or less in numeric value because the pseudowords have two or three sounds. In spite of the fact that at the middle of first grade, the weighting of CLS is far heavier in the Composite Score than the WWR, teachers will want to make sure that students can read CVC words blended by this point in the year so that they can continue making progress in reading connected text.

The components included in the Composite Score change from the middle to the end of grade 1. Only the NWF-WWR is factored into the Composite Score and its value is doubled with the use of the multiplier of 2. The NWF-CLS is measured but not included in the Composite Score at this time period. This same calculation also applies at the beginning of grade 2, the last time NWF is assessed. The Benchmark Goal for WWR for both those time periods is 13, so a benchmark score doubled would add 26 to the Composite Score (see *Table 3.9*).

In comparing a DORF Words Correct benchmark score of 47 or 52 for those same time periods, the WWR Composite Score of 26 is less than half the value of DORF Words Correct. This signals that as DORF words read correctly increase across the grade levels, the impact of the WWR in the composite will be minimized. Over time, students move beyond reading simple CVC words, and that skill is almost subsumed in their reading of passage text where there are

Giving the NWF indicator at the beginning of second grade provides a safety net to identify any student who may be reading words more from sight yet is unable to apply letter-sound correspondences when coming across a word she doesn't already know.

many other patterns of words as well as sight words. Giving the NWF indicator at the beginning of second grade provides a safety net to identify any student who may be reading words more from sight yet is unable to apply letter-sound correspondences when coming across a word she doesn't already know. This enables teachers to flag a student who might otherwise slip by with weak decoding skills, which will impair her text reading at later grade levels.

The second area to discuss is that the DORF Accuracy Value is heavily weighted in the Composite Score. If a student at the end of first grade reads the Benchmark Goal number of 47 words at the goal of 90% accuracy, 75 points would be added to the Composite Score based on the Accuracy Value chart; that's nearly twice as many points for reading accurately (75) as for the number of words read correctly (47). As the goal for words read correctly increases over time, the balance between words and accuracy become more even. If a student reads words 100% accurately in grade 1, the accuracy value is 98 points increasing to a maximum of 120 points for perfectly correct reading from mid-second grade through sixth grade.

The third interesting area regarding the Composite Score is the relationship of the Daze score to the Retell score. Both Daze and Retell are ways to measure comprehension. The multiplier for the Retell score is 2, and the multiplier for the Daze score is 4. *Table 3.10* shows how each indicator contributes to the total Composite Score.

Notice that there is a difference at the end of first grade between the sum of the parts included in the composite calculation of 148 versus the Composite Score benchmark for that period of 155. This is because the Composite Score benchmark was not created by adding up the components.

Table 3.10

Grades 3–5 End-of-Year Composite Scores and Contributing Indicators

Indicator	Grade 3—EOY	Grade 4—EOY	Grade 5—EOY
DORF Words Correct	100	115	130
Retell Score × 2	(30 × 2) = 60	(33 × 2) = 66	(36 × 2) = 72
Daze Adjusted Score × 4	(19 × 4) = 76	(24 × 4) = 96	(24 × 4) = 96
Accuracy Value	96	104	112
TOTAL of Components	332	381	410
Benchmark Composite Score	330	391	415
Note: Accuracy Percentage	97%	98%	99%

As you can see from *Table 3.10*, when a student scores at exactly the Benchmark Goal level on all indicators, Daze is weighted more heavily than Retell.

Uses of the Composite Scores

Figuring out where the Composite Score falls in the continuum between the Cut Point for Risk and the Benchmark Goal gives the teacher one overall indicator of where a student's reading stands at a point in time. According to the authors of *DIBELS Next*, the Composite Score enables an even stronger predictor of student performance than not using it. At the *DIBELS* Summit in February 2011, Dr. Roland Good said, "You can get 8%–17% more predictability or confidence from using the Composite Score. ORF is very good as a predictor of risk, and the Composite Score is even better."

The educational rationale for using the Composite Score is very compelling when examining what it is measuring. For grades 3 and above, the *DIBELS Next* Composite Score contains three things:

1. The student is reading at a high degree of accuracy. This is measured by the combination of the DORF Words Correct and the DORF Accuracy Value.

2. The student can tell you orally about what they just read aloud. This is measured by Retell.

3. The student is reading for meaning while reading silently. This is measured by the Daze indicator.

So overall, when a student reaches the Benchmark Goal on the Composite Score, it indicates that he is reading for meaning at an adequate rate with a high degree of accuracy.

So how can Composite Scores be used? It is possible to discuss whether a group of students improved over time on the Composite Scores; this can be done through the percentage of students in the three categories (*at benchmark, below benchmark,* and *well below benchmark*). For example, a principal could say that students in third grade are reading better overall when there were 50% at or above the composite Benchmark Goal in the fall, and there are now 75% in the winter that are at or above the goal. Similarly, if a student moved from below the composite benchmark in the fall to above it in the winter, his reading has improved.

One caution about using Composite Scores: The scores themselves are not comparable across time. Because the calculation of the score varies across time and grade level, the scores can be compared only during a period within one grade level but not across time periods. It is not possible to say that a Composite Score was better in one period versus another just because the number increased. If a student's Composite Score was 40 at the beginning of the year and rose to 70 by the middle of the year, this sounds like an improvement. However, this statement may not be correct because there are four indicators added into the Composite Score at the middle of the year and only two at the beginning of the year. Additionally, because the number of indicators drops to three at the end of the year, the Composite Score Benchmark Goal declines from 122 at the middle of the year to 119 at the end of the year. *Table 3.11* illustrates how the Composite Score changes over time.

Table 3.11

Kindergarten Composite Score Across the Year—Student at Benchmark Goal Level

Indicators	Beginning of the Year	Middle of the Year	End of the Year
FSF	X	X	
LNF	X	X	X
PSF		X	X
NWF-CLS		X	X
TOTAL Composite Score	26	122	119

Consistency in Readability Levels of DORF Passages

While working with schools throughout the country, one of the most predictable things teachers complained about in the 6th Edition was their perception that some passages were much more difficult than others. If a list were compiled of the ten most disliked passages, a few titles that would surely make the list would be "Keiko the Whale" and "Meals on Wheels." Teachers could show data indicating that an entire school of second-grade students dipped in performance on a particular passage. Luckily, the median score was the one that was recorded, which helped somewhat in buffering teachers' concerns. However, concern about passage variability was a topic that caused a lot of frustration. The research team has corrected this issue in *DIBELS Next*. This is perhaps one of the most significant changes from the 6th Edition to *DIBELS Next*.

In a Response to Intervention (RTI) framework, oral reading fluency passages are used in making decisions about a student's improvement in reading based on the core and intervention instruction. Therefore, passage consistency is important not only on benchmark passages, but also on progress monitoring passages. Educators often graph the results of three progress monitoring passages to look at slopes of lines of improvement to determine whether to make changes to a student's intervention plan. If students are progress monitored weekly and the variability of the passages is an issue, the graphs will not provide reliable data. Within the context of RTI, the use of progress monitoring data addressing the issue of passage variability was critical for the success of *DIBELS* as a valued assessment tool.

The research team did several things to assure that the readability of the passages would be more consistent across a grade level. These actions included:

- Wrote all new passages—some of the 6th Edition passages perhaps contained a few things that were outdated after more than ten years.

- Measured the readability of passages using a formula developed by DMG.

- Field-tested the passages with students (this was not done in previous editions of *DIBELS* and, therefore, *DIBELS Next* has made a major improvement over previous editions).

- Arranged the passages in triads so that each benchmark set would include an easier, medium, and harder passage.

- Designed the triads for a specific grade-level mixture of narrative and expository text. In grades 1 through 3, it's two-thirds narrative, and, in grades 4 through 6, the mix changes to two-thirds expository.

- Computed coefficients of new DORF passages against a 6th Edition benchmark passage and a standard fourth-grade reading passage used in the National Assessment of Educational Progress (NAEP) 2002 Special Study of Oral Reading to make sure the difficulty of the *DIBELS Next* passages was in line with both.

A research study on readability of the new passages was completed and is available online at the DMG Web site (www.dibels.org). The title of the publication is *DIBELS Next Oral Reading Fluency Readability Study* by Kelly Powell-Smith and Roland Good from DMG, and Trent Atkins from the University of Montana. It is labeled *Technical Report #7*. The research team's goal was to have a highly consistent set of benchmark and progress monitoring oral reading fluency passages for *DIBELS Next*, which they have achieved.

Summary of the Research Project

The research team began with several research questions:

- What is the average number of words read correct on a DORF passage at each grade level (mean grade level)?

- Which are the best performing 32 passages (29 for first grade) at each grade level where students performed closest to the grade level mean and the passages are most reliable and valid?

- What are some common patterns in the passage characteristics or qualitative features of the best passages?

- How do the new DORF passages compare to the 6th Edition passages?

- How do the DORF passages correspond to a standard fourth-grade passage used in the National Assessment of Educational Progress (NAEP) 2002 Special Study of Oral Reading (Daane, Campbell, Grigg, Goodman, and Oranje 2005)?

The participants in the study were 140 students from two Title I eligible schools in the Mountain West region of the United States: one elementary school and one middle school. The students were from 6 grade levels (first through sixth) with 23 to 25 students per grade level. All students were receiving their reading instruction in English, and students with disabilities and English language learners were included if they had the capability to respond. The study design was that 13 university students (all but one at the graduate level) assessed all the students for the entire study. The university students were trained in a 2-hour webcast, and there were observations to make sure that procedures were followed.

Each participant read a total of 42 passages:

- 40 *DIBELS Next* passages at his grade level.

- 1 Spring Benchmark 6th Edition passage at his grade level.

- 1 passage (198 words) used in the fourth grade NAEP 2002 Special Study of Oral Reading, which was used as a read-aloud passage.

Each student participant was tested in eight to ten testing sessions, one-on-one, over two to four weeks in the spring of 2009. Each time a student was assessed, it took about 8 to 10 minutes. Assessors also took qualitative notes in several areas:

- Challenging words, difficult proper names, difficult sentence structures

- Topics that had positive, negative, or no influence on student's fluency

- Topics seemed appropriate and of interest to students in that grade level

After the data were collected, the research team identified the best 32 passages by developing a regression line to compare them by subtracting predicted score versus actual score on each passage. In order to remove the effects of individual reading differences, it was important to look at passages and rank order them by their relative difficulty for each student. Cumulating the scores on an individual passage across all readers would not be effective. If a weaker reader's average score was 50, then a score of 60 on a passage would place it as an easier passage. That score could not be compared to a stronger reader's score of 80 on a passage when his average is 90. This process enabled the team to rank order passages by relative difficulty first by student, and then within each grade level, so they could identify the best passages and to find outlier passages. The team selected the best 32 passages from the original 40 passages for each grade level based on looking at how individual students did on a passage given their own personal performance on other passages, as well as correlation of each passage with the 6th Edition and NAEP passage.

Once the 32 best passages were identified, they were organized into groups (see *Figure 3.3*):

- 10 slightly easier
- 12 medium difficulty
- 10 slightly harder

For first grade, since DORF begins in the middle of the year, only 29 passages were needed. There were 9, 11, and 9 in the three subgroups for the first-grade passages. Then the passages were rank ordered within those groups. The middle four passages were assigned to the three benchmark periods (B1–B3) plus a *DIBELS Next Survey* passage. *DIBELS Next Survey* is a tool for determining the instructional level of *DIBELS Next* materials for a student who is not reading at grade level—using this tool enables the teacher to test back down in grade level to find the appropriate reading level for a student's instruction and progress monitoring. It will be especially useful in assessing students in special education on IEPs. *DIBELS Next Survey* is available in print form from Cambium Learning® Sopris (www.soprislearning.com).

Figure 3.3

Grades 2–6 Passages

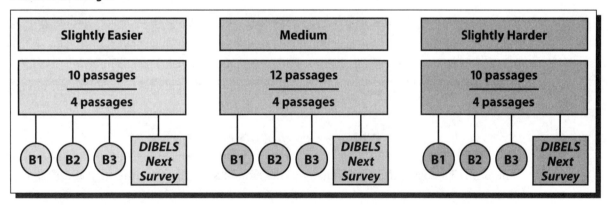

Within the triads for the three benchmark passages in *DIBELS Next*, there is a very tight range of scores. According to the readability study publication (Powell-Smith, Good, and Atkins 2010), for most points in time, there is typically a mean difference of about two words read correct from triad to triad. They also report that there is slightly increased variability in third, fifth, and sixth grade compared to the grade 1, 2, and 4 passages. *Figure 3.4* (next page) shows the mean for the passages on the left and the mean for the triad of the passages on the right. As you can see, arranging the passages in carefully constructed triads results in tighter readability levels.

Passage Variability

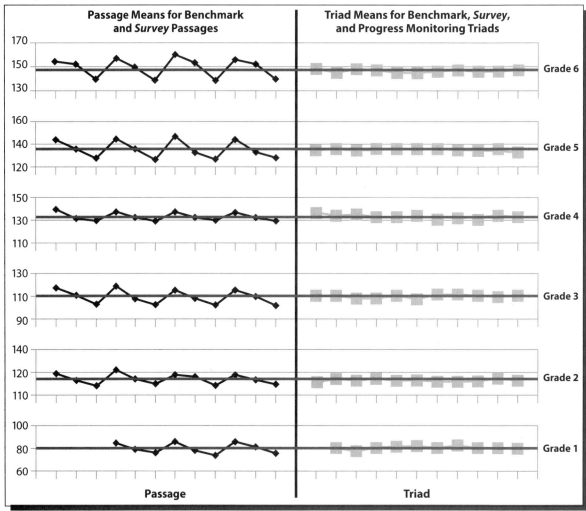

Passage Means for Benchmark and *Survey* Passages | Triad Means for Benchmark, *Survey*, and Progress Monitoring Triads

Grade 6 · Grade 5 · Grade 4 · Grade 3 · Grade 2 · Grade 1

Passage | Triad

DMG Passage Difficulty Index

The DMG Passage Difficulty Index was developed to assess the difficulty of *DIBELS Next* passages. It is a robust measure that uses semantic difficulty, syntactic difficulty, and word difficulty as criteria to determine passage readability difficulty. Many readability formulas combine two indicators and provide a single result, which means that the individual indicators are not examined in isolation. Unlike many formulas, the DMG formula examines these three values individually and as a composite.

The three criteria for the DMG Passage Difficulty Index are made up of different indicators. DMG calculates word difficulty using the value of the decoding difficulty of the passage. The decoding difficulty is made up of the following four measures:

1. Characters per word

2. Percentage of words with three or more syllables

3. Percentage of words with seven or more characters

4. Number of syllables per word

After the scores have been determined, the four scores are weighted equally and compiled into a composite decoding difficulty score.

DMG finds semantic difficulty by using the percentage of rare words, and the syntactic difficulty is calculated using median words per sentence. To determine the DMG Passage Difficulty Composite, the values of word, semantic, and syntactic difficulty are weighted equally and combined. In the readability study, the difficulty index was used to compare the difficulty of passages in the 6th Edition to those in *DIBELS Next*.

Because oral reading fluency assessments are used in many districts within the RTI framework, it is important that the data are as reliable as possible. The *DIBELS Next* design of arranging passages in triads for text type and difficulty is a major change that improves its use in a decision-making RTI framework. With the improvement in consistency of readability of the *DIBELS Next* passages, teachers can be more confident that increases in scores indicate growth in reading ability rather than variation in passage difficulty. Now that the passages have been selected with empirical data, the use of the median DORF score for benchmark periods improves the quality of the data. Additionally, schools are encouraged to use a band of three data points from consecutive progress monitoring scores to determine whether a student is improving while receiving intervention instruction. It's important for teachers to administer progress monitoring passages in order rather than picking and choosing out of order given the design of positioning passages as triads, even in the progress monitoring passages.

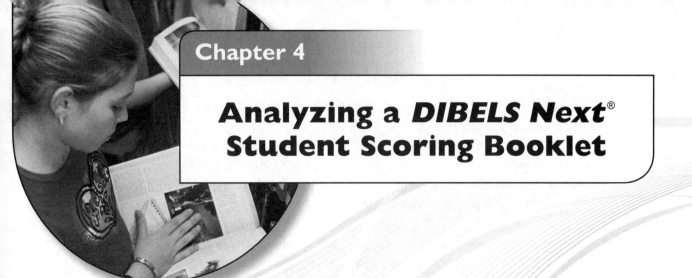

Chapter 4

Analyzing a *DIBELS Next*® Student Scoring Booklet

> *The information gained from looking through the student's booklet is the key to unlocking the door of reading for the individual child. The student's deficits or possible areas of concern are easily identified from looking through the booklet. Making decisions about the student's reading success must come from more than looking at the score on the front cover. Without the use of* DIBELS®, *we would continue to do the same old thing and get the same old results.*
>
> Reading Coach

Introduction and Purpose for Analyzing Error Patterns

The purpose of this chapter is to discuss a procedure for analyzing a student's *DIBELS Next*® data in order to make informed instructional decisions for that student. Other uses of *DIBELS* data will be covered in different chapters, including reviewing progress of an entire classroom or grade level and determining the effectiveness of tiers of instruction. This chapter is about an individual student rather than a more systems-wide view. Throughout this chapter, sample probes with scoring marks are shown for purposes of discussion; these probes were written by the author for this book and are not actual *DIBELS Next* probes.

DIBELS Next student scoring booklets offer much more than numerical scores. An analysis of the student's responses in the student scoring booklet can help determine whether to administer a diagnostic assessment or to conclude that there is enough information to place a student directly into an intervention group. Looking inside the booklet at the scoring details can also reveal if a benchmark student exhibits desirable reading behaviors or if the student met the benchmark level but has potential problems, such as responding quickly but with a low accuracy rate.

In order to make informed decisions about students, teachers need to analyze the *DIBELS Next* student scoring booklets. In fact, teachers should be encouraged to write all over their students' scoring booklets and note what the student said when making errors, if possible, as long as it doesn't interfere with the standardized scoring procedure. The *DIBELS Next* student scoring booklets not only have a space for examiner's notes (like the 6th Edition), but now also contain new common error check boxes at the bottom of the scoring page. This feature was not included in the 6th Edition student scoring booklets. The time spent analyzing the errors is valuable because teachers cannot afford to waste any time reteaching a skill that the student has mastered or, worse yet, missing a skill that is critical. Analyzing the pages of the student's scoring booklets gives invaluable insights as to which skills the student may be missing. Although reviewing error patterns in the *DIBELS* indicators is useful, this approach is not as thorough as using the data from a diagnostic screener. It is best to consider *DIBELS* as the first step in a two-step process; *DIBELS* identifies who needs a diagnostic assessment and then diagnostic screening reveals what to do to intervene. Diagnostic screener data provide more information about the skills a student has mastered and those they still are lacking.

The process for analyzing a *DIBELS Next* student scoring booklet outlined in this chapter helps teachers learn as much as possible from having given the *DIBELS* assessment. As you spend more time studying your own students' scoring booklets, you may develop your own process, including new questions to ask and additional observations to make. The process in this chapter will help you get started with your detailed analysis of error patterns so that you can use information from *DIBELS Next* to inform your decisions about data-driven intervention instruction.

Steps for Analyzing a *DIBELS* Next Student Scoring Booklet

The procedure outlined in this chapter includes four steps:

Step 1: Review the Composite Score.

Step 2: Review the Indicator Scores.

Step 3: Analyze Each Indicator Scoring Page.

Step 4: Record Observations on Summary Sheet.

Each step is outlined in detail in *Figure 4.1*.

Figure 4.1

Overview of Process to Analyze a Student Scoring Booklet

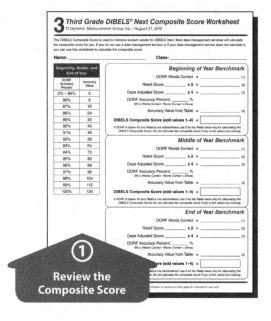

①
Review the Composite Score

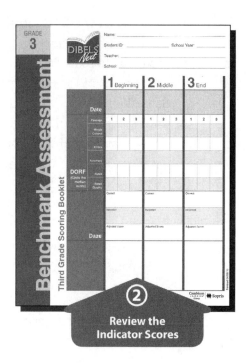

②
Review the Indicator Scores

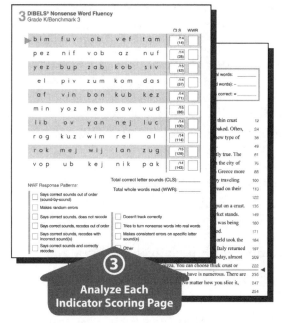

③
Analyze Each Indicator Scoring Page

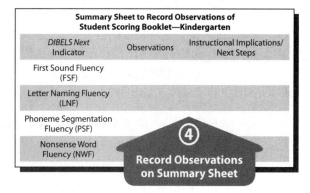

④
Record Observations on Summary Sheet

Step 1: Review the Composite Score

The first step in this procedure is to compare a student's Composite Score to the Composite Score Benchmark Goal. The Composite Score gives an overall indication, by looking at all the indicators together, of how well the student is acquiring literacy skills at that time point. It tells the teacher whether the student is on track overall. Meeting the Composite Score Benchmark Goal level tells the teacher that, considering the information known at this time period, the student is predicted to read well at a later time point. This step can be completed by looking at the cover of the Benchmark Assessment Scoring Booklet or at the Composite Score Worksheet, which is in the *DIBELS Next Assessment Manual* (available from Cambium Learning® Sopris, www.soprislearning.com). The purpose of this step is to get an overall sense of how well the student is doing before diving into the details to look for any concerns or weaknesses.

Step 2: Review the Indicator Scores

In this step, the focus is on the individual indicator scores. This step can be completed by looking at the summary chart on the front of the student benchmark booklet.

Look for any areas where the data are inconsistent. Inconsistencies occur when a higher-level skill develops before an underlying one or when related skills are not equally strong or weak. Several examples of inconsistencies are described below:

- **PSF above benchmark, FSF low**. Normally, the ability to segment and identify initial sounds develops before a student can segment all the sounds in a word.

- **High NWF, low PSF and LNF**. Generally, students with a high NWF will have already developed a strong fluency with phoneme segmentation and letter naming.

- **High DORF Words Correct per minute with high accuracy, low NWF**. Typically, students with DORF scores above benchmark are proficient in applying letter-sound correspondences in reading nonsense CVC words.

- **High Retell, low Daze**. This would be unusual because both indicators measure reading comprehension. For most students it's easier to comprehend while reading silently (Daze) than to comprehend while reading aloud (Retell).

By identifying these inconsistencies first before diving into the student scoring booklet, the process of studying the scoring pages for each of the indicators will be more directed toward seeking answers to inconsistencies and questions.

Step 3: Analyze Each Indicator Scoring Page

> DIBELS Next *has helped me to be more specific with error patterns, such as leaving off ending sounds, vowel sounds, and hearing sounds but not knowing they come together.*
>
> First-Grade Teacher

This step takes more time, but it's worth every moment. In Step 2, we gained a sense of the student's skills by comparing his individual indicator score to the indicator Benchmark Goals for each measure that was given and generating questions. Now the analysis turns to the details. Study each page of the student scoring booklet and look at the mistakes the student made. Start by looking at the student's accuracy and fluency rates on the individual indicator. Then look at the student's mistakes and try to identify any error patterns. What part is the student consistently getting right? What is he consistently getting wrong? From this, some conclusions can be reached about possible deficit areas and whether diagnostic screening is recommended for a student who is below benchmark.

Step 4: Record Observations on Summary Sheet

Teachers often like to use a chart to summarize observations from their analysis. *Table 4.1* shows a blank template of a sample sheet with a place to note observations on each indicator, implications for instruction, and next steps.

Table 4.1

Summary Sheet to Record Observations of a Kindergarten Student Scoring Booklet

DIBELS Next Indicator	Observations	Instructional Implications/Next Steps
First Sound Fluency (FSF)		
Letter Naming Fluency (LNF)		
Phoneme Segmentation Fluency (PSF)		
Nonsense Word Fluency (NWF)		

Source: 95 Percent Group Inc. (2011). Reprinted with permission. All rights reserved.

Summary sheets for other grades, similar to the kindergarten chart above, are provided at www.IDNWnext.com.

One of the conclusions you may reach is that a student's performance on *DIBELS Next* seems inconsistent or difficult to interpret. Assessment results with young students may be unreliable. When in doubt, reassess to check the reliability of the results. Remember that confidence from a pattern of performance is higher than from a single score.

Example of Analyzing a Kindergarten Student Scoring Booklet

In order to describe an approach for analyzing a student scoring booklet, we'll start with kindergarten and use example student booklets to describe the approach. Sometimes it's helpful to look at two booklets together in order to highlight different error patterns. For kindergarten, we'll analyze the booklets of Melissa and Fernando (see *Table 4.2*).

Table 4.2

Summary of Scores of Two Kindergarten Students (Melissa and Fernando)

Kindergarten DIBELS Next Indicator		Melissa		Fernando		Benchmark Goals	
		Middle	End	Middle	End	Middle	End
FSF		17		34		30	
LNF		56	57	39	38		
PSF		9	30	20	46	20	40
NWF	CLS	14	29	31	36	17	28
	WWR						
Composite Score		96	116	124	120	122	119

Melissa and Fernando are both imaginary kindergarten students who are in the same classroom. These scores are from the middle- and end-of-the year benchmark screening. In the spring of kindergarten, *DIBELS Next* consists of three indicators that were also given in the middle of the year (LNF, PSF, and NWF). First Sound Fluency (FSF) is not assessed at the end of the year.

Step 1: Review the Composite Score

As of the end of kindergarten, Melissa is below benchmark on the Composite Score and Fernando is just above benchmark. Although Melissa is further behind, there are some areas of concern for Fernando, as well. Melissa's Composite Score was below benchmark at both the middle of the year and the end of the year. Fernando, on the other hand, was slightly above benchmark (124 versus 122) at midyear and remained just barely above benchmark at the end of the year (120 versus 119).

It is important to note that it's not appropriate to compare Composite Scores from one time period to another. For example, Melissa's Composite Score went from 96 in the winter to 116 in the spring—it is not possible to conclude that Melissa's reading performance improved because of the 20-point gain in the Composite Score. There are two reasons that reaching this conclusion isn't valid. First, in many cases, the number of indicators changes from one time period to another. For example, in kindergarten there is one less indicator in the spring (three instead of four because FSF is not assessed in the spring). Second, the benchmark expectations are different in every period. In the case of Melissa, the expectation for PSF is higher in the spring than in the winter, so it's impossible to know whether the gains are adequate. Comparing the Composite Score at an assessment period to the benchmark Composite Score for that same time period is the best way to use these composites. They take into account the Benchmark Goals for all the individual indicators and consolidate them into one score. It's possible to look at whether a student closed the gap between her score and the benchmark. For example, a student whose score was way below the composite benchmark in one period and just barely below it in the next benchmark is most likely improving.

Composite Scores can be compared at a single point in time. For students in the same grade level, it's acceptable to compare one student's score to another in the same period and know whose reading performance is stronger overall.

Step 2: Review the Indicator Scores

Melissa's Composite Score was below benchmark in the winter and spring. This merits examining her scores on each indicator. Melissa's winter scores are as follows:

- **FSF: 17**—Below the Cut Point for Risk; Likely to Need Intensive Support

- **LNF: 56**—(LNF is a risk indicator and not an instructional benchmark)

- **PSF: 9**—Below the Cut Point for Risk; Likely to Need Intensive Support

- **NWF-CLS: 14**—Between the Cut Point for Risk and the Benchmark; Likely to Need Strategic Support

Melissa exhibited strong Letter Naming Fluency at the middle of the year with an LNF score of 56. Although this score stayed about the same at the end of the year, both are fairly strong. It's possible that Melissa was taught about letter names at home or in preschool, or she gained letter naming knowledge from instruction in the kindergarten classroom between September and January. In spite of her strong letter naming scores, there is reason to be concerned about her phonological awareness skills. At the middle of the year, her First Sound Fluency (FSF) score of 17 was well below the Benchmark Goal of 30. Phoneme Segmentation Fluency (PSF) was also low at midyear. Both scores are well below benchmark, indicating that she is behind where we'd like her to be in phonemic awareness.

Melissa's *DIBELS Next* scores indicate that she may need intensive support in phonological awareness because she scored below the Cut Point for Risk in both FSF and PSF. Additional diagnostic assessments can validate this recommendation and inform her teacher about what she has learned in the area of phonological awareness. Is she aware of syllables or onset-rime units in words? Her NWF score was relatively higher than her phonemic awareness scores. It's possible that her higher letter naming skills enabled her to perform comparatively better on NWF-CLS than would have been expected from her low phonemic awareness scores. This is a common pattern in student's scores because of the similarity of many letter sounds and names.

Melissa's PSF score did improve over the second half of the year, increasing from 9 to 30. In spite of improvement, she did not perform well enough to reach the Benchmark Goal of 40 at the end of the year. Since her score at the middle of the year indicated a need for intensive support, she should have been placed in an intervention group to receive help with phonological awareness. Given that she has not reached benchmark at year-end, it is critical to know more about the type of phonological awareness instruction she was receiving in both the Tier 1 core as well as while participating in any Tier 2 or Tier 3 group for intervention. It's important to know about the type of instruction she was receiving and how the other students in the group performed. If they caught up and she didn't, this is a red flag that Melissa is at risk of later difficulties. Some of the questions to ask include:

- How much phonological awareness was taught in the Tier I curriculum? How explicit was it? Which skills were taught?

- How many minutes of instruction did she receive weekly outside of Tier I in phonological awareness instruction (e.g., 30 minutes a day, 5 days a week would be 150 minutes weekly)?

- What size was her intervention group?

- Was the curriculum organized and delivered in an explicit, systematic, and sequential manner?

- Are there progress monitoring data to review? How often was her progress monitored?

- Was the instruction intensity increased? If so, in what way?

Fernando's Composite Score indicates that he is just above benchmark at both the middle and the end of the year. His phonemic awareness indicators of FSF and PSF are both above benchmark, although not by a lot. At the middle of the year, his FSF was 34 compared to a benchmark of 30, and at the end of the year his PSF was 46 compared to a benchmark of 40. It would be necessary to study the scoring marks to see if there are any areas of concern. One question from the scoring booklet cover is his NWF-CLS. It was way above benchmark at midyear (31 versus 17) but proportionately not as much above at the end of the year (36 versus 28).

Step 3: Analyze Each Indicator Scoring Page

In Step 2, we noted Melissa's lack of phonological awareness, below-benchmark level of letter-sound associations, and high letter naming skills. The next step is to open the booklet and study each page.

First Sound Fluency (FSF)

The first page in the kindergarten benchmark student scoring booklet is First Sound Fluency (see *Figures 4.2a* and *4.2b*). Some questions to guide the analysis of the student's performance on this indicator follow the figures.

- **How accurate is the student with initial sounds?**
  Melissa had difficulty with this skill in the middle of the year. Her score of 17 placed her not only below the Benchmark Goal of 30, but also below the Cut Point for Risk of 20. The next step is to calculate an accuracy rate for segmenting initial sounds. For purposes of this step, we'll assume that accuracy is defined as getting the maximum possible 2-point score by answering with a single phoneme sound. The accuracy rate is calculated by dividing the correct points by the maximum number of points possible if she had answered all attempted words with a 2-point correct response. In 1 minute, Melissa attempted 16 words and would have earned 32 points if all of her responses had contained only the correct initial sound segment with no other sound attached to it. Melissa's accuracy rate is her FSF score divided by the maximum number of points she could have gotten if all her answers had been 2-point responses (16 × 2 points for each response):

---

17 points / 32 possible maximum points = 53% accuracy

This is a low accuracy rate.

Figure 4.2a

Hypothetical First Sound Fluency (FSF) Probe Melissa (MOY)

1 DIBELS® First Sound Fluency
Grade K/Benchmark 1

Test Items	Correct/2 points	Correct/1 point			Incorrect
1. map	/m/	(/ma/)			0
2. chirp	/ch/	/chir/			⊘
3. plate	/p/	/pl/	(/plai/)		0
4. jump	(/j/)	/ju/			0
5. blink	/b/	/bl/	(/bli/)		0
6. moon	/m/	/moo/			⊘
7. drive	/d/	/dr/	(/dri/)		0
8. creep	/k/	/kr/	(/kree/)		0
9. strand	/s/	/st/	/str/	(/stra/)	0
10. wait	/w/	(/wai/)			0
11. nest	(/n/)	/ne/			0
12. stand	/s/	/st/	(/sta/)		0
13. home	/h/	(/ho/)(long o)			0
14. grill	/g/	/gr/	(/gri/)		0
15. bird	/b/	(/bir/)			0
16. faith	(/f/)	/fai/			0
17. street	/s/	/st/	/str/	/stree/	0
18. scrap	/s/	/sk/	/skr/		0
19. shirt	/sh/	/shir/			0
20. flip	/f/	/fl/	/fli/		0
21. scrub	/s/	/sk/	/skr/	/skru/	0
22. mush	/m/	/mu/			0
23. trim	/t/	/tr/	/tri/		0
24. belt	/b/	/be/			0
25. spring	/s/	/sp/	/spr/	/spri/	0
26. west	/w/	/we/			0
27. dunk	/d/	/du/			0
28. flick	/f/	/fl/	/fli/		0
29. wink	/w/	/wi/			0
30. string	/s/	/st/	/str/	/stri/	0
31. dim	/d/	/di/			0
32. flop	/f/	/fl/	/flo/		0

Accuracy Rate 17/32 = 53%

Fernando's score of 34 is above the Benchmark Goal of 30. Without studying his student scoring booklet, everything appears to be fine. Let's calculate his accuracy rate. With 31 words attempted, the maximum possible score is 62 if all his answers earned the 2-point score. Fernando's accuracy rate is:.

---

34 correct / 62 maximum possible = 55% accuracy

This low accuracy rate signals the need to take a close look at how he achieved this score. He attempted 31 words in 1 minute, yet he earned only three 2-point scores. Therefore, upon closer examination, his pattern of being fast but rarely isolating and naming solely the initial sound is not the pattern that good readers should

Figure 4.2b

Hypothetical First Sound Fluency (FSF) Probe Fernando (MOY)

1 DIBELS® First Sound Fluency
Grade K/Benchmark 1

Test Items	Correct/2 points	Correct/1 point			Incorrect
1. map	/m/	/ma/			0
2. chirp	/ch/	/chir/			0
3. plate	/p/	/pl/	/plai/		0
4. jump	/j/	/ju/			0
5. blink	/b/	/bl/	/bli/		0
6. moon	/m/	/moo/			0
7. drive	/d/	/dr/	/dri/		0
8. creep	/k/	/kr/	/kree/		0
9. strand	/s/	/st/	/str/	/stra/	0
10. wait	/w/	/wai/			0
11. nest	/n/	/ne/			0
12. stand	/s/	/st/	/sta/		0
13. home	/h/	/ho/ (long o)			0
14. grill	/g/	/gr/	/gri/		0
15. bird	/b/	/bir/			0
16. faith	/f/	/fai/			0
17. street	/s/	/st/	/str/	/stree/	0
18. scrap	/s/	/sk/	/skr/	/skra/	0
19. shirt	/sh/	/shir/			0
20. flip	/f/	/fl/	/fli/		0
21. scrub	/s/	/sk/	/skr/	/skru/	0
22. mush	/m/	/mu/			0
23. trim	/t/	/tr/	/tri/		0
24. belt	/b/	/be/			0
25. spring	/s/	/sp/	/spr/	/spri/	0
26. west	/w/	/we/			0
27. dunk	/d/	/du/			0
28. flick	/f/	/fl/	/fli/		0
29. wink	/w/	/wi/			0
30. string	/s/	/st/	/str/	/stri/	0
31. dim	/d/	/di/			0
32. flop	/f/	/fl/	/flo/		0

Accuracy Rate 34/62 = 55%

exhibit. It suggests that he may be at risk of not achieving the PSF goal by the end of the year if he doesn't receive instruction in this skill.

- **How fluent is the student with initial sounds?**
  Melissa reached 16 words in a minute. The Benchmark Goal for the middle of the year is 30, which can be earned with a combination of 1- and 2-point answers. If a student earns a score entirely with 1-point answers, she would have to attempt 30 words in 1 minute to meet the Benchmark Goal. Melissa reached 16 of the 30 words, so she is also not particularly fluent at this skill.

Fernando is very fluent because he reached 31 words in 1 minute; this is slightly better than 2 seconds per word. His fluency compensated for a lack of accuracy in isolating only the initial sound away from other consonants or vowels that follow it.

- **What percentage of the responses earned a 2-point answer?**
  Melissa earned a 2-point score for only 3 of the 16 words she attempted before the minute was up. Melissa's performance on naming only the initial sound is:

  ---

  3 words earning 2-point scores / 16 total words attempted =
  19% of points from initial sound isolation

  This indicates that she is not segmenting solely the initial sound in very many of her answers.

  Fernando earned a 2-point score in only 3 of the 31 words he attempted in the minute. Fernando's success in isolating solely the initial sound is:

  ---

  3 words earning 2-point scores / 31 total words attempted =
  10% of points from initial sound isolation

  This indicates a red flag for initial sound segmentation in spite of his above-benchmark score.

- **For all attempted words that have blends, in what percentage of responses was the initial sound segmented?**
  Of the 16 words that Melissa attempted, 7 contained initial consonant blends of either two or three sounds (*plate*, *blink*, *drive*, *creep*, *strand*, *stand*, *grill*). She never isolated the initial phoneme sound from the other sound in any of these seven words, so her percentage would be 0%. She always added the vowel sound onto the consonant blend in her answer. This performance shows that she is unable to segment just the initial consonant sound from the sounds that follow it. This foreshadows difficulty with PSF, where she will be asked to segment all the sounds, since, at the middle of the year, she is isolating only the onset from the rime most of the time.

  Fernando did not successfully extract the initial single consonant sound from a blend in any of the 15 words he attempted that began with blends. He does not understand how to segment the sounds in blends.

- **What percentage of the words attempted included the vowel along with one or more consonants?**

  Melissa attempted 16 words. There were no answers in the 1-point column where she included the consonant blend but not the vowel after it. One of the 16 words she got incorrect, so it will be excluded from this calculation. Therefore, 11 of the 15 responses, or 73% of the time, Melissa added the vowel sound in her response.

  Here's a quick summary of Fernando's performance:

  - Attempted: 31 words

  - Incorrect: 0 words

  - Segmented initial sound only: 3 words

  - Initial consonant sound plus one or more consonants: 7 words

  - Initial consonant sound plus a vowel: 15 words

  - Initial consonant sound, another consonant, plus a vowel: 8 words

  This shows that Fernando didn't have just one error pattern. Sometimes he gave both consonants in a blend, while other times he added consonants plus the vowel. The directions asked him to give the initial sound; he doesn't seem to know what that means or how to separate the initial consonant sound from the other consonants in a blend. He also doesn't separate the initial consonant from the vowel. My recommendation is to provide Fernando the opportunity to work in a small group where the instruction is on how to isolate and segment the initial consonant from all other sounds that follow it. If this isn't done now, Fernando may have trouble with spelling words because of confusion about the individual sounds and how to map letters to sounds. This is an example of a student whose score fell above the benchmark level, but he is actually not successfully demonstrating the intended skill in the measure. He was inaccurate but fast.

- **Are there any other unusual error patterns?**

  One possible pattern to observe is whether the student performed better on two-consonant blends than on three-consonant blends. This pattern was not present for Melissa as she did as poorly on initial blends that had two consonants as she did on those with three consonants. Other possible patterns include scoring lower on the more difficult items that contain continuant sounds at the beginning of the word versus stop sounds, which are easier to isolate. Stop sounds include /b/, /d/, /p/, /t/, /k/, and /g/. Continuant sounds are those that can be said until running out of breath, such as /s/, /m/, /n/, /f/, and /z/. Some students find it easier to segment a stop sound from the vowel that follows it versus a continuant sound, which feels a bit more like it runs into the vowel. There weren't any noticeable patterns on Melissa's scoring sheet regarding continuant or stop sounds.

In Fernando's case, there are so many other errors to work on first that it's not important to review length of blend or stop versus continuant sounds at this point. Maybe after some intervention, and if he makes progress with simply learning to isolate the single initial sound, this more granular analysis would make sense.

Letter Naming Fluency (LNF)

The second indicator for the kindergarten benchmark is LNF (see *Figure 4.3*).

Figure 4.3

LNF for Melissa and Fernando

Hypothetical Letter Naming Fluency (LNF) Probe Melissa (MOY)

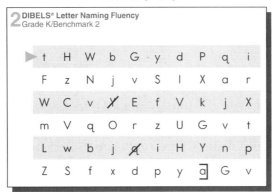

Accuracy Rate
56/58 = 97%

Hypothetical Letter Naming Fluency (LNF) Probe Melissa (EOY)

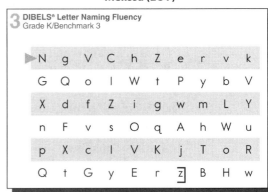

Accuracy Rate
57/57 = 100%

Hypothetical Letter Naming Fluency (LNF) Probe Fernando (MOY)

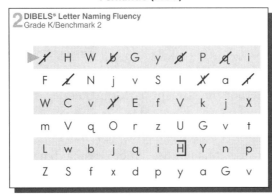

Accuracy Rate
39/47 = 83%

Hypothetical Letter Naming Fluency (LNF) Probe Fernando (EOY)

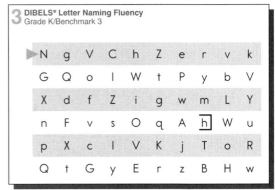

Accuracy Rate
38/38 = 100%

- **How accurate is the student in letter naming?**
  In the middle of the year, Melissa got 56 correct out of the 58 letters that she attempted to name. Melissa's accuracy rate can be calculated as follows:

  ---

  56 correct letters / 58 letters attempted = 97% accuracy rate

  ---

  At year-end, she attempted 57 and got them all correct for 100% accuracy. She is accurate in letter naming.

  Fernando got about the same number of letters correct in the middle of the year as he did at the end of the year (39 versus 38). However, his accuracy rate improved, as follows:

  MOY: 39 correct letters / 47 letters attempted = 83% accuracy rate
  EOY: 38 correct letters / 38 letters attempted = 100% accuracy rate

  ---

- **How fluent is the student in naming letters?**
  At the middle of the year, Melissa attempted 58 letters in 1 minute, which is a relatively fast time for that point in the year. At year-end, she attempted just one less letter and got them all correct. Letter naming fluency is an area of strength for Melissa.

  Because he attempted 47 letters midyear and then only 38 at year-end, more research should be done on why there was a decline in Fernando's rate. Sometimes students slow down to become more accurate, and he did go from eight errors to no errors.

- **Is there a pattern of missing letters that are harder because they are used infrequently (harder letters include those used infrequently such as *q, v, w, x, y,* and *z*)?**
  At the middle of the year, Melissa missed *y* and *q*, both of which are less frequently used letters. She didn't miss any letters at year-end.

  Fernando missed eight letters at midyear, yet only half of these were infrequently used letters. He missed the very common letters *t, b, d,* and *r*. At year-end, he got them all correct.

- **Did the student miss more lowercase letters than uppercase letters?**
  Of the two letters Melissa missed at midyear, one was uppercase and the other was lowercase. Therefore, there is no pattern of missing more lowercase letters than uppercase ones as is the case with some students.

  At midyear, Fernando missed six lowercase and only two uppercase letters. He should be further assessed to determine whether he is having more trouble recognizing lowercase letters. At year-end, he got them all correct.

- **Does the student get any letters correct one time and incorrect another time?**

  Melissa missed only two letters, and they were different ones. This error pattern is not present for her.

  At midyear, Fernando did get lowercase *r* incorrect at the end of the second row and then correct later on in the middle of the fourth row.

- **Does the student correctly name the letters in her own name?**

  All of the letters in Melissa's name appeared in this assessment before the minute was completed, and she got all of these correct.

  Interestingly, two of the eight letters Fernando missed at the middle of the year (the letters *r* and *d*) are in his name. This is unusual.

- **Did the student skip more than one row or not read across the row left to right?**

  Neither Melissa nor Fernando skipped any rows while completing the letter-naming task in *DIBELS Next*. Since adding the lines to the student materials, skipping a line should occur less frequently in *DIBELS Next* than in the 6th Edition. Losing track of place or sequence multiple times may signal a problem with left-to-right tracking.

Melissa is accurate and fluent with letter names. Fernando's rate is a little lower. One of the important differences between *DIBELS Next* and many other non-CBM early literacy screening instruments is that in *DIBELS Next*, the indicators are timed. Timing is critical because there is no other way to determine whether a student recognizes the letters automatically. Students who automatically recognize and can name the letters have an advantage once they begin phonics instruction because they don't have to devote any attention to thinking about letter identity. Students can then dedicate all their attention to associating the sound with the letter symbol. Students can go unnoticed as candidates for extra help in letter naming unless fluency counts. It's important to compare the benchmark pages to see what improvements a student has made from the instruction received throughout the kindergarten year.

Phoneme Segmentation Fluency (PSF)

PSF is the third indicator given at the middle and end of the kindergarten benchmark assessments (see *Figure 4.4a* and *Figure 4.4b*, next page).

The main focus of our analysis will be on whether the student fully or partially segments the sounds in words. First, we'll look for evidence that the student understands the concept behind segmentation. Does the student know how to segment, or does she simply repeat the whole word back? A score of 0 can indicate two different things. First, it may indicate that the student repeated the entire word back in the first five words; if this was the case, each word would be circled and the score of 0 would be recorded. The second option is that the student attempted to segment but was unsuccessful on all items. If this happened, the student scoring booklet would look different. Instead of circles around all words, there would be slash marks through each of the sounds for the first five words and a score of 0 correct would

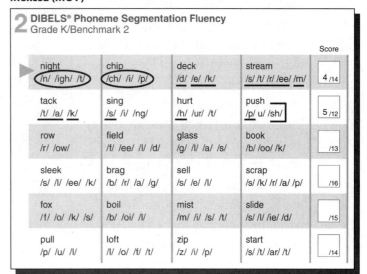

Figure 4.4a

Hypothetical Phoneme Segmentation Fluency (PSF) Probe Melissa (MOY)

Accuracy Rate 9/26 = 35%

Hypothetical Phoneme Segmentation Fluency (PSF) Probe Melissa (EOY)

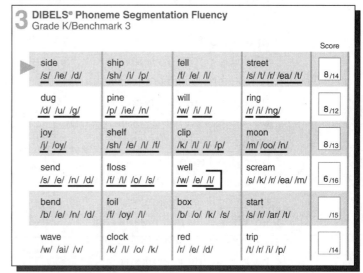

Accuracy Rate 30/50 = 60%

also be recorded. If a student gets a score of 0, the teacher needs to look inside the booklet to see whether she repeated words back or attempted to give sounds but got them all incorrect.

After confirming that the student understands how to segment, look to see whether the student partially or fully segments. Partial segmentation is indicated when there are lines under some individual sounds, yet other segments include several sounds together. Sometimes students don't segment consonant blends (e.g., *st*, *pr*, *cl*, and *br*), or they segment by onset and rime (e.g., *s-at*, *br-ush*) without going to the phoneme level. In analyzing the results, it's important to note whether the student demonstrated proficiency in initial sounds, ending sounds, and middle vowels.

- **Does the student know how to segment phonemes?**

  Melissa appears to know how to segment because there are lines under the individual phonemes. At the middle of the year, she struggled a bit at the beginning of the assessment; note that the first two words (*night* and *chip*) are circled, which means that she repeated the whole word back instead of segmenting any sounds. Because she began segmenting with

Figure 4.4b

Hypothetical Phoneme Segmentation Fluency (PSF) Probe Fernando (MOY)

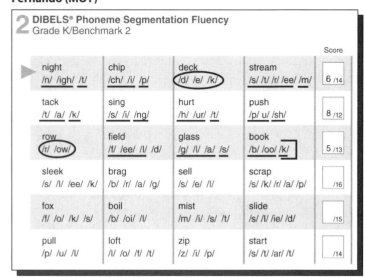

Accuracy Rate 18/39 = 46%

Hypothetical Phoneme Segmentation Fluency (PSF) Probe Fernando (EOY)

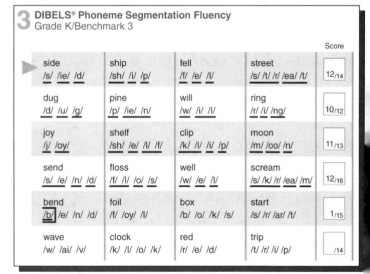

Accuracy Rate 46/56 = 82%

the third word and didn't resort back to repeating whole words, she may simply have been confused at the outset about the task. She segments some sounds in the other six words she reached. Her score of 9 was well below the Benchmark Goal of 20 and just below the Cut Point for Risk of 10. By year-end, she had improved to 30 and moved above the Cut Point for Risk of 25, but she remained below the Benchmark Goal of 40. She didn't repeat any whole words at year-end.

As of the middle of kindergarten, Fernando was gaining some awareness that one-syllable words can be segmented into parts. Out of the 12 words he attempted in 1 minute, he repeated back two of them. For the other 10 words, he partially segmented at the onset-rime level (the *onset* is the initial sound or sounds before the vowel, and the *rime* is the vowel and all sounds that follow it). By the end of the year, this had changed; now his scoring booklet shows that sometimes he segmented at the onset-rime juncture, yet occasionally he segmented at the phoneme level.

- **How many times does the student partially segment rather than completely segment the word?**
  At both the middle and end of the year, Melissa demonstrated partial segmentation consistently. Of the 15 words she attempted at year-end, only once did she fully segment each sound in the word. Many times she segmented at the onset-rime level. Additionally, she always kept consonant blends together. Because many teachers teach blends as units, it's not uncommon to see this error. While blends are taught as a unit for spelling, it's important to teach them as separate sounds for phonemic awareness. With direct, systematic instruction, most students quickly learn how to segment consonant blends into the two or three separate sounds.

  At the middle of the year, Fernando doesn't segment at all for two words and then partially segments all the rest. He never completely segments any words at that assessment period. Then at the end of the year, he completely segments eight words, partially segments eight other words, and only has time enough to segment the initial sound in the last word. This shows progress from the middle of the year, but this skill should be mastered by year-end; therefore, Fernando has not made enough progress. Because neither Melissa nor Fernando achieve the year-end goal of complete phoneme segmentation, it's worth examining the rest of the class' scores to see whether the Tier 1 core curriculum didn't provide enough opportunities for students to master this skill.

- **How accurate is the student in segmenting phonemes?**
  Melissa's accuracy is an issue because, at the middle of the year, she got only 9 correct out of the 26 phonemes she attempted. Her accuracy rates are:

MOY: 9 correct / 26 attempted = 35% accuracy rate
EOY: 30 correct / 50 attempted = 60% accuracy rate

Although her accuracy rate improved from 35% to 60% by the end of the year, it's still too low.

Fernando's accuracy rate improved substantially from the middle of the year to the end of the year:

MOY: 18 correct / 39 attempted = 46% accuracy rate
EOY: 46 correct / 56 attempted = 82% accuracy rate

In spite of the improvement, this is still not a high enough accuracy rate.

- **How fluent is the student in segmenting phonemes?**
Fluency is determined by whether the student's pace allowed him to attempt at least the required number of items so that if they were all correct, the score would have been at benchmark. At the middle of the year, Melissa was fluent enough because she attempted 26 phoneme segments in 1 minute. If she were 100% accurate with a score of 26, she would exceed the benchmark of 20. At the end of the year, her fluency is acceptable, based on attempting 50 phonemes, because the benchmark is 40.

Fernando is fluent enough during both time periods in that he attempted more than the 20 at midyear and 40 at year-end. Because he reached 39 in the winter and 56 in the spring, if his accuracy rate had been much better he would have had no problem benchmarking. Fluency is not an issue for Fernando.

- **How accurate is the student's knowledge of initial sounds?**
Melissa demonstrates a strong awareness of the initial sound in words. She got all the initial sounds correct in the words she was given.

Fernando does not have any errors on initial sounds at either time period.

- **How accurate is the student's knowledge of ending sounds?**
Melissa is also accurate in ending sounds.

Fernando didn't miss any ending sounds at either time period.

- **How accurate is the student's knowledge of vowels?**
For Melissa, accuracy of letter-sound correspondence is not an issue for any sounds, even medial vowel sounds.

At both time periods, Fernando did not make errors on any medial sounds. His issue is not in saying incorrect sounds. His challenge is partial segmentation instead of full segmentation.

Nonsense Word Fluency (NWF)

Nonsense Word Fluency (see *Figure 4.5a* and *Figure 4.5b*, next page) is not given at the beginning of kindergarten so the middle of the year is the first time that students are assessed with this measure. Although the student scoring booklet has a spot for it and it's helpful to calculate both the WWR (Whole Words Read) scores in kindergarten, there is no benchmark for WWR until first grade. Kindergarten students are increasingly learning letter-sound correspondences, which is what is measured in Correct Letter Sounds (CLS). Many kindergarten curricula don't expect students to blend sounds to read whole words in CVC patterns by the end of kindergarten; although, if your curriculum does teach this and mastery is expected, it may be useful to create a local norm for NWF-WWR for kindergarten end of year. Even if you don't create a local norm, it still may be helpful to look at WWR to identify any students who are well above benchmark and can be reading simple texts.

Figure 4.5a

Hypothetical Nonsense Word Fluency (NWF) Probe Melissa (MOY)

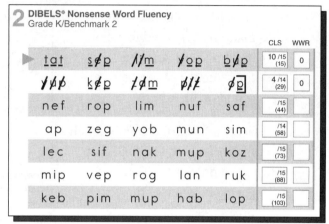

Accuracy Rate 14/29 = 48%

Hypothetical Nonsense Word Fluency (NWF) Probe Melissa (EOY)

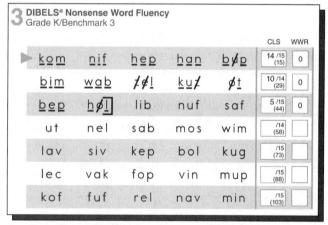

Accuracy Rate 29/35 = 83%

- **How accurate is the student's knowledge of letter-sound correspondences?**

  Melissa is struggling at the letter-sound correspondence accuracy level, as measured by NWF-CLS. Let's examine her accuracy rates at both the middle and end of year:

  MOY: 14 correct / 29 attempted = 48% accuracy rate
  EOY: 29 correct / 35 attempted = 83% accuracy rate

Even with an accuracy rate of 83%, this is not strong enough. Accuracy rates should be above 95% to elicit no concerns in this area. Melissa's intervention instruction should focus on building accuracy and then fluency at associating sounds with letters.

Fernando started from a much higher level of NWF-CLS at the middle of the year and got even better as the year progressed.

His accuracy rates are:

MOY: 31 correct / 41 attempted = 76% accuracy rate

EOY: 36 correct / 39 attempted = 92% accuracy rate

Although his end-of-year score of 36 was above the benchmark of 28, it was not as far above as at the middle of the year when his score of 31 was almost twice the benchmark of 17 at that time.

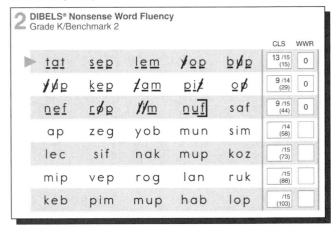

Figure 4.5b

Hypothetical Nonsense Word Fluency (NWF) Probe Fernando (MOY)

Accuracy Rate 31/41 = 76%

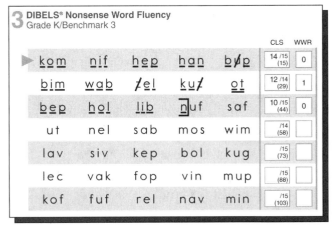

Hypothetical Nonsense Word Fluency (NWF) Probe Fernando (EOY)

Accuracy Rate 36/39 = 92%

- **How fluent is the student in reading nonsense words?**

  Fluency in NWF is not a problem for Melissa at either benchmark time period. At the middle of the year, she attempted 29 letter-sound correspondences, which is almost twice the 17 CLS-per-minute benchmark. At the end of the year, she reaches 35 phonemes, which is also still above the benchmark for CLS of 28. Looking at this adequate level of fluency focuses the attention even more on accuracy.

  Fernando's attempted scores of 41 and 39 are above the benchmarks at both time periods; therefore, fluency is not an issue for him. It's interesting to note that he appears to have slowed down a little at the end of the year in order to say more letter sounds accurately. This was probably a good choice on his part, and shows that he is monitoring his own performance and gauging his rate based on how accurate he is.

- **How accurate is the student's knowledge of initial letter sounds?**
  At the middle of the year, Melissa struggles with initial sounds in six of the ten words attempted. By the end of the year, this improves as her letter-sound correspondence is much stronger. She misses only one initial sound, which is /z/. Looking back at the LNF probe, she did not miss the letter z on it. There were no words beginning with z in the PSF, so we don't know whether she's having trouble with the sound of /z/.

  Fernando misses four initial sounds at the middle of the year, and then only one initial sound at the end of the year. He missed /z/ at the end of the year, which is a harder sound. Since both Melissa and Fernando missed /z/ at year-end, it's possible that the Tier 1 classroom instruction on the sound /z/ was limited.

- **How accurate is the student's knowledge of final letter sounds?**
  At the middle of the year, Melissa missed two letters in the final position: p and z. The only final letter-sound correspondence that Melissa missed at the end of the year was z, which she also missed midyear in the final position and when it appeared in the initial position.

  Fernando missed only one letter-sound correspondence at both time periods. There is no particular concern in this skill.

- **How accurate is the student's knowledge of middle vowel sounds?**
  Melissa had more difficulty with middle vowel sounds than with consonants. She missed the medial vowels in eight of the ten words she attempted at the middle of the year. She didn't consistently get any vowel sound correct. At year-end, she improved with only four vowel errors.

  Fernando had less trouble with vowels than Melissa did. He missed four at midyear; he missed i once, u twice, and o once. At year-end, he missed only u, which is typically the last vowel letter sound for students to master. Because he'll receive plenty of Tier 1 classroom instruction on it in first grade, I wouldn't be worried about it yet.

Step 4: Record Observations on Summary Sheet

Based on the *DIBELS Next* data, which skills appear to be a concern? Melissa is below benchmark on FSF and PSF. Because Melissa had accuracy issues on phonemic awareness, she is a candidate for additional diagnostic assessment in the area of phonological awareness. It's hard to tell from these data exactly where to begin her intervention instruction. Intervention will need to include more rapid and automatic identification and pronunciation of the initial phoneme in a target word. However, she may be struggling with syllables and onset-rime segmentation, blending, and production as well. Diagnostic screening would help pinpoint exactly which skills she has mastered and which she is still struggling to learn. If her FSF score had been below benchmark at the beginning of the year, this would have been the perfect time to assess her with a phonological awareness diagnostic screener. When kindergarten students are weak at the beginning of the year in FSF, then there is time to provide intervention at lower levels of phonological awareness including syllable and onset-rime. However, if the student moved into a school after the midpoint of the kindergarten year, it's critical to feel a sense of urgency to move from syllables and onset-rime to instruction at the phoneme level as quickly as possible.

If your school doesn't have a phonological awareness screener, one quick way to validate the results of the *DIBELS Next* assessment is to begin working on activities emphasizing these skills. Informal observation of a student's response to instruction should corroborate the assessment findings. By observing errors on repeated progress monitoring assessments of the FSF and PSF indicators, the teacher can continue to observe the pattern of responses and confirm any original impressions about appropriate intervention instruction.

Fernando could benefit from some additional instruction on Letter Naming Fluency. His phonological awareness skills appeared to be higher than they were with closer examination. He moved quickly to answer, and his rate covered up his accuracy issues. He would benefit from additional instruction in phonemic awareness, despite the fact that his FSF score was at benchmark and his PSF scores looked strong. His NWF-CLS scores do not show any need for additional support on this skill at this time.

Example of Analyzing a Third Grade Student Scoring Booklet

The process of analyzing a *DIBELS Next* student scoring booklet for a third-grade student is similar to that of a kindergarten student. We will use a third-grade sample student scoring booklet from the beginning of the year as an example. There are many precursor skills that should be in place well before third grade. Some of these include:

- FSF of 30 first sounds per minute (FSPM) by the middle of kindergarten and PSF of 40 by year-end

- NWF of 43 correct letter sounds per minute (CLSPM) and 8 whole words read (WWR) by the middle of first grade

- DORF of 47 at the end of first grade and 87 at the end of second grade

- DORF accuracy increasing from 90% at the beginning of second grade to 97% at the end of the year

- Retell quality of 2

Throughout third grade, there are only two measures assessed: DORF including Retell, and Daze. Students are assessed with DORF and Retell in earlier grades, but the first time Daze is given is at the beginning of third grade. Even though there are only two measures, there are five data points to monitor. In addition to DORF Words Correct, the other factors are DORF Accuracy Rate, Retell Score, Retell Quality, and Daze.

Just like with the kindergarten example, we'll analyze two fictitious students who, for ease of discussion, have been named "Jason" and "Maria." *Table 4.3* (next page) shows a summary of their scores. All the student probes were written by the author and are not actual *DIBELS Next* probes. They are similar to the oral reading fluency passages and maze passages in assessments but may not look exactly like the reading level of *DIBELS Next* third-grade passages because they have not been reviewed using the readability calculation. The objective of including student probes in this chapter is to be able to discuss a review process and specific questions. Because *DIBELS Next* is a standardized assessment, I prefer to create probes for the book rather than use actual *DIBELS* passages in order to protect them from extensive visibility.

Table 4.3

Summary of Scores of Two Third-Grade Students (Jason and Maria)

Grade 3 Beginning of Year		Jason			Maria			Benchmark Goals
	Date	9/14/2012			9/14/2012			Beginning of Year Grade 3
DORF (median score is circled)	Passage	1	2	3	1	2	3	
	Words Correct	102	(106)	112	71	84	(78)	70
	Errors	(19)	18	22	3	5	(4)	
	Accuracy	106/(106 + 19) = 85%			78/(78 + 4) = 95%			95%
	Retell	14	(16)	21	(25)	20	27	20
	Retell Quality	1	(2)	2	4	2	(3)	2
Daze	Correct	6			12			
	Incorrect	8			2			
	Adjusted Score	6 − (8 × .5) = 2			12 − (2 × .5) = 11			8

We'll use the same four-step process for analyzing a student scoring booklet as outlined earlier in this chapter.

Step 1: Review the Composite Score

The Composite Score for the students would be calculated on a worksheet from the *DIBELS Next Assessment Manual* if you are not using a data-management system that calculates the score for you. *Table 4.4* provides a Composite Score calculation for Jason and Maria.

Table 4.4

Composite Score Calculation for Jason and Maria

Composite Score Calculation	Jason	Maria	Benchmark Goal—Beginning of Year Grade 3
DORF Words Correct	106	78	
Retell Score × 2	16 × 2 = 32	25 × 2 = 50	
Daze Adjusted Score × 4	2 × 4 = 8	11 × 4 = 44	
DORF Accuracy Value*	0	80	
Composite Score	146	252	Benchmark 220/Cut Point for Risk 180

*From lookup table on Composite Score Worksheets. 85% accuracy for Jason = 0 accuracy value.
95% accuracy rate for Maria = 80 accuracy value.

Based on the Composite Scores, Maria is above the Benchmark Goal and Jason is below the Cut Point for Risk, which is 180. Our next step is to try to figure out why.

Step 2: Review the Indicator Scores

Jason's DORF Words Correct score was about 30 points more than Maria's. Although his reading rate was higher, his accuracy rate was lower. He read more words than Maria but retold fewer. Additionally, his Retell Quality was lower than hers. Jason's Daze data show that he had a lot of errors. In general, Jason moves more quickly through the text but makes a lot of mistakes. Maria's reading behavior can be described as adequate rate with accuracy.

Step 3: Analyze Each Indicator Scoring Page

In this section, we'll analyze each indicator using a set of analysis questions.

DORF

- **What is the student's accuracy rate on all three passages?**
  A student's accuracy rate in the Composite Score is calculated from the median words read correctly and median errors. It's sometimes helpful to see whether there's a wide or narrow range around the median for an individual's performance. *Table 4.5* provides a calculation of the accuracy rate on all three passages:

Table 4.5

Calculation of the Accuracy Rate for Jason and Maria

Passage Reading Accuracy Rate	Jason			Maria		
	Passage 1	Passage 2	Passage 3	Passage 1	Passage 2	Passage 3
Words Read Correctly	102	106	112	71	84	78
Total Words Read	121	124	134	74	89	82
Accuracy Rate	84%	85%	84%	96%	94%	95%

Jason's accuracy rate was actually quite close for all three passages at 84%, 85%, and 84%. Maria's accuracy rate is also very close with 96%, 94%, and 95%.

- **Did the student perform differently on narrative versus expository passages?**
  Passages 1 and 3 were narrative and Passage 2 was expository (see *Figures 4.6a– 4.6c*, pages 106–108). Jason performed similarly on all three passages, so there doesn't seem to be a pattern here.

  Maria had higher accuracy rates on the two narrative passages (1 and 3) than the expository passage. Although she had a lower accuracy rate on the expository passage, she read at a higher reading rate on that passage. For some reason, she read more words but made more errors on the expository passage, which was about eclipses.

Figure 4.6a

DIBELS Oral Reading Fluency Grade 3 Benchmark 1.1—Jason

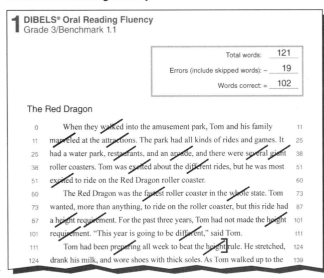

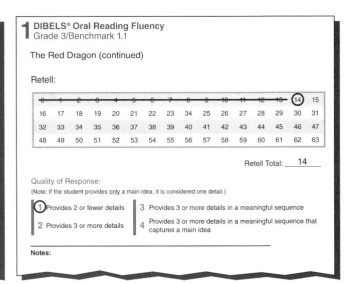

DIBELS Oral Reading Fluency Grade 3 Benchmark 1.1—Maria

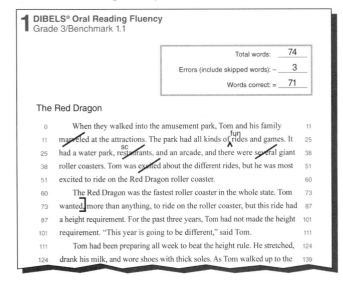

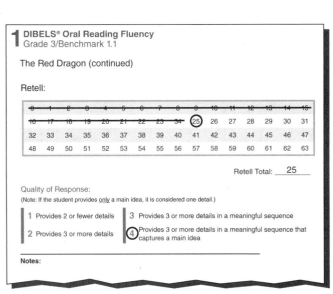

Figure 4.6b

DIBELS Oral Reading Fluency Grade 3 Benchmark 1.2—Jason

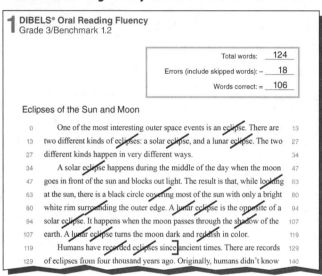

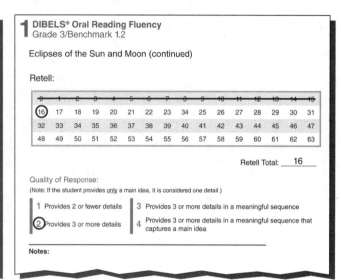

DIBELS Oral Reading Fluency Grade 3 Benchmark 1.2—Maria

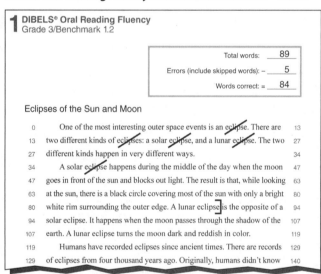

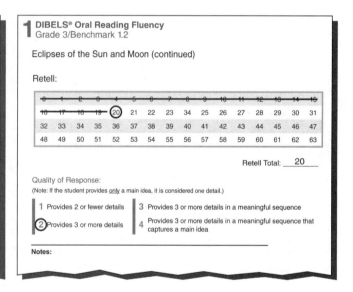

Figure 4.6c

DIBELS Oral Reading Fluency Grade 3 Benchmark 1.3—Jason

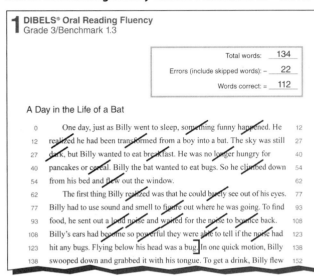

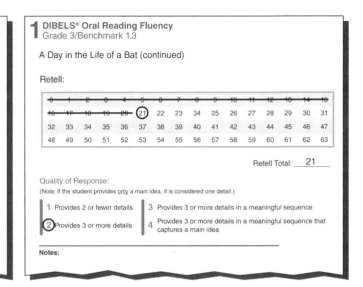

DIBELS Oral Reading Fluency Grade 3 Benchmark 1.3—Maria

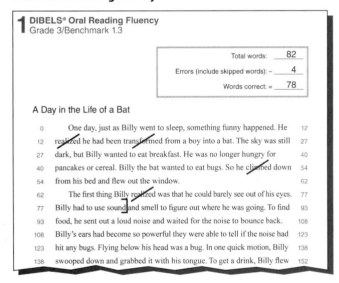

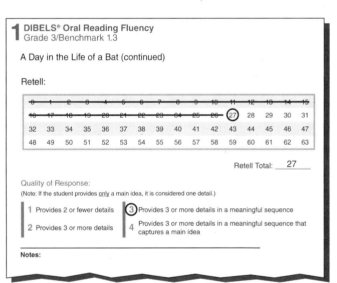

- **Are there any patterns in the student's errors?**

  Jason missed many multisyllable words, as well as words with endings. He didn't miss any short sight words or phonetically regular one-syllable words.

  On the first fiction passage about an amusement park, Maria inserted one word on the first passage; however, because this only occurred once, it's not a pattern. She missed four words and self-corrected one of those errors. The three errors were all multisyllable words. On the second passage about eclipses, she missed five words, but it was the word *eclipse* all five times. In the last passage about the boy dreaming he was a bat, she missed four words. Each of these errors was a multisyllable word with the past tense ending *-ed*.

Retell

- **Is there consistency or variability in the student's Retell percent of DORF?**

  To answer this question we'll reference *Table 4.6*.

Table 4.6

Retell Percent of DORF for Jason and Maria

Retell Percent of DORF Words Correct	Jason			Maria		
	Passage 1	Passage 2	Passage 3	Passage 1	Passage 2	Passage 3
DORF Words Correct	102	106	112	71	84	78
Retell Score	14	16	21	25	20	27
Percent	14%	15%	19%	35%	24%	35%

Jason's retell score is only 14%–19% of his DORF Words Correct score, compared to Maria, whose retell was more substantial at 24%–35% of her DORF Words Correct score. Maria's accuracy rate was higher, so it makes sense that her Retell score was a higher percentage of the words she read correctly.

- **Is the student's Retell Quality score consistent or variable?**

  Jason had a Retell Quality score of 2 on two passages and a score of 1 on the other passage. This means that his retell included some details, but they weren't in any particular sequence and didn't include a main idea.

  Maria's Retell Quality score is a higher quality than Jason's retell. She received Retell Quality scores of 2, 3, and 4, so, clearly, her retell included details in sequence and a main idea.

Daze

- **What is the student's accuracy rate on Daze responses?**

  Accuracy rates on Daze (see *Figure 4.7*) can be calculated as number correct divided by the number of items attempted. Both students' accuracy rates are as follows:

Jason: 6 correct / 14 attempted = 43% accuracy

Maria: 10 correct / 12 attempted = 83% accuracy

This calculation reveals that Maria's accuracy rate on Daze responses is nearly twice that of Jason's.

Figure 4.7

Jason and Maria's Daze Passages

Daze Grade 3/Benchmark 1—Jason

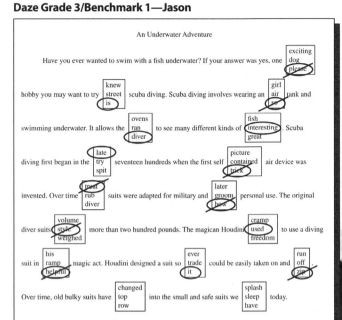

Daze Grade 3/Benchmark 1—Maria

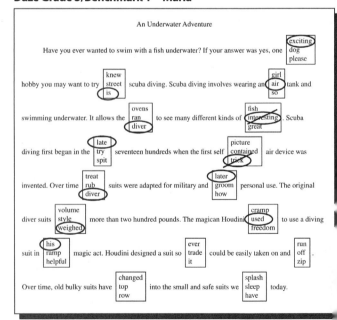

Step 4: Record Observations on Summary Sheet

Jason's Words Read Correctly scores in the range of 102–112 (see *Table 4.5*, page 105) place him well above the Benchmark Goal of 70 for the beginning of third grade. However, there is much more to the picture than this. Jason read at a faster rate but really struggled with errors. His low accuracy rate of 84% suggests a possible decoding issue. It's interesting to notice that Jason's low accuracy rate of 84% gave him 0 points in the Composite Score compared to Maria's 80 points (see *Table 4.4*, page 104). Both comprehension measures are low. His comprehension appears to have suffered from making many errors in decoding words. The next step for Jason is to assess his decoding skills with a phonics diagnostic screener. It appears that he is missing some phonics skills and would benefit from intervention in phonics.

Maria's Words Read Correctly scores in the range of 71–84 also place her above the Benchmark Goal of 70. Although she didn't read nearly as many words correctly as Jason (78 versus 106 on median scores), what she did read was considerably more accurate than Jason's reading. Although Jason's reading looked better than Maria's on Words Read Correctly alone, her slower reading rate with higher accuracy means that she has a stronger overall reading performance. At this time, Maria's reading appears to be on track and there are no real issues to address. She will need to continue to make progress in her reading rate in order to make the Benchmark Goal of 86 at midyear and 100 at the end of the year. Continued practice in reading text and responding to it should keep her at benchmark.

Chapter 5

Process for Grouping Students

The resources facilitate a continuous cycle of instruction and assessment that has the needs of children at its core. This combination provides a much-needed road map for teachers to use to intervene and support children before concerns become major roadblocks to literacy.

Curriculum Specialist, Regional Office of Education

DIBELS Next® data have many uses. These uses tend to fall into a couple of categories, including systems-wide information and student information. Examples of systems-wide purposes include measuring:

- the percentage of students who are at benchmark at various grade-levels;

- the growth in percentage of benchmark grade-level students from one period to the next; and

- the effectiveness of Tier 2 through observing the number of students starting the period below benchmark who have moved up to benchmark.

Student-based purposes include identifying which students may be struggling and sorting struggling readers for next steps in determining what type of extra support is needed. The focus of this chapter is on individual students and alternative processes to use *DIBELS Next* and other data to determine appropriate group placement. While grouping decisions should be based on a portfolio of information, *DIBELS*® results can be one of these pieces of information because they provide data that help identify possible skill deficiencies for below-benchmark students.

Educators today are hearing a great deal about "data-driven instruction." I prefer to view the *DIBELS* data as *informing* instruction rather than driving instruction; the teacher is driving the instruction based on analysis of data and careful observations about the student's response to instruction. The data can help teachers identify deficit areas, select which students need further diagnostic assessment, and monitor whether the student's skills are improving with instruction. The goal of carefully grouping students is motivated by the substantial gains possible when there is perfect alignment between the student's deficient skills and the instruction provided to the group.

Below-benchmark students in Tier 2 or Tier 3 groups do best where the instruction focuses on one or two key skill areas taught in homogeneous groups. *DIBELS* data in grades K–2 are helpful for identifying areas of need because many of the indicators assess the student's abilities in precursor or underlying skills in reading, including phonemic awareness (FSF and PSF) and early phonics (NWF-CLS and WWR). *DIBELS* data can be used to identify possible deficit areas, and then the teacher needs to validate this deficit and define it better. One of the most effective ways to validate and pinpoint missing skills is to give a diagnostic screener.

In this chapter, the term *small group* means three to five students for most skills and slightly larger groups for a few skill areas such as passage fluency. For students who are below benchmark, small groups are more effective than whole class instruction because the instructor can provide immediate corrective feedback on errors, along with follow-up explanations and guided practice, until the student learns the skill. This type of instruction is simply not possible when working with an entire class of 20 to 30 students. It is impossible to overstate the importance of fully utilizing all instructional time to improve skills of students at risk, especially those valuable minutes when the student is receiving instruction in a small group. This is one of the reasons that groups need to be formed in an analytical rather than incidental manner, resulting in skill groups that are tight and cohesive.

Keep in mind that the *DIBELS Next* data are only one type of data used in making these grouping decisions. Other sources of data are the teacher's observations of the student's errors, additional informal assessments including diagnostic screeners, student writing samples, and student text reading levels. No matter which approach a school uses for grouping, the goal is for each student in an intervention group to receive the maximum benefit from this critical instruction.

Factors to Consider When Forming Groups

There are many factors to consider when determining the groups, including how intervention groups will be delivered. Some schools have intervention take place in each classroom while others group across classrooms to enable more specific skill groups. At most points in time, there is more than one important indicator to consider. The balancing of several indicators at once is one reason that forming groups is complex. Each of these topics is covered in this section.

Grouping Students Is Not Always Straightforward

Teachers often find that the task of grouping students for intervention instruction is challenging and somewhat less straightforward than they expect. One thing that would greatly simplify grouping decisions would be using scores on only one

DIBELS measure. This process would be simple because teachers could construct a list of all the students who are below benchmark on a single indicator, decide how many groups to form, and then assign the students to groups. For example, if six students in a class were below benchmark in Phoneme Segmentation Fluency (PSF) and the teacher decided to have two groups of three students, then the students with the lowest PSF scores might be grouped together and the ones closer to benchmark might be placed in the second group.

There are two problems with grouping based on a single indicator. First, sometimes a student's scores on another indicator influence the decision about the student's overall needs. Grouping on the basis of a single indicator fails to acknowledge the link between many early literacy skills. For example, grouping beginning-of-year first-grade students only on their Nonsense Word Fluency (NWF) scores is not as informative as also considering their scores on the other indicators, including PSF. Students who are above benchmark in phoneme segmentation skills may make quicker progress from instruction in letter-sound correspondences than students whose PSF scores are below benchmark, an indicator that they may not be able to manipulate phonemes in words heard orally.

The second problem with single-indicator grouping is that it includes an assumption about a less-than-optimal delivery model. If students are grouped based on only one indicator, what happens if a student is showing deficiencies in several areas? Teachers are already pressed for time and this would make scheduling even more difficult because they would have to find time for some students who are missing more than one skill to work in several groups. Additionally, this approach wouldn't recognize that instruction in reading skills is often blended. For example, in September, a first-grade student who is below benchmark in PSF and well below in NWF would benefit from some blended instruction.

> *. . . it is worth the extra time and effort to assign groups based on the whole picture of the student's needs rather than single-skill grouping and rotating students to multiple groups when they are deficient in more than one skill.*

Teaching phoneme segmentation, even though it should have been mastered by the end of kindergarten, is useful because it's important for later reading skills. Research shows that adding letters once the student has an adequate level of phonemic awareness can actually aid in developing phonemic awareness. For these reasons, it is worth the extra time and effort to assign groups based on the whole picture of the student's needs rather than single-skill grouping and rotating students to multiple groups when they are deficient in more than one skill.

Although first-grade students whose phoneme segmentation scores in the fall are below benchmark benefit from additional instruction in this area, they also need to be making progress in letter-sound connections. Instruction on phonemic awareness must be accelerated and must rapidly build to letter sounds because these mid-first-grade students have multiple goals to accomplish if they are going to get back on track. With first-grade students who are well below benchmark in NWF at midyear, there is no time to waste. There is an urgency to teach phonics and word-level fluency reading at the phrase, sentence, and text level.

What makes the decision for grouping students challenging is that often there is interplay between indicators, and several indicators must be studied at the same time before a group can be formed. When students' scores are similar for one indicator but different for another, deciding on an appropriate group placement can be complicated. When this is the case, it helps to remember that students most often need to be grouped with recognition of the development of skills along the continuum (see *Figure 5.1*).

Figure 5.1

Learning-to-Read Skills Continuum—*DIBELS* 6th Edition

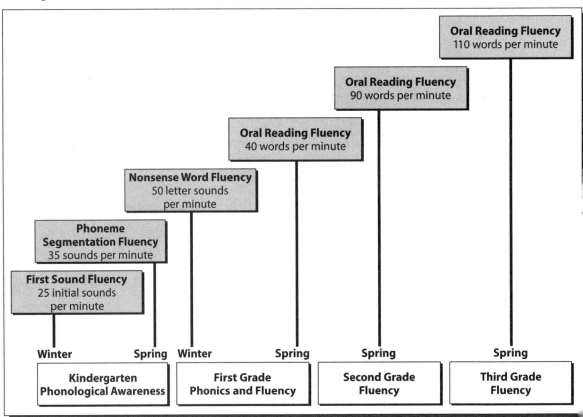

The learning-to-read continuum in *Figure 5.1*, which is from 6th Edition, reinforces the sense of urgency for progress when students are missing precursor skills (see *Figure 6.3* for the *DIBELS Next* version). Delay in reaching a key *DIBELS* indicator in grades K–1 is a red flag that the student is at risk. We don't have to wait for the middle of first grade to tell that a student is not on track in reading. Meeting each benchmark on all indicators is the only way to ensure that the student will read well later.

One significant change from the 6th Edition to *DIBELS Next* is that there are no longer terminal levels for these precursor reading skills. In the 6th Edition, the PSF goal was 35 by the end of kindergarten and the NWF goal was 50 letter sounds by the middle of grade 1. Even though PSF was supposed to be mastered by the end of kindergarten, it was measured at all three benchmark assessment periods in first grade. The Benchmark Goal for the beginning, middle, and end of grade 1 remained 35 because that was the terminal point for PSF when it was supposed to be mastered at the end of kindergarten. In *DIBELS Next*, there are no longer terminal points; but instead, each benchmark is empirically-derived for specific time periods. Notice that NWF-CLS continues to change from the middle of grade 1 through the beginning of grade 2. Instead of using the terminal Benchmark Goal of 50 for the goals for all three periods, the *DIBELS Next* Benchmark Goals for NWF-CLS now are as follows:

- Grade 1 Middle of Year (MOY): 43

- Grade 1 End of Year (EOY): 58

- Grade 2 Beginning of Year (BOY): 54

The research that was completed in the design of *DIBELS Next* pointed to how critical it is for students to reach all the goals measured in these early time periods to be on track; when determining what instruction a student needs, the focus must be on reaching all the critical skills instead of one critical skill that will reach its terminal point at the next period. It's no longer correct to assume that NWF-CLS is measured at mid-year kindergarten just to begin to see how well a student is doing, and that as long as he reaches the terminal goal by the middle of first grade, all is well. Staying on track means reaching the Benchmark Goal for each skill each period.

The focus on the importance of all the skills doesn't mean that they have to be taught in every lesson but that the student's instructional plan has to account for getting up to benchmark in all areas. Previously, it may have been easier to be lulled into celebration that the student finally reached the Benchmark Goal, when actually, by reaching the goal several months later than the recommended time, the student may already be behind in the next skill.

This change in *DIBELS Next* means that it is more important than ever to take into consideration how a student is performing on all major indicators when determining group placement and the instructional focus he needs to reach benchmark. The focus may need to be on achieving two or three goals within a reasonable time period for students to catch up. For example, a beginning of year first grade group may need to reach the following three goals for the students to have odds in their favor of reaching benchmark on the next indicator:

- Improve letter-sound correspondence so that they reach 43 on NWF-CLS by midyear.

- Improve blending of simple words with short vowels to reach 8 on NWF-WWR by midyear.

- Work on reading accuracy and fluency so that rate in connected text is 23 DORF-Words Correct with at least 78% accuracy.

How to Consider Letter Naming in Grouping Decisions

Letter naming is an intriguing skill, and one that merits further discussion. In spite of the fact that this skill is a powerful predictor of which students will struggle in learning to read, there are mixed messages about whether to provide instruction on this skill. Research does not show with certainty whether difficulty in letter naming is correlated with difficulty in reading or is related to other things that cause difficulty. Some researchers have hypothesized that a low letter naming score could actually measure low speed in cognitive processing or deficiencies in rapid automatic naming. Another possibility is that fluency with letter names may actually be an indirect measure of parental involvement (Good et al. 2003).

The *DIBELS* research team advises that teaching letter names is not necessarily going to raise later reading outcomes. However, students still need to know letter names for spelling and it may be an underlying foundation that makes learning letter sounds easier. Even though the *DIBELS* team positions letter naming as a risk indicator instead of a learning-to-read skill, this doesn't mean that some students wouldn't benefit from strategic instruction in letter naming when this skill is low. Phonemic awareness and letter-sound correspondences are clearly more important skills to teach than letter naming, but can we really ignore letter knowledge? Letter naming knowledge may be important in serving as an anchor for students as they connect sounds with letters. Fluency in letter recognition may help students so that they simply don't have to spend any time thinking about which letter they are looking at.

The key is to clarify where letter naming instruction fits in terms of instructional priorities. Letter naming should not be placed in the limelight as a main focus, yet it is acceptable to teach it when needed as long as it's not given a large amount of instructional time.

It is not recommended to form a group whose sole focus is on improving letter naming fluency during the 30-minute intervention block. However, teachers can strategically instruct in letter naming with a group whose focus is on phonemic awareness or letter-sound correspondences. Sometimes teachers pull a small group for an extra 5 to 10 minutes during the day to work on letter names so that the entire 30-minute intervention block can be dedicated to other skills.

Homogenous Groups Are a Necessity

When all students in a group have the same skill deficit, the teacher can select instructional strategies that are targeted on one or two key skills. The more alike the students in the group are in terms of skills they lack, the more likely that each student in the group is benefiting from the strategies and practice activities introduced during group time. A student who is proficient in a skill should not be in a group that is practicing that skill.

Some teachers raise concerns about homogeneous grouping. This is understandable because in the past homogeneous grouping has been denigrated, especially if it led to "tracking." In spite of concerns about tracking, it is imperative that students are homogeneously grouped by their skill deficits for intervention instruction. Remember that intervention time is generally half an hour and rarely longer than 1 hour. Most educators agree that it is not appropriate to group students homogeneously for the entire day or even the entire language arts block. However, during this short portion of the school day, the teacher must explicitly teach specific missing skills and not rely on students to learn from other students who cannot be expected to fully understand the instructional needs of at-risk students. Many students who are at risk failed to learn skills necessary for reading during the whole classroom instruction already provided or by observing their peers who answered ahead of them.

> *In spite of concerns about tracking, it is imperative that students are homogeneously grouped by their skill deficits for intervention instruction.*

At-risk students benefit from a smaller group where their attention can be focused and they can receive extra wait time before answering, if needed. Another important characteristic of intervention group instruction is that students receive immediate and appropriate feedback on errors when the group size is small. Additionally, students will be provided as many repetitions of a strategy, or variations in explanations, as needed until they master the skill being taught. Only by placing together students who need the same type of instruction can teachers maximize instructional time for everyone in this group.

Benefits of the Walk-to-Intervention Model

Many schools implementing RTI are using an approach to delivering small groups that we've named "Walk to Intervention," whereby during the intervention block time, students walk to the location of their group, which may not always be in their classroom. In any classroom of 18 to 28 students, there will be students who need intervention in many different skill areas. It's not practical for a teacher to try to schedule time to meet with five to eight different groups. If the teacher tries to meet with all these groups within the classroom, a couple of things might occur. The teacher may combine groups with the result that the instruction cannot be as targeted and students will get instruction on skills they already know or are too high for them. Additionally, the teacher may not meet with each group daily, which also will diminish the success of the intervention groups.

One possible solution is to have one or more staff members help in the classroom who will teach groups while the teacher works with another group. In the perfect situation, the teacher would need to have as many staff members in the room as number of groups. Because it's not uncommon to have five to eight different skill groups (or more) to meet the needs of all the students in a class, it's very difficult for schools to have enough staff to accomplish this. The best solution is to have a common intervention block time for a grade level and have teachers form groups across the grade level. In order to have group sizes small enough for effective intervention instruction, it's necessary to have at least 50% more support staff than the number of classroom teachers. For example, if there are four teachers at a grade level, there would need to be at least two support staff joining them so there can be six groups.

Let's look at how this might work with a third-grade team that has four classroom sections. Assume that the school's master schedule includes a 30-minute intervention block for third grade from 10:30 to 11:00 a.m., just after the 90-minute reading block. During the intervention block, the four classroom teachers are joined by three other staff members to help teach small groups. *Table 5.1* shows a possible grouping of the 84 students at this grade level (21 per classroom).

Table 5.1

Example of Third Grade Walk-to-Intervention Model

Group Number	Number of Students	Teacher	Skill
1	3	Special Education	**Short Vowels**—Grouped by deficit on diagnostic phonics screener
2	5	Reading Specialist	**Long Vowel Silent-*e***—Grouped by deficit on diagnostic phonics screener
3	5	Classroom Teacher 1	**Vowel Teams**—Grouped by deficit on diagnostic phonics screener
4	8	Classroom Teacher 2	**Vowel-*r***—Grouped by deficit on diagnostic phonics screener
5	12	Title I Teacher	**Multisyllable Word Strategies**—Based on phonics screener
6	21	Classroom Teacher 3	**Fluency**—Mini-lessons on fluency skill followed by paired reading
7	30	Classroom Teacher 4	**Comprehension and Enrichment**—for above-benchmark students
Total	84		

In this example, 33 of the 84 students entering third grade were weak in decoding skills that should be mastered in third grade. Those in the lowest skills (Groups 1–3) were in the smallest groups in order to give them the most intense instruction possible. The students closest to benchmark in Group 6 didn't have phonics issues but were provided assistance in developing their fluency. These students can be identified directly from the *DIBELS Next* data; they will have very high accuracy rates (95% on BOY passages, 96% on MOY passages, and 97% on EOY passages), yet they didn't read the Benchmark Goal number of words correct per minute. Their reading rate was low even though their accuracy was high.

One important advantage of the walk-to-intervention approach is that it serves all students and not just those who are below benchmark. We are so accustomed to using *DIBELS* to identify the at-risk students that sometimes we forget to look for students at the other end of the exceptionality profile—those who are way above benchmark for their age. Look back at the benchmark students again and identify any students whose scores place them above the 80th or 90th percentile. As the size of the benchmark group grows, it's possible to divide it into sections so that the really high readers get more enriched sessions with peers reading and responding to text that is above grade level.

Skill Focus Is Critical

> *If instruction is to be targeted, the plan must be explicit. It is not enough to say the group needs to work on medial vowel sounds. The plan must explicitly list the medial vowels the students will work on in the lesson. The explicit language the teacher will use to model the sounds should either be in the plan or "routinized" through training.*
>
> State Department of Education

Schools that have achieved the greatest gains in reading have grouped students for intervention groups based on skill deficits. As you can see from the example in *Table 5.1* on page 121, the third-grade students are placed in groups for the 30 minutes of intervention to receive instruction in a specific needed area. It's best not to pull students from the 90-minute core Tier 1 reading block for their intervention time.

The whole point of the intervention block is to offer differentiated instruction. It's not differentiated if all groups receive the same curriculum. While there has been a great deal of discussion about fidelity to the program and the benefits of using a standard curriculum, my experience with several hundred schools over the past ten years has taught me that one-size fits-all in Tier 2 does not lead to gains as strong as with a more differentiated approach. Schools benefit from using a uniform curriculum for Tier 1 and possibly for Tier 3 but not for Tier 2. In Tier 1, it's important that all components of reading instruction are covered in a comprehensive, sequential, and systematic manner. In Tier 3, it makes sense that students who are struggling with reading and who have not responded to Tier 2 will need a more comprehensive program that covers all the skills taught systematically and at a pace that enables them to master one skill at a time. Students in Tier 3 generally are provided intervention for more minutes than those in Tier 2; for example, a typical schedule is to have 30 minutes daily for Tier 2 groups and an hour daily for Tier 3 groups (the hour doesn't have to be delivered in one sitting). When evaluating whether it's possible to deliver a comprehensive standardized program during Tier 2, consider that if it takes 90 minutes a day to deliver a core program that covers all five components of reading instruction, how can that be done in 30 minutes?

Tier 2 is different from Tiers 1 and 3. The students needing Tier 2 have gaps in their skills. They have mastered some skills and can read somewhat but are having difficulty because they are missing selected skills. They aren't like students who need Tier 3 who are far behind and are missing many skills. To use a comprehensive program in Tier 2 where the teacher follows lessons 1 to 99 doesn't make sense. Most students in Tier 2 don't need a portion of those lessons. They need specific skills and differentiated instruction to help them master what they are missing.

One critical assumption about the approach advocated here is that the groups are flexible. A student stays in a skill group for only one or two cycles and is moved to the next missing skill group as soon as possible. This way, she can receive instruction in missing decoding skills, then fluency work, and finally comprehension through moving up the continuum of skill groups. Sometimes a student's reading rate is low because she is struggling with decoding. Once the decoding issue has been addressed and the student has made major gains in single-word reading, her passage reading rate increases to the point that there is no longer a fluency issue. Similarly, some students whose Retell and Daze are initially low will show improvement in these comprehension measures after improving their decoding skills. This means that teachers will be reassessing some skills along the way to make sure intervention it still needed.

Sometimes a group covers more than one skill, but the focus is always clear. Having a clear focus keeps the time allocation aligned to the purpose. If the focus of a group is teaching phoneme isolation, at least 20 minutes of a 30-minute group should be dedicated to that skill. If the data show that all the students placed in that group also would benefit from additional help with letter naming, the instructor can either begin or end the lesson by spending about 5 minutes on letter naming. It's completely acceptable for a teacher to make sure students know the meanings of words in their word lists or passages during a decoding group. Vocabulary is always valuable. When a student finishes reading a passage the teacher should ask a question about what the text meant even though the focus of the lesson was decoding. The key is that the time spent should be aligned with the focus skill. If the focus of the lesson is on phonics, then spending half the time on vocabulary and comprehension wouldn't be a wise choice. Reading is a complex process and the reading components are intertwined. Instruction will intersect other components naturally just in the course of providing focused instruction in one specific area.

> *Sometimes a group covers more than one skill, but the focus is always clear. Having a clear focus keeps the time allocation aligned to the purpose.*

Because our approach is to provide intervention on targeted missing skills, scheduling intervention outside of the reading block is critical so that students don't miss instruction on all the components of reading that are covered during the core. If a student's intervention is in decoding, he needs to be present for the vocabulary and comprehension instruction in the core because his intervention will not cover those skills.

Group Size

One of the factors that contributes to accelerating progress for below-benchmark students is determining an appropriate group size for instruction. The lowest-performing students need to be in the smallest groups so they get the most corrective feedback and maximum time to practice the skill. Try groups of three for the lowest-performing students, and change to groups of two, if needed, for the students who aren't making enough progress. Groups of five students may be effective for the highest of the intervention students. Groups with more than five students tend to be less effective because the instructor cannot see and respond to each error. These suggested group sizes are ideal; in some schools, there are so many students needing intervention instruction that resource limitations lead to larger group sizes. Additionally, if 80% of the students in a class have scores in the intensive range, the type of instruction provided to the whole class will mirror some of the explicit and systematic characteristics of intervention instruction.

Alternative Approaches for Grouping Students

Schools use a variety of approaches to grouping students for intervention instruction depending on whether they use a data-management system or not. Some of the options include the following:

- **Grouping within a data-management system.** Some data-management systems provide grouping. Providers of data-management systems include VPORT by Cambium Learning® Sopris, DIBELS.net by DMG, University of Oregon, and Wireless Generation.

- **Grouping with data from *DIBELS* and a diagnostic screener.** Many schools have experienced success by using data from *DIBELS* as a universal screener to identify students at risk and then administering diagnostic screeners to pinpoint needs of students at risk.

- **Grouping with data from *DIBELS* only.** This can include grouping with spreadsheets, grouping boards or folders, or through reports on a school server.

- **Dynamic Measurement Group's (DMG)** *DIBELS Next* **Initial Instructional Grouping Suggestions Worksheets.** These are a set of grouping worksheets that can be downloaded from the DMG Web site for use with initial grouping.

The grouping reports available within data-management systems vary depending on the provider. Generally, the grouping functions are available only to schools that use the data-management services and there are fees for these services.

In this chapter, two approaches will be discussed in depth because they are available to anyone without extra cost: the DMG grouping worksheets and an approach the author and her company, 95 Percent Group, have developed. The grouping ideas included in this chapter are designed to help teachers who are beginning to use *DIBELS* data have an efficient way to form groups for targeted instruction. If you have been working with *DIBELS* data and use an approach that differs from the process outlined in this chapter, continue using your approach if it has been successful. An approach is successful when the students in groups are making improvements and closing the gap, as measured by *DIBELS* progress monitoring.

Grouping With Data From *DIBELS* and Diagnostic Screeners

Many schools use *DIBELS* as a universal screener to assess the skills of all students three times a year to track the reading progress of students, to evaluate the effectiveness of tiers of instruction, and to identify below-benchmark students who may be at risk of later difficulties. *DIBELS* and *DIBELS Next* are excellent tools for universal screening, yet they are not diagnostic instruments. It is critical not to try to use *DIBELS Next* data to conclude where to begin intervention instruction when only certain skills are assessed. For example, *DIBELS* assesses NWF, which only provides information about a student's ability to decode words with the CVC pattern but not long vowel, vowel team, or vowel-*r* patterns. It's difficult to conclude when a student misses the word *elderly* in a DORF passage whether she had trouble with the *r*-controlled vowel or the suffix *-ly*.

Informal diagnostic screeners are individually administered, brief, informal assessments of a skill. The word informal in this context means that it is not a standardized test, so directions and practice items can be given in any way the assessor feels the student will understand the task. Although it's fine to restate the directions in other words and give extra practice items, it's recommended that the assessor refrain from coaching the student during the test items or the results may overstate the student's skills. Informal diagnostic screeners typically are not norm referenced. They are usually criterion referenced by indicating that a specific percentage correct is recommended, such as 90%. Most of the time, these recommended percentages are not necessarily empirically derived but are based on expectations that students who have mastered the skill should be able to get that number correct. Generally, informal diagnostic assessments are not timed because their purpose is to assess accuracy, or mastery of a skill, and not fluency.

> DIBELS *helped me to determine which students I needed to assess further. I administered the PSI™ (Phonics Screener for Intervention™) to the students who had many miscues on* DIBELS. *I was then able to see which syllable patterns they need to be taught.*
>
> Third-Grade Teacher

The purpose of a diagnostic assessment is that it pinpoints which skills a student has mastered and which are still deficit. It gives much more detailed information about what a student can and cannot do. Effective diagnostic screeners:

- measure one skill at a time;

- are easy to administer and interpret;

- enable administering part of, rather than all of, the assessment, at any given time;

- have alternate forms (at least three forms); and

- are time efficient.

The last characteristic, time efficiency, is critical. Ideal screeners give enough examples to show whether a student can do the skill but not too many because then they take too long to administer. The test items should be carefully chosen to allow the assessor to observe how the student can handle word patterns containing that skill. Diagnostic screeners often have one, two, or three of the following: lists of pseudowords, lists of real words, and example real words in context.

My recommendation is to look for diagnostic screeners that have pseudowords and real words in context. The lists of real words are not as useful as the other two items, and are not necessary if the instrument contains the other two types of test items. Pseudowords that contain a specific pattern are the best. *Table 5.2* shows the design of the skills assessed in one phonics diagnostic screener followed by a sample student scoring sheet for one skill (see *Figure 5.2*).

Table 5.2

Skills Measured in the Phonics Screener for Intervention (PSI)

Level of Phonics	Skill Number	Phonics Skill Description	Grade Level Typically Mastered (minimum—can be earlier)
Basic	1	Letter Names and Sounds—consonants and vowels	Kindergarten
	2	CVC—consonant-vowel-consonant	Grade 1
	3	Consonant Blends—short vowels	
	4	Consonant Digraphs—short vowels	
	5	Long Vowel Silent-*e*	
Advanced	6	Predictable Vowel Teams—predictable pronunciation	Grade 2
	7	Unpredictable Vowel Teams—multiple common pronunciations	
	8	Vowel-*r*	
	9	Complex Consonants (e.g., dge, tch, silent letters)	
Multisyllable	10	Closed Syllable	Grade 3
	11	Long Vowel Silent-*e* Syllable	
	12	Open Syllable	
	13	Vowel Team Syllable	
	14	Consonant-*le* Syllable	
	15	Vowel-*r* Syllable	

Figure 5.2

Sample PSI Student Scoring Sheet

Skill 3: Consonant Blends					
<u>tri</u>z	fl<s>ug</s> vug	<u>bl</u><s>et</s> plit	mo<u>nd</u>	ga<u>mp</u>	# Correct
str<s>om</s> stom	sp<s>let</s> sprit	<u>pr</u>ant	<u>br</u>u<u>nd</u>	gr<s>ust</s> prest	5/10
<u>Fred</u> was <u>glad</u> to <u>swim</u> to the <u>raft</u> at <u>camp</u>.					# Target Words Correct
<u>Brad</u> <u>held</u> on to the <u>strap</u> so he could <u>jump</u> off the <u>stilts</u>.					10/10

As you can see from the example of the scoring sheet, the phonics skill of reading words with consonant blends and short vowels is isolated. The pseudowords used are simple and don't contain many other word patterns like the suffix -*ed* or -*s*. Notice that the consonant blend is underlined in each pseudoword. This is to indicate to the assessor the part that counts for the point. If a student misses the short vowel but gets the consonant blend correct, it's important to recognize that the error was not in reading the blend but in the short vowel. Some diagnostic screeners don't make this clear and the result is that students may be incorrectly grouped.

Selecting a phonics screener that is easy to administer is also important so that many people can administer it and the results will be consistent between assessors. If it's too complex, even if it's more efficient, there is a risk that it may not be used appropriately. Schools appreciate diagnostic screeners that are straightforward so that they can be administered by many staff members, including classroom teachers, reading specialists, reading interventionists, and paraprofessionals. One consideration in selecting who will assess is that the individual can distinguish when a student is giving the proper pronunciation of the sounds in the words.

The alternate forms are critical for using the diagnostic screener for progress monitoring to ensure that the student doesn't remember the prompts when the assessment is administered within a short time frame. It's ideal to have three alternate forms, commonly called Forms A, B, and C. Most schools use Form A for placement and then Forms B and C for progress monitoring, as needed. When schools have a diagnostic screener, they typically use it for progress monitoring a student's mastery of a specific skill rather than using the *DIBELS* progress monitoring assessments. *DIBELS* is ideal for monitoring groups focused on improving reading fluency using DORF progress monitoring passages. However, *DIBELS* is not ideal for progress monitoring phonological awareness, phonics, or comprehension groups because it doesn't measure these skills in a finite enough manner. *DIBELS* measures CVC words in NWF but not any other phonics patterns. If a group is working on the long vowel silent-*e* skill, it's not effective to give a student a DORF passage to monitor their progress in learning this skill. There may not be many long vowel silent-*e* words in one passage, and even if there are some, the word may contain another pattern, such as a suffix ending, so it's impossible to know whether the student missed it because of the target pattern or the suffix.

If using Form A for initial assessment, a student will be placed in an intervention group for the lowest missing skill. After a reasonable period of time (1 to 3 weeks), the student can be assessed with Form B of only the skill that is the focus of instruction. If the student fails to reach the mastery level of 90%, then she remains in that skill group for another intervention cycle and is assessed with Form C at the end of the next intervention cycle. On the other hand, if she passes the skill in Form B, then the assessor can go back to Form A and continue administering skills up the list until she fails another skill. This process for progress monitoring is very efficient because assessment on each skill takes less than 1 minute.

Many schools use a grouping worksheet in a spreadsheet program to keep track of student scores and groups. *Figure 5.3* shows an example of a grouping worksheet for a phonics diagnostic screener. All students at a grade level whose DORF accuracy rate was below the benchmark DORF Accuracy Rate have been assessed with the phonics screener, and their scores are recorded on the spreadsheet. Each student is placed in the group that will focus on their lowest missing skill in the continuum from Skill 1 to Skill 15. The shading of the names shows which students will work in each group.

Figure 5.3

PSI Grouping Worksheet Example

	Beginning Phonics Skills						Advanced Phonics Skills				Other
Student Name	**1a: Letter Names**	**1b: Letter Sounds**	**2: VC/CVC**	**3: Consonant Blends**	**4: Consonant Digraphs**	**5: Silent-e**	**6: Vowel Teams (Predictable)**	**7: Vowel Teams**	**8: Vowel-r**	**9: Complex Consonants**	**Sight Words**
Maximum Points	**26**	**21C/5V**	**10/10**	**10/10**	**10/10**	**10/10**	**10/10**	**10/10**	**10/10**	**10/10**	**/220**
Brian			10/10	7/10	7/10	2/10					
Hadley			10/10	7/4							
Becca			6/10	7/7	6/7						
Alyssa			10/10	9/9	9/10	7/7					
Mercedes			9/9	9/10	7/8	8/10					
Kristi			10/10	9/10	8/7	7/10					
Quinn			9/9	9/9	7/9	6/8					
Jed			9/10	9/7	6/8	7/6					
Jordan			9/9	9/10	9/10	4/10					
Brittanie			9/10	10/10	9/9	1/8					
Sommer			10/10	9/10	10/9	6/10					
Shandra			9/10	10/10	9/9	7/9					
Jaden			9/10	10/10	9/10	7/8					

Source: 95 Percent Group Inc. (2011). Reprinted with permission.

One thing that schools have done that helps all staff know when to assess is to prepare a schedule for the intervention cycles at the beginning of the year. *Table 5.3* on the next page shows an example of one such schedule.

Table 5.3

Intervention Cycle Schedule Example

Cycle #	Period	Assessment Dates	Data Team Meeting Dates (Thursdays)	New Groups Begin (Monday)
1	Beginning of Year Benchmark	September 6–15	September 15	September 19
2	PM	October 3–6	October 6	October 10
3	PM	October 24–27	October 27	October 31
4	PM	October 14–17	November 17	November 21
5	PM	December 12–15	December 15	January 2
6	Middle of Year Benchmark	January 3–12	January 12	January 16
7	PM	January 30–February 2	February 2	February 6
8	PM	February 21–23	February 23	February 27
9	PM	March 12–15	March 15	March 19
10	PM	April 9–12	April 12	April 16
11	End of Year Benchmark	May 7–17	May 17	End of Year

In the example above, the grade level team would give *DIBELS* to all students as a universal screener during a two-week time frame for the three benchmark periods at the beginning, middle, and end of the year. For all students below benchmark in phonological awareness and phonics, a diagnostic screener would be given next to determine group placement. These intervention students would then be assessed with an alternate form of the diagnostic screener only on the specific skill or skills they were taught to make sure they have mastered them and can be moved up to their next missing skill. The progress monitoring assessment can be administered the last few days of the three-week cycle just before the scheduled grade-level team meeting when all teachers bring their data and the students are regrouped. In this sample schedule, the meetings occur on Thursdays and the new groups begin meeting the following Monday, which gives all staff time to prepare for their new groups.

Grouping Without Diagnostic Screeners

When schools don't have a diagnostic screener for phonological awareness and phonics, there are other approaches they use for grouping. This section includes some ideas for how to group based on *DIBELS* data when diagnostic screener data are not available.

The first step is to figure out which students are considered at benchmark and which are not based on the Composite Score. We think about student reading behaviors falling into four categories:

- **Fast and Right**—Students who read at a sufficient rate to benchmark, plus their accuracy meets expected levels. At grades K–2, these students also are able to demonstrate that their phonological awareness, letter-sound correspondence, and early phonics skills are accurate and fluent enough to not be at risk of later difficulties.

- **Slow and Right**—Students who read accurately but perform at a rate that is not sufficient to meet expected levels of performance. For students in grades 2 and above, this category will include students whose accuracy is above benchmark on DORF, but who don't meet the accuracy goals.

- **Fast and Wrong**—Students who read at a fast rate, but their accuracy is not high enough to meet expected levels.

- **Slow and Wrong**—Students who read at a slow rate, and their accuracy is also below benchmark.

Each classroom teacher can complete an initial sorting form using these four categories to determine which students are ready for grouping and which ones will need additional diagnostic assessment. *Figure 5.4* shows an example for grade 3. The other grade levels are available on 95 Percent Group's secure Web site at www.IDNWnext.com.

Figure 5.4

Initial Sorting Form Example for Grade 3

	Fast and Right DORF	Slow and Right DORF	Fast and Wrong DORF	Slow and Wrong DORF
	BOY/MOY/EOY Words Correct Above: 52/72/87 Accuracy Above: 95%/96%/97%	**BOY/MOY/EOY** Words Correct Above: 52/72/87 Accuracy Above: 95%/96%/97%	**BOY/MOY/EOY** Words Correct Above: 52/72/87 Accuracy Above: 95%/96%/97%	**BOY/MOY/EOY** Words Correct Above: 52/72/87 Accuracy Above: 95%/96%/97%
Next Steps	Evaluate Comprehension Skills (Retell, Retell Quality, and Daze)	Fluency Instruction	Assess with a Phonics Diagnostic Screener	Assess with a Phonics Diagnostic Screener
Lesson Format	Comprehension and Vocabulary Focus	Fluency Focus	Phonics Focus	Phonics Focus
Progress Monitor		*DIBELS* DORF	Phonics Diagnostic Screener	Phonics Diagnostic Screener

DORF, Retell, and Daze are names of *DIBELS Next* Measures.
Source: 95 Percent Group Inc. (2011). Reprinted with permission. All rights reserved.

Grouping With Dynamic Measurement Group's Initial Grouping Worksheets

DMG has provided initial grouping worksheets that can be downloaded from their Web site. The version available at the time this book was written is dated April 2011. There may be more recent updated versions available now. The directions on the first page emphasize that DMG views these worksheets as initial suggestions for grouping and they advise that the teacher should consider other information available on the student. They suggest that validating the need for support is an important step and that additional information to validate can be gathered by retesting with alternate forms of the corresponding *DIBELS* measure or by using other assessment data including that from a brief diagnostic assessment.

The DMG grouping forms are a set of worksheets with one sheet per grade level per benchmark time period. The Benchmark Goals are printed on the forms on the column headers for the groups. Each worksheet has four groups, as follows:

- Group 1 is benchmark.

- Group 2 needs support on one skill at that time period but not both skills.

- Group 3 needs support on the other skill.

- Group 4 (lowest group) needs support on both key skills at that period.

There are two indicators considered for grouping at most time periods. These indicators are summarized in *Table 5.4*.

Table 5.4

Indicators Used for Grouping on DMG's Initial Grouping Worksheets

DIBELS Indicator	Kindergarten BOY	Kindergarten MOY	Kindergarten EOY	Grade 1 BOY	Grade 1 MOY	Grade 1 EOY	Grade 2 BOY	Grade 2 MOY	Grade 2 EOY	Grades 3–6 BOY	Grades 3–6 MOY	Grades 3–6 EOY
Composite Score	X											
FSF	X											
PSF		X	X	X								
NWF–CLS		X	X	X								
NWF–WWR					X	X	X					
DORF Words Correct					X	X	X	X	X	X	X	X
DORF Accuracy Rate								X	X	X	X	X
DORF Retell								Check benchmark group		Check benchmark group		

The DMG initial grouping approach has some positive features. First, it's simple because there are only four groups for initial grouping and these are focused on the most important indicators at a given time period. As DMG states in the cover sheet of their *Initial Instructional Grouping Suggestions*, the grouping worksheets "provide an initial focus on the two most salient core components at each assessment time." (Dynamic Measurement Group 2011d). They recommend validating that a student needs support, which can be done by administering an alternate form or a brief diagnostic assessment. Also, if too many students fall into Groups 2–4, review the core instruction to consider supplementing it to address missing skills.

There are some cautions to using the DMG initial grouping worksheets. First, teachers may be tempted to think that only four groups are necessary. Most schools have more than four groups, and it's preferable to have even more specific skills. It's possible to subdivide a group by looking more closely at other *DIBELS* indicators not listed as the two most important, in combination with other information available on a student. However, this may be more difficult and less accurate than using diagnostic screener data for gathering more specific information in the areas of phonological awareness and phonics.

Another caution involves grades 2 and above. These grouping worksheets focus on DORF Words Correct and DORF Accuracy. The following instructional recommendations for the groups are provided on the worksheets:

- **Group 1: Benchmark**. Students in this group are at or above the Benchmark Goal in DORF Words Correct, Accuracy, and Retell. The recommendation is that they are likely to continue to make progress with core support only.

- **Group 2: Fluency**. This group of students is above benchmark on Accuracy and below on number of Words Correct. The instructional recommendation is to provide support on fluency in reading connected text.

- **Group 3: Accuracy**. Students in this group are at or above benchmark in Words Correct but below in Accuracy. The recommendation is to provide support on accurate reading of text.

- **Group 4: Accuracy and Fluency**. Students placed in this group have DORF Words Correct and Accuracy scores below or well below benchmark. The instructional recommendation for this category is listed as "Additional support on the accurate and fluent reading of connected text levels."

My concern with these grouping worksheets is that Groups 3 and 4 will include students with too many different types and degrees of issues for the instruction to be effective within the same group. There are too many different causes of low accuracy. Students would be placed in Groups 3 and 4 with Accuracy Rates anywhere from only somewhat below the 90%–98% Benchmark Goal levels (depending on the grade level and time of year) to way below. For example, at fifth grade, where the accuracy Benchmark Goals are 98%–99%, it's possible that Group 3 would include students with a 97% accuracy rate and others with a 70%

accuracy rate (or lower). This is a very wide range of accuracy issues, but even subdividing by degrees of accuracy rates wouldn't help the teacher determine the instruction needed. Students falling in this category could have difficulty only in reading multisyllable words, while others still might be struggling even at the single-syllable level. Some students may have trouble with only *r*-controlled vowels, while others may have more pervasive confusions even about long and short vowels. These groups would include students not accurately reading nonphonetic sight words, and there would be other students who read these words well but have trouble with other reading patterns. There are just too many reasons for students to read inaccurately, and it's nearly impossible to figure out how to provide appropriate instruction just by knowing that they are inaccurate. Accuracy issues signal that there's a phonics issue, but there are over a dozen major phonics patterns and many more minor patterns.

For both Groups 3 and 4, the instructional recommendation of increasing DORF Accuracy is going to be hard for teachers to provide without more diagnostic data on exactly which word patterns the students are lacking. Additional diagnostic information is essential to make good instructional decisions. Our experience is that grouping by phonics skill deficit regardless of reading rate is best. Some students that would be listed under the criteria for Groups 3 and 4 can be grouped together for phonics instruction; both groups are inaccurate and the only difference is that Group 4 also has a slow reading rate. Often after a student masters the phonics pattern, his reading rate improves dramatically so that fluency at the word level addresses the issue at the passage level.

Most schools are identifying students who read accurately and fluently but whose comprehension is not strong. Therefore, my recommendation is that it is necessary to have a group for these students. In DMG's four-group worksheets, these students are not identified and listed. *Table 5.5*, here and on the following page, summarizes DMG's initial instructional grouping suggestions.

Table 5.5

Summary of the Initial Instructional Grouping Suggestions of DMG

Indicator:	Kindergarten—BOY		Indicator:	Kindergarten—MOY		Indicator:	Kindergarten—EOY	
	Group 1	Group 2		Group 1	Group 2		Group 1	Group 2
FSF	10+	10+	PSF	20+	20+	PSF	40+	40+
Comp	26+	0–25	NWF-CLS	17+	0–16	NWF-CLS	28+	0–27
Instruction	Core	PA + Letter-Sound	**Instruction**	Core	AP + Basic Phonics	**Instruction**	Core	PA + Basic Phonics
Indicator:	**Group 3**	**Group 4**	**Indicator:**	**Group 3**	**Group 4**	**Indicator:**	**Group 3**	**Group 4**
FSF	0–9	0–9	PSF	0–19	0–19	PSF	0–39	0–39
Comp	26+	0–25	NWF-CLS	17+	0–17	NWF-CLS	28+	0–27
Instruction	PA	PA + Letter-Sound	**Instruction**	PA	PA + AP + Basic Phonics	**Instruction**	PA	PA + AP + Basic Phonics

Based on *Initial Instructional Grouping Suggestions Worksheets*, © Dynamic Measurement Group, Inc./January 2011
Source: 95 Percent Group Inc. (2011). Reprinted with permission. All rights reserved.

Table 5.5

Summary of the Initial Instructional Grouping Suggestions of DMG

Indicator:	Grade 1—BOY		Indicator:	Grade 1—MOY		Indicator:	Grade 1—EOY	
	Group 1	Group 2		Group 1	Group 2		Group 1	Group 2
PSF	40+	40+	NWF-WWR	8+	8+	NWF-WWR	13+	13+
NWF-CLS	27+	0–27	DORF wrc	23+	0–23	DORF wrc	47+	0–46
Instruction	Core	AP + Basic Phonics	Instruction	Core	Accurate & Fluent reading of text	Instruction	Core	Accurate & Fluent reading of text
Indicator:	Group 3	Group 4	Indicator:	Group 3	Group 4	Indicator:	Group 3	Group 4
PSF	0–40	0–40	NWF-WWR	0–7	0–7	NWF-WWR	0–12	0–12
NWF-CLS	27+	0–26	DORF wrc	23+	0–22	DORF wrc	47+	0–46
Instruction	PA	PA + AP + Letter-Sound	Instruction	AP + Basic Phonics	AP + Basic Phonics + text reading	Instruction	AP + Basic Phonics	AP + Basic Phonics + text reading

Based on *Initial Instructional Grouping Suggestions Worksheets*, © Dynamic Measurement Group, Inc./January, 2011

Indicator:	Grade 2—BOY		Indicator:	Grade 2—MOY		Indicator:	Grade 2—EOY	
	Group 1	Group 2		Group 1	Group 2		Group 1	Group 2
NWF-WWR	13+	13+	DORF	72+, 96% +	96%+ accur.	DORF	87+, 97% +	97%+ accur.
DORF wrc	52+	0–51	DORF	Retell 21+	0–71 wrc	DORF	Retell 27+	0–86 wrc
Instruction	Core	Accurate & Fluent reading of text	Instruction	Core	Accurate & Fluent reading of text	Instruction	Core	Accurate & Fluent reading of text
Indicator:	Group 3	Group 4	Indicator:	Group 3	Group 4	Indicator:	Group 3	Group 4
NWF-WWR	0–12	0–12	DORF	0–95% accur.	0–95% accur.	DORF	0–95% accur.	0–96% accur.
DORF wrc	52+	0–51	DORF	72+ wrc	0–71 wrc	DORF	87+ wrc	0–86 wrc
Instruction	AP + Basic Phonics	AP + Basic Phonics + text reading	Instruction	Accurate & Fluent reading of text	Accurate & Fluent reading of text	Instruction	Accurate & Fluent reading of text	Accurate & Fluent reading of text

Based on *Initial Instructional Grouping Suggestions Worksheets*, © Dynamic Measurement Group, Inc./January, 2011

Indicator:	Grades 3–6—BOY		Indicator:	Grades 3–6—MOY		Indicator:	Grades 3–6—EOY	
	Group 1	Group 2		Group 1	Group 2		Group 1	Group 2
DORF	Retell 20+	13+	DORF	Retell 26+	96%+ accur.	DORF	Retell 30+	97%+ accur.
DORF	70+, 95%	0–51	DORF	72+, 96%	0–71 wrc	DORF	87+, 96% +	0–86 wrc
Instruction	Core	Accurate & Fluent reading of text	Instruction	Core	Accurate & Fluent reading of text	Instruction	Core	Accurate & Fluent reading of text
Indicator:	Group 3	Group 4	Indicator:	Group 3	Group 4	Indicator:	Group 3	Group 4
DORF	0–12	0–12	DORF	Below 96% accur.	Below 96% accur.	DORF	Below 97% accur.	Below 97% accur.
DORF	52+	0–51	DORF	72+ wrc	0–71 wrc	DORF	87+ wrc	0–86 wrc
Instruction	AP + Basic Phonics	AP + Basic Phonics + text reading	Instruction	Accurate & Fluent reading of text	Accurate & Fluent reading of text	Instruction	Accurate & Fluent reading of text	Accurate & Fluent reading of text

Based on *Initial Instructional Grouping Suggestions Worksheets*, © Dynamic Measurement Group, Inc./January, 2011
Source: 95 Percent Group Inc. (2011). Reprinted with permission. All rights reserved.

Other Tips for Grouping

For more than ten years, I've been using another grouping process that teachers like. It's a format that makes the grouping process visible to a group of teachers, such as a grade-level team, and facilitates the grouping decisions by making it visible to all participants in a meeting. It involves using a place to list categories as column headers and then moving self-stick notes representing below-benchmark students until the optimum groups are formed. Grouping is a balance between the number of staff members available to teach small groups, the number of students needing intervention, and the specific skills missing for each student. The process is started by listing category names across the top of a whiteboard or a science project board. The categories define the range of scores on the important indicators for that time period. Teachers then place the name of each student in their classroom on a self-stick note, along with pertinent data in different corners of the self-stick note. Students are placed in groups temporarily by larger categories and then subgrouped based on refinements within the major categories.

The needs of the top and bottom groups are typically quite distinct from one another and form an obvious contrast. Students in the highest group are often at, or nearly at, benchmark in one or more indicators yet lacking on the more advanced skill measured. Because of the contrast, there will be a cohesive group at the bottom and a cohesive group at the top. This makes it easier to group from each end first, and then place all the middle students as a final step for dealing with intervention students. It can be more obvious where to place students whose scores fall in the middle of the rank order list after the obvious high and low groups have been identified.

In about 2003, while teaching workshops on using the 5th and 6th Edition *DIBELS* data, I created a series of grouping mats for each grade level and time period. Back when the 5th Edition had *DIBELS* measures only for grades K–3, we handed out mats for each grade level for the beginning, middle, and end of the year. The mats were printed on 11 × 17 paper, color-coded by grade level to match the colors of the *DIBELS* student scoring booklets printed by Sopris, at that time (green for kindergarten, red for grade 1, blue for grade 2, and orange for grade 3). We had sample classroom reports and participants used small self-stick notes to complete a classroom placement during the workshop. This process is still useful. Copies of these mats, which have been updated for *DIBELS Next*, are available for download at www.IDNWnext.com.

Record Keeping for Grouping and Regrouping

The grouping board process described in the preceding paragraph is very helpful the initial time teachers go through grouping. Then after the initial grouping, the boards are not needed as much because the regrouping is mostly moving some students up a skill. At that point, the question is more about group size and staffing constraints. Sometimes two skills have to be combined because there are so few students needing those skills as students begin moving up the continuum. Later, the challenge is subdividing the benchmark/enrichment group as it grows in size. At this stage, the process can be done on paper. Often teachers submit updated progress monitoring data to a coordinator (often the grade-level team leader or the reading coach) by a cut-off time before the next meeting. The coordinator then does the regrouping and passes out a sheet with the suggested regrouping for confirmation by the teachers.

Most schools that use our phonological awareness and phonics diagnostic screeners do their grouping and regrouping by updating the student data on the spreadsheet and passing out lists of the new groups at grade-level team meetings. These spreadsheets are often posted on the school server so all intervention teachers can post their scores into one file. If there are minor changes in between the three-week cycle to move a couple of students, the coordinator can send out an email with the link and let everyone know of the groups affected. After about the first three months, the regrouping process generally becomes very automated and doesn't need to be the focus of collaboration time.

Summary on Placing Students in Groups

Using data from *DIBELS Next* as part of the grouping process is a complex process. It's tempting to believe that it's possible to group from these data alone, but the best results are achieved when using *DIBELS Next* data to identify which students are at risk and then assessing those students with diagnostic screeners to determine group placement. Just remember that whatever decisions you make about groups is temporary. This generally gives teachers a sense of relief that any incorrect placement decisions can be corrected when students are regrouped. After you begin progress monitoring, students will be moved between groups anyway. Some students will make considerable progress within about six to nine weeks of working in the intervention groups. Scores of others will not respond much at all, and these students may need to receive more intense intervention.

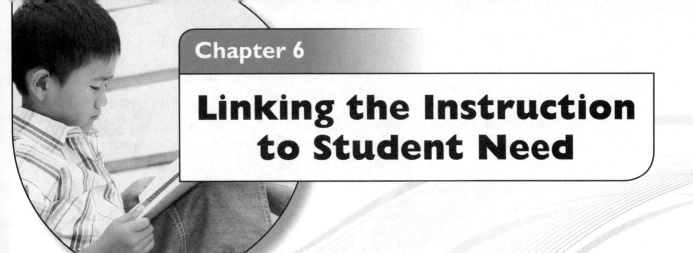

Chapter 6

Linking the Instruction to Student Need

> *One of the most important things that we've had to remember is to teach the skill and not the test. This is something that is often difficult for teachers, as we always want students to succeed.*
>
> Third-Grade Teacher

A critical step in planning data-informed intervention is to carefully select lessons for intervention instruction that address the specific skill the student lacks. The closer the link between student needs and instruction, the more effective the intervention will be. Teachers must analyze their available materials to identify exactly which skill each one teaches. Even if a school has purchased an intervention curriculum that provides lesson plans, teachers still need to know how to link skill deficits and activities to appreciate why they are teaching a particular lesson, and so they can constantly evaluate the effectiveness of a particular curriculum for their students. All the work invested in analyzing the student scoring booklet to determine student needs may be for naught if this step is not done well.

The topic of this chapter is how to map appropriate instructional strategies to student needs. This information is the bridge between analyzing the *DIBELS Next®* data in a student scoring booklet and preparing a lesson plan. (Preparing lesson plans will be discussed in the next chapter.) Intervention instruction is most effective when teachers can take any instructional strategy or practice activity and clearly pinpoint which skill it is teaching. Both sides of the equation have to be equally strong. Without a strong perception about what an activity is teaching, all the in-depth analysis to appropriately group students and to see error patterns in the *DIBELS Next* student scoring booklet may not result in maximum student improvements.

Intervention Instruction Is Intensive and Focused

Intervention instruction should be intensive and focused. Intensive, focused instruction allows the struggling reader to practice a limited set of skills while the instructor gives immediate corrective feedback to errors. Working in small groups not only enables students to respond to more questions than would be possible in a classroom setting, but also allows the teacher to tailor a follow-up question based on whether the student answered correctly or incorrectly. Teachers can explicitly teach a skill and then give the students a chance to immediately apply the skill. It is the targeted question-error-question loop that makes it different from whole class instruction.

Intervention instruction is not intended to serve as the entire reading curriculum, but rather it is intended to address a small number of essential skills at a time. Each lesson typically covers one primary skill and one to two secondary skills. It is not advisable to cover all five components of reading instruction during an intervention group time, which typically is planned for one 30-minute session daily. Although a lesson may include a couple of different skills, it typically focuses on one main area such as phonological awareness or reading words with short vowel patterns. For kindergarten students, the lesson may be focused primarily on phonological awareness with strategic instruction in letter-sound correspondence for some groups that have deficiencies in both areas. For a first-grade intervention group, a phonics lesson might include a phonemic awareness review at the beginning and fluency at the word and phrase level. For example, if the primary focus that day is on associating the /sh/ sound with the consonant digraph *sh*, most of the time would be spent practicing reading and writing words that include *sh*. However, at the beginning of the lesson, the instructor may integrate a phonemic awareness routine such as thumbs up for words that contain the /sh/ sound in the initial or final position as a warm-up activity. But time is too short in one phonics lesson to spend too much time on other skills, such as spending 15 minutes on vocabulary. Briefly discussing the vocabulary that will be in the passages is always a good idea, yet it should be brief and not take the focus away from the phonics concept. Attempting to thoroughly teach too many skills at a time can split the short intervention time too many ways, which risks diminishing its effectiveness. Many skills can be briefly reinforced, but not become a focus. Different skills can be taught over time but not all within the same lesson.

> *Intervention instruction is not intended to serve as the entire reading curriculum, but rather it is intended to address a small number of essential skills at a time. Each lesson typically covers one primary skill and one to two secondary skills.*

The focus of each group's instruction should be articulated, preferably at the top of the lesson plan. For example, assume a teacher is preparing lessons for a group of mid-year first-graders whose scores showed they were at risk on PSF and NWF, and their DORF was also very weak. Even though these students have low DORF scores, the instruction would not initially focus on developing fluency at the passage level. Their low PSF and NWF scores indicate that the deficit is at a far lower developmental level than connected text in passages. In general, the intervention instruction would begin at the lowest deficient skill and move up. However, since these students are already in the middle of first grade, time is of the essence to get them back on track. The teacher needs to accelerate their development of phonemic awareness and focus on mastering letter-sound correspondences. This group will work at mastering their ability to understand sounds in words and to apply letter-sound knowledge while decoding consonant-vowel-consonant words accurately before moving to reading sentences and passages for fluency.

For the first-grade intervention group just described, the initial intervention lesson would include a brief review of phonemic awareness with a focus on mastery of early decoding of simple CVC words. Very little time would be spent on other areas, such as vocabulary instruction. In fact, not all the students in this group may need help with vocabulary. The students in this group were placed together because of their common need for help in decoding phonetically regular CVC words as measured by their low NWF scores. Although sometimes an interventionist may be able to include some explicit vocabulary instruction while working on phonemic awareness, most of the time, it doesn't happen. The words that are initially used for learning how to segment and manipulate sounds typically contain only three or four sounds, and, therefore, are very common words that are part of the student's oral vocabulary. If a student's vocabulary is especially low, there needs to be a plan for her oral language development. Low oral vocabulary is a major red flag, and, if not addressed, can impair the student's fluency and comprehension even after her decoding skills are improving.

Intervention Instruction Should Not Replace the Core Reading Curriculum

Because intervention instruction suggested in this book focuses on only a couple of skills at a time, it's critical that students attend intervention group at a time when it won't interfere with them being present for the entire language arts instruction time. Students must continue to receive vocabulary, fluency, comprehension, and writing instruction in the core program while intensively working on their weak skills in intervention group. Intervention instruction must be in addition to, rather than replace or supplant, the core reading instruction.

This suggestion that intervention instruction supplements, but does not replace, the core instruction is also emphasized in a publication by the Center for Reading and Language Arts at University of Texas called *Three-Tier Reading Model*. As expressed in this publication, "For some students, focused instruction within the regular classroom setting is not enough. To get back on track, these students require supplemental instruction in addition to the time allotted for core reading instruction" (University of Texas Center for Reading and Language Arts 2003).

The Three-Tier Reading Model

The University of Texas' Center for Reading and Language Arts (UTCRLA) advocates a "Three-Tier Model" for reading whereby there are alternative layers of instruction for students. The three "tiers" of reading instruction are described in their publication as:

- **Tier 1**—The core reading instruction that all students receive, generally 90 to 120 minutes daily.

- **Tier 2**—30 minutes of daily small-group reading instruction that students who do not score at benchmark on the screening assessment receive. This instruction is in addition to the core reading instruction.

- **Tier 3**—60 minutes of daily small-group reading instruction that students who do not make adequate progress with Tier 2 instruction receive. The 60 minutes can be delivered in two daily 30-minute intervention sessions and is in addition to the core reading instruction.

Under the Three-Tier Model, any student who is not making adequate progress in achieving early literacy skills with the core program receives supplemental instruction to enhance the classroom instruction. Students whose skills don't progress after a reasonable time in the Tier 2 level of intervention receive more intense intervention. Only after a student doesn't make adequate progress with both Tier 2 and Tier 3 intervention is he referred for testing for reading disabilities. This model is depicted graphically as a triangle in *Figure 6.1*.

Figure 6.1

The Three Tier Model

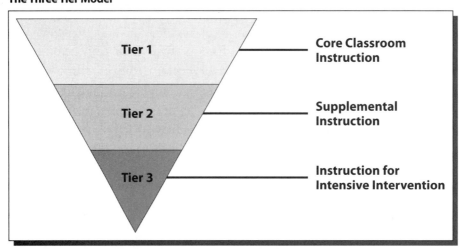

Source: *Three-Tier Reading Model: Reducing Reading Difficulties for Kindergarten Through Third Grade Students,* University of Texas Center for Reading and Language Arts 2003.

The Three-Tier Model was widely discussed and studied by states and districts as they implemented the Reading First program. Increasingly, schools are aware of the Three-Tier Model, or a variation of the model, through their state's rollout of training related to Response to Intervention. The Three-Tier Model and some of the studies of the model are discussed in this section.

The effectiveness of a strong classroom-level comprehensive core reading program (CCRP) has been extensively researched, resulting in the finding that students become better readers with a CCRP. One summary of several research studies suggests that with a strong core curriculum program "only about 6% or less of students should be expected to experience reading problems requiring secondary intervention" (Denton and Mathes 2003).

Tier 2 is the first line of intervention in a tiered model of reading instruction. Students who are below benchmark in *DIBELS*® or another early literacy assessment are placed in a group of three to five students for 30 minutes of instruction provided by a teacher or aide in the classroom or in a group that is taught during an intervention block. The model calls Tier 2 "supplemental instruction." Districts usually establish a schedule for progress monitoring Tier 2 groups every two or three weeks to see whether the students are benefiting from the instruction. After a reasonable period in a Tier 2 group, the student who achieves benchmark on *DIBELS* scores may stop intervention and be working in an enrichment group during the differentiation block. Students who make good progress but are not yet scoring at benchmark can continue in Tier 2 for another round of instruction. Students who show little or no progress with the first round of Tier 2 instruction, as well as students who do not achieve benchmark scores after two rounds of Tier 2 instruction, are moved to Tier 3.

> *Districts usually establish a schedule for progress monitoring Tier 2 groups every two or three weeks to see whether the students are benefiting from the instruction.*

Five studies on the effectiveness of Tier 2 have been summarized. The researchers concluded that when the lowest 12%–18% of students were given intervention, approximately 70%–90% of these intervention students were reading at grade level, depending on the intensity and duration of the intervention (Denton and Mathes 2003).

Tier 3 intervention is the most intense level. Students whose skills are not demonstrating adequate progress after more than one round of Tier 2 intervention are moved to Tier 3 typically after discussion in a problem-solving meeting. Tier 3 is sometimes called "Intensive Intervention." The UTCRLA recommends that Tier 3 students receive a total of 1 hour of small-group intervention broken into two slots of 30 minutes each. A few states define Tier 3 as special education, but most states advise districts that Tier 3 takes place within general education and is a more intense layer of instruction. They also suggest that the materials can be the same as for Tier 2, or they may be different, depending on the needs of the students in the group.

In this book, the term *intervention instruction* is used to designate both Tier 2 and Tier 3 instruction. Although the Three-Tier Model is a very effective framework to articulate that groups are flexible and intervention is provided at varying levels of intensity depending on student need, in practice, the lines may blur more than this model suggests. Increasing levels of intensity can be accomplished in a gradual step-like fashion as the needs of the students in the group merit.

Increasing Intensity and Complexity of Intervention Over Time

Increasing Intensity of Instruction

What differentiates Tier 3 from Tier 2 instruction is that the intervention is more intensive. Greater intensity can be achieved in several ways:

- Reduce the size of the group to enable more corrective feedback.

- Increase the time spent in intervention instruction.

- Change the instruction so that it is more systematic, sequential, multisensory, or provides more repetitions by using a different material or instructor, or both.

Instructional intensity is also adjusted by providing more examples, a wider range of examples, breaking a task into smaller steps, spending longer time on a task, and by asking the student to move along a continuum in type of response (see *Table 6.1*) (Good, Kame'enui, Simmons, and Chard 2002).

| Table 6.1 |

Ways to Adjust Instructional Intensity of Responses

Low Intensity	Medium Intensity	High Intensity
Yes/no response	Oral response	Oral independent response (no choices offered)
Point to correct answer	Multiple-choice response	Written response

Complexity of Instruction Varies

An effective intervention instructor must be knowledgeable about how to change the complexity of the instruction. When an interventionist begins to design instruction, it may be necessary to think through how to adjust instruction from simpler to more complex. Eventually these shifts need to become so intuitive that the interventionist can make these adjustments on the spot during a lesson without formal preplanning.

Intervention lessons follow a progression from simple to more complex. For example, most students learn to isolate the initial sound in a word, then the final sound, and lastly the middle sounds. The medial vowel sound is generally the most difficult for students to isolate. Therefore, the obvious order of instruction in teaching phoneme identification would be initial, ending, and medial sound.

Another way to increase complexity is by distinguishing between open and closed sorts. Generally, a closed sort is easier than an open sort. For this reason, it is best to use a closed sort when first teaching students a new feature of a word, such as how to focus on the initial sound. In word sorts, students discover patterns as they figure out how words are alike or different by examining words with and without the feature. If the interventionist is asking students to sort between two options, and all the words fit into one of the two categories, this is a closed sort. An open sort is more difficult because students have to decide whether a word belongs in either of the two categories or whether it is another unspecified possibility.

Two examples of thoughtful progressions from easier to more complex intervention instruction follow in *Table 6.2*.

Table 6.2

Examples of Thoughtful Progression of Intervention Instruction

	Example 1: Teaching Sounds	**Example 2: Teaching Reading and Writing Words With Short Vowel Sounds**
Strategy	Students are learning to categorize words by initial sound. Teacher uses picture cards to sort words in columns by initial sound.	Students are learning to apply sound-letter correspondence in spelling and reading CVC words with short vowels.
First Level (Easiest)	All the pictures begin with the target sound and can be placed in the same column. For example, the target sound is /h/ in the initial position and all the pictures begin with /h/. Examples: *hill, hat, house*.	Students pick a picture from a small set of choices and place it on a box in the middle of a word strip that already has the beginning and ending letters. For example, the student places the picture of a pan on the strip with p_n.
Second Level (Middle)	This is a closed sort with two initial sounds that are distinctly different—an /h/ column and an /m/ column. All the pictures fit on one column or the other.	Students pick a picture from a bag, place it on the middle box for the vowel, and then write the beginning and ending consonant. For example, the strip has three empty boxes. The student places the picture of a pan in the middle box and then writes the letter *p* in the first box and the letter *n* in the last box.
Third Level (Hardest)	This is an open sort with three sounds that are close in articulation—an /n/, /m/, and /ng/ column (all three nasal sounds are similar). This is a sort based on ending sounds. Additionally, some pictures don't fit in any of the three columns. The pictures could include *ring, lamb,* and *sun*, which would be placed in the columns, and *knife, leaf,* and *mouse,* which would not be placed in any column.	Students look at a picture and spell CVC words in boxes (Elkonin box technique) using a moveable alphabet such as magnetic letter tiles. The picture of the word helps the student remember what he is supposed to be writing, and the three boxes indicate the number of letters needed to spell the word. The student chooses the letters from a selection of five consonants and two vowels. For example, the letters might be *m, t, b, f, p, a, o.* The pictures could be *bat, top,* and *fat*.
Fourth Level		Students spell CVC words with a moveable alphabet. Student has to find the letters from a board with all the letters of the alphabet and spell a spoken CVC word without any lines to tell him how many letters are needed to spell the word and without a picture reference.
Fifth Level		Students write the words from dictation.

The Focus of the Intervention Changes Over Time

For any given intervention group, the focus of instruction will evolve as time passes. Once the students demonstrate mastery at one skill level, the lesson will focus on a skill that is more complex. For example, imagine that just after the kindergarten benchmark a classroom teacher identifies that eight students in her class have FSF scores below the benchmark of 10. She assesses these eight students with a phonological awareness screener and based on their skill deficits, places them in two groups. The data show that for the lowest four students, not only are they unaware of phonemes, but these identified kindergartners also don't have awareness of syllables or onset-rimes. A kindergarten intervention group is formed just after the fall benchmark and they begin working on developing awareness of syllables, hoping to prepare the students to hear and be able to isolate, segment, and manipulate individual phonemes.

> *Once the students demonstrate mastery at one skill level, the lesson will focus on a skill that is more complex.*

The kindergarten teacher uses lessons that teach students to work with syllables using picture cards of compound words that are cut lengthwise in half. While working with this small group the teacher pulls the left half of the rainbow to a line while saying *rain* and then pulls the right half of the rainbow down while simultaneously saying *bow*. She slides her finger below the line saying the entire word, rainbow. Students answer with the teacher during the "We Do," and then they receive split pictures of compound words and mats for the "You Do" portion of the lesson. After the students have mastered blending and segmenting syllables with the split pictures, they work with rectangles and finally orally by clapping syllables. Because this group also had very low scores on Letter Naming Fluency, the teacher spends about 5 minutes of the 30-minute intervention block working on letter naming—sometimes they work on letter naming as a warm-up to focus the students; whereas, other times the teacher inserts a letter-naming activity that gets the students up and moving as an attention break so they can refocus on phonological awareness.

Once the group has mastered syllable blending and segmenting, they continue to work on more complex syllable manipulation skills. They learn to delete, add, and manipulate syllables in compound words. Then they count syllables and sort picture cards into columns for two, three, or four syllables. The sequence of instruction continues with words that are not compound until students in the group can blend, segment, and manipulate noncompound words successfully. At this point, the teacher assesses the students with an alternate form of the phonological awareness diagnostic screener; she verifies that the entire group has mastered the syllable level and is ready to move on to onset-rimes.

The teacher demonstrates segmenting and blending onsets to help students learn that the onset is all the sounds before the vowel, and the rime is the vowel and the sounds that follow it. Then she focuses the students on recognizing that it's the rime that is different in rhyming words. Using a progress monitoring probe from the diagnostic screener, the teacher verifies that all the students have developed a strong level of rhyming. Since many students have improved in letter naming, the teacher now uses the 5 minutes on letter-sound correspondence to break up the phonological awareness lessons.

Next, instruction moves to initial sound phoneme isolation, the skill which is measured by the FSF indicator in *DIBELS Next*. Because the students have become adept at isolating, blending, segmenting, and manipulating both syllables and onset-rimes, they make quick progress in learning to isolate initial sounds in words. Having learned to count syllables, they can more easily count phonemes in three- and four-phoneme words. The teacher continues her lessons to demonstrate and model these skills with manipulatives. She gives a progress monitoring assessment with Form B or Form C of the phonological awareness diagnostic screener after completing each subskill within phonemic awareness. By December, she is dedicating about 10 minutes to letter-sound correspondence and the other 20 minutes to phoneme skills. After the mid-year benchmark screening, she'll determine whether to discontinue playing a letter-naming game on Fridays. She'll also look at that time allocation and either split the time equally between phonological awareness and letter-sound correspondence, or even slightly favor the letter-sound work. The teacher always teaches an explicit lesson and then uses activities like the ones found in Part II of this book to provide students the opportunity to practice what they have been working with during the "I Do, We Do, You Do" portions of the lesson.

Decisions About When to Exit a Student or Refer for Testing

Teachers often ask many questions about how to know when it's time to exit a student from an intervention group. They also have many questions about how to determine when a student should be referred for possible testing for a learning disability. Both of these topics will be discussed in this section.

When Do Students Exit an Intervention Group?

A general guideline for when a student is ready to exit an intervention group is when his score on the focus skill reaches benchmark and stays there for at least two progress monitoring periods. Most schools administer progress monitoring assessments every two or three weeks. It is important to consider where a student is in relation to the skills that are supposed to be established by the next *DIBELS* benchmark period, not just what was supposed to be established at the last benchmark assessment date. The expectations continue to grow across the year, as evidenced by increasing benchmark goals.

If, for example, a student is in intervention in the middle of first grade and is lacking in both NWF-CLS and NWF-WWR, she would not be exited until both her NWF scores reach their respective benchmarks, even though initially instruction would be focused only on getting letter-sound correspondences correct. Once a student shows progress on letter-sound correspondences, then instruction can shift to teaching her to successfully blend CVC words. Once this skill is mastered, then she is ready to exit this particular skill group, but whether she can exit intervention altogether depends on whether she has mastered all the skills. The other skills for middle of the year first grade are passage reading accuracy and rate, as measured by DORF accuracy and fluency. If she can meet the benchmarks for words correct and percent accuracy in DORF passages, she is ready to be released from intervention groups at this time. It's critical to make sure that a student is maintaining the gains, so it is recommended that she has to receive above benchmark scores on two or three progress monitoring assessments to validate the achievement and show that she can maintain it. This is shown on the progress monitoring chart by whether the student's scores are on or above the aimline.

When schools first begin implementing intervention groups, one of the most common occurrences is that the teachers are hesitant to move a student out of an intervention group. This reluctance is normal because it is hard to know whether the student will retain the gains he has made. Most of the time when we catch students up, as evidenced by benchmark scores on *DIBELS*, they will not need extensive intervention again. If teachers are reluctant to exit a student, they can be reminded that it is always possible to continue to monitor the progress of a student after he exits the intervention group. If scores fall below benchmark, the student can be placed back into an intervention group.

Referral for Special Education Testing Is Recommended After Lack of Response to Intervention

When we began to systematically screen and identify students lacking in critical skills early and applying targeted interventions, we were able to reduce the number of students referred for special education by 78%.

Arkansas Department of Education employee

Students who have completed at least one round of Tier 3 intervention and whose skills are still not improving are candidates for further diagnostic testing. These students are easiest to spot by graphing progress monitoring scores for a group on the same graph and comparing the rates of progress of the students in a group. What is shown in *Figure 6.2* is that two of the students in the group are making significant progress. Then there is the third student, whose slope of improvement is too flat, especially in contrast to her peers, who started at approximately the same level and received the same intervention instruction. Clearly, the intervention is working with two of the students, but the third student's scores are not responding to the instruction. In this case, the third student would be referred for more extensive diagnostic testing and possibly referral for special education services.

Figure 6.2

Progress Monitoring Chart Showing One Student Is Not Responding

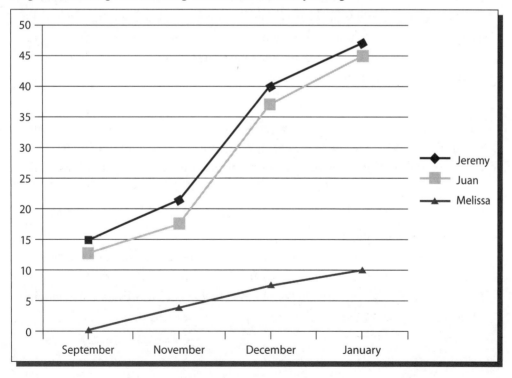

Planning Intervention Instruction

The topic of this section is alternative sources for curriculum materials for intervention groups. Teacher-designed and purchased materials will be discussed.

Purchasing or Designing an Intervention Curriculum

There are more than 200 intervention curriculum programs available today. Only a few intervention programs have a broad focus; most are designed to develop only one skill, such as phonemic awareness or building fluency in reading text passages.

There are many good programs, and schools typically purchase a variety of programs so that they have materials for each of the five essential components. A school might select a program for each of the following areas:

- **A phonemic awareness and early phonics program.**
  This material is for use with the lowest kindergarten and first-grade students whose deficiencies are extensive and are in multiple areas. This type of program usually integrates instruction in phonological awareness, letter recognition, and the alphabetic principle in a well-designed set of lesson plans. These programs vary in cost and materials provided.

- **A systematic and sequential phonics intervention program.**
  Some first-grade groups that are close to benchmark in phonemic awareness and letter recognition but need extensive work in the alphabetic principle may benefit from this type of program. The program provides the teacher with scripts to explicitly teach the sound and letter correspondence, lists of words to use for reading and writing, and decodable text for students to practice applying the concepts taught.

- **A fluency program.**
  When groups of students have mastered the individual phonics concepts and can apply them in reading words accurately but are not fluent at the passage level, a fluency program is helpful. These programs provide sets of leveled passages that you can use for repeated, timed oral readings, which you then use to chart progress.

- **A vocabulary program.**
  Some students have extremely low levels of oral language and need to work in small groups using a systematic program to introduce and use oral language. Typically, students who are English language learners or others with deficient vocabularies work on vocabulary throughout the entire year.

Following are some of the many benefits of purchasing intervention programs:

- The program provides a set of designed lesson plans that are systematic and sequential. It is difficult for teachers to prepare well-designed intervention lessons for each group. In some areas, such as phonics, it is complex to develop the sequence of instruction and write appropriate text that builds on the previously taught concepts.

- The program includes scripts or sample instruction. Depending upon the teaching expertise of the intervention group instructor, scripts are critical. If instructional aides who have more limited training and experience teach the groups, lesson plans with scripts or sample instructions help provide scaffolding for this instruction.

- The program is validated with research. The validation should be focused on justification for the instructional strategies used in the program.

- Materials are provided. Programs that provide most or all the materials will save teachers time and make program implementation fidelity higher.

- Documentation is easier. When intervention groups are taught by Title I teachers or instructional aides, it is easier for the classroom teacher to understand what was taught if the instructor is following a program and writing in a log the lessons that were covered each week.

Appropriate Use of Purchased Programs

Although there are many advantages of purchased intervention programs, it is critical to know how and when to use them. Ideally, the school will have a portfolio of programs to use, although not all intervention groups should be placed in a program. For Tier 2 groups, the materials need to have lessons labeled by the skills taught and the ability to use some lessons without having to teach each and every one. If teachers are using the *DIBELS* data to analyze student needs and place students in groups, it will be apparent that some groups have more pervasive needs than other groups. For the groups that have gaps in their knowledge, using lessons that teach only what is missing is more effective for the students. Failure to use the data to inform instruction—placing all groups at the beginning of an intervention program and teaching every lesson—is inconsistent with the meaning of differentiated instruction.

One reason that some of the intervention programs are not right for every group is that they combine instruction in several skills and are not particularly flexible. One excellent intervention program commercially available that focuses on building early phonological awareness and phonics skills is Scott Foresman's *Early Reading Intervention* program. This program was designed by researchers at the University of Oregon who are colleagues of the developers of *DIBELS* and was previously marketed by the reading center at the University of Oregon under the name of *Optimize*. Some advantages of using this program include that it is research based, includes all the materials needed, and provides specific instructions that enable use by instructional aides. It is excellent for kindergarten students who are extremely low in both phonological and letter knowledge. Two disadvantages are that this program is expensive—over $1,000 per set—and it may be inflexible. It is designed to be taught by following the lessons in order from the first lesson through the ending lesson, although there is a placement test to assist in starting a group later in the sequence. This sequential series of lessons is especially helpful for students who are extremely deficient in the entire skill area of focus. However, it may not lend itself well when the instructor wishes to customize the lessons to exclude the skills the student already has mastered and to concentrate only on the missing skills.

Even the *Early Reading Intervention* program doesn't cover all the intervention needed for every student deficit at the kindergarten through third-grade level; rather, it is more focused on the kindergarten or first-grade student who lacks phonemic awareness and early phonics. Most schools will need a set of different program materials to use for teaching phonemic awareness, phonics, fluency, vocabulary, and comprehension. At any time within a school, there is likely to be at least one group working on each of these skill areas; therefore, instructors need an assortment of program materials to use in instruction.

The area that is most challenging to develop teacher-designed lessons is phonics. It is possible to design intervention lessons in phonics, but teachers need a deep knowledge to link the development of sound-letter correspondence with practice at the word and text level. The presentation of letter-sound correspondences must be systematic, and the words and books students use for applying their letter-sound knowledge must be well correlated to the sequence. Therefore, most schools choose to use a structured program for intervention lessons focused on phonics. The money invested in purchasing a good program for phonics is well spent.

Deciding Where to Begin Intervention

Intervention starts at the lowest skill that is deficient and addresses this skill before moving up the continuum. Some examples include:

- Teaching a student to accurately and rapidly read individual words before working on building fluency in reading passages.

- Providing intervention on missing phonics pattern skills before intervening on below-benchmark comprehension skills.

- Making sure that the student demonstrates some proficiency with recognizing and expressing the initial sound in words before teaching the student to segment all the sounds in a word.

- Verifying that the student has an adequate level of phonemic awareness before associating sounds with the letters (adding letters helps after some point).

The most efficient and effective way to determine where to start intervention instruction for a specific student is to place him in a group for a specific skill along a phonological awareness or phonics continuum. These phonological awareness and phonics continuums define the order of instruction. Schools can adopt generic continuums or create their own from studying their core curriculum and outlining the sequence of instruction. If your school would like to see a generic phonological awareness and phonics continuum, they are available on the following Web site: www.IDNWnext.com. Sometimes teachers ask whether it's a concern that the generic continuum may teach skills in a slightly different order than their core program. This is not an issue because the intervention instruction is provided to students after they fail to reach mastery with the core alone. It's fine that the student's intervention instruction teaches consonant blends before digraphs even though the order of these two skills may be reversed in their core program because they've both already been taught in the core. Students in intervention groups are receiving reteaching on skills they are still lacking and should have previously mastered.

Stepping Stone Skills Are Sequential

> DIBELS *has forced me to look at how my children learn. I firmly believe in the stair-step model of learning to read. I have been more conscious of where my students "sit" on those stairs.* DIBELS *has been a kind of shot in the arm.*
>
> Teacher

DIBELS Next indicators incorporate a progression that DMG sometimes refers to as the "stepping stones to early literacy." The order in the *DIBELS Next* indicators follows; however, keep in mind that although the Benchmark Goal is listed for one period of time in this list, it's important for students to reach Benchmark Goals on these indicators in several periods and not just the one listed.

- **FSF**—30 initial sounds per minute by the middle of kindergarten.

- **PSF**—40 phoneme segments per minute by the end of kindergarten.

- **NWF-CLS**—28 correct letter sounds by the end of kindergarten and 43 by the middle of first grade.

- **NWF-WWR**—8 whole words read by the middle and 13 by the end of first grade.

- **DORF**—47 words per minute by the end of first grade, 87 by the end of second grade, 100 by the end of third grade, 115 by the end of fourth grade, 130 by the end of fifth grade, and 120 by the end of sixth grade—Retell averaging 29% of words read correctly throughout these periods (from 25%–32%).

- **Daze**—19 by the end of third grade, 24 by the end of fourth grade, 24 by the end of fifth grade, and 21 by the end of sixth grade.

There are no longer terminal points for these skills; however, from an instructional viewpoint, we recommend that students need to reach these levels by these time periods (see *Table 6.3* and *Figure 6.3*).

Table 6.3

Benchmark Progression of Early Literacy

	FSF	PSF	NWF-CLS	NWF-WWR	DORF	Daze
Benchmark Time/ Established Benchmark Level	30 initial sounds per minute— Kindergarten MOY	40 phoneme segments per minute— Kindergarten EOY	28 correct letter sounds— Kindergarten EOY 43 correct letter sounds— Grade 1 MOY	8 whole words read— Grade 1 MOY 13 whole words read— Grade 1 EOY	47 words per minute— Grade 1 EOY 87 words per minute— Grade 2 EOY 100 words per minute— Grade 3 EOY 115 words per minute— Grade 4 EOY 130 words per minute— Grade 5 EOY 120 words per minute— Grade 6 EOY	19—Grade 3 EOY 24—Grade 4 EOY 24—Grade 5 EOY 21—Grade 6 EOY

Figure 6.3

Benchmark Highlights—Progression of Early Literacy (K–6)

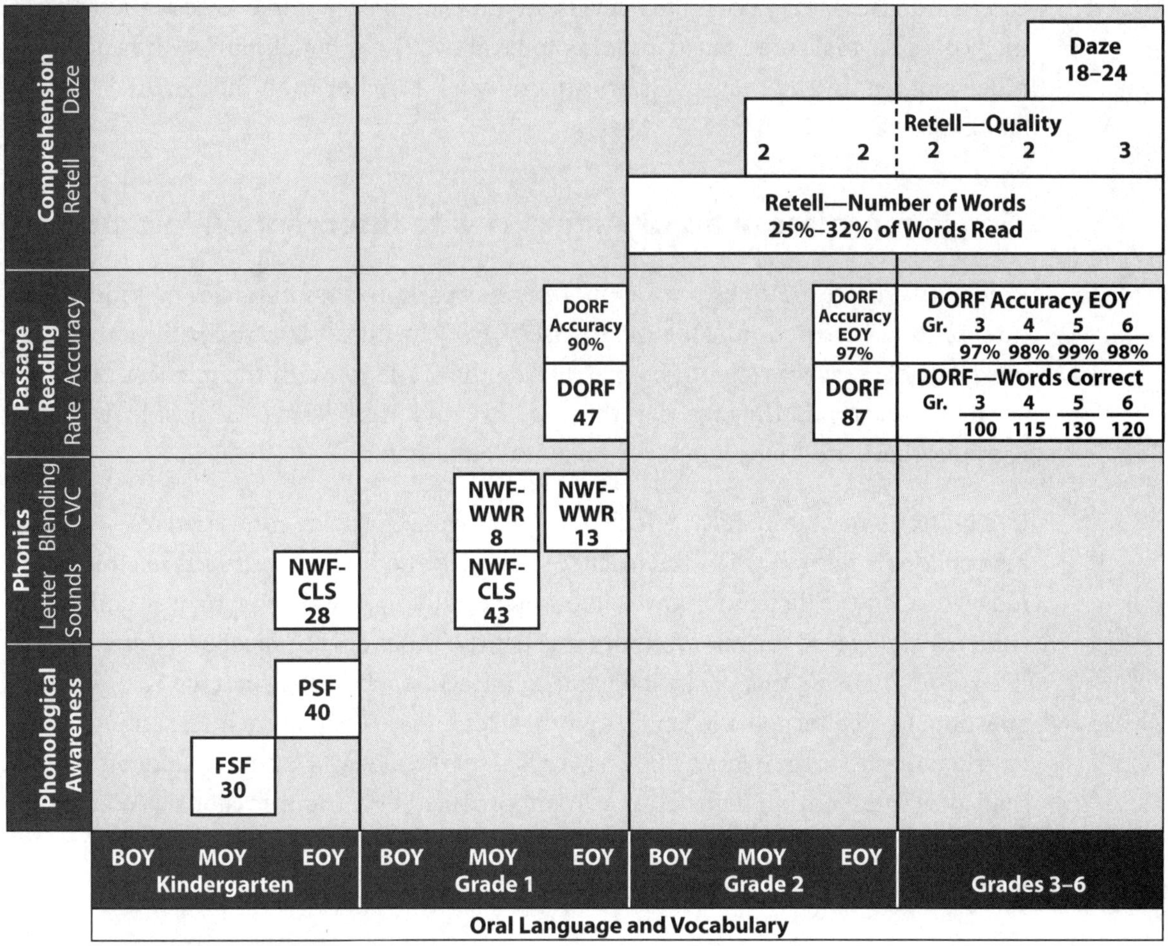

	BOY MOY EOY Kindergarten	BOY MOY EOY Grade 1	BOY MOY EOY Grade 2	Grades 3–6
Comprehension (Daze / Retell)				**Daze 18–24**
			Retell—Quality: 2 2 2 2 3	
			Retell—Number of Words 25%–32% of Words Read	
Passage Reading (Rate Accuracy)		DORF Accuracy 90% / DORF 47	DORF Accuracy EOY 97% / DORF 87	**DORF Accuracy EOY** Gr. 3 4 5 6 / 97% 98% 99% 98% — **DORF—Words Correct** Gr. 3 4 5 6 / 100 115 130 120
Phonics (Letter Blending CVC / Sounds)	NWF-CLS 28	NWF-WWR 8 / NWF-CLS 43 — NWF-WWR 13		
Phonological Awareness	FSF 30 / PSF 40			
			Oral Language and Vocabulary	

Numbers equal Benchmark Goals as of this printing.

Many of the learning-to-read skills (see *Table 6.3*) are sequential and cumulative. The sequential skills are phonemic awareness, phonics, and accurate reading of text. For example, a student who masters phonemic awareness and letter-sound correspondences in kindergarten generally does well in early reading instruction and can decode unfamiliar words as well as read words that are in her sight vocabulary. Reading rate typically improves after accuracy is achieved, and it is measured by words read. Important literacy skills, such as vocabulary and comprehension, develop concurrently with decoding. Because of this sequential learning pattern, data can be used to determine the lowest point of a student's deficit.

DIBELS Next Benchmarks Are Minimums Rather Than Goals

In *DIBELS Next,* the benchmark levels are minimum acceptable levels rather than the goal. The goal is for most students to be above these benchmarks. In fact, other oral reading fluency levels are generally a bit higher than the *DIBELS Next* benchmarks.

Can Paraprofessionals or Aides Provide Intervention Instruction?

Frequently, there are questions about whether paraprofessionals can provide intervention instruction. This issue arises because educators often believe that the most capable teachers should be instructing the students with the greatest needs. While it is certainly the case that the neediest students deserve the best instructors possible, there are times when this may not be possible.

In a perfect world, only fully certified teachers would provide intervention instruction. However, given the teacher shortages and budget shortfalls in education today, this isn't realistic in many schools. Especially in schools where over half the students are flagged for intervention, it is nearly impossible to meet every student's needs by only using highly certified and columned teachers. So then we face a critical question: Is it better to have smaller group sizes and provide more intervention instruction rather than less? The answer is a set of tradeoffs, and one tradeoff is that some intervention instruction is often provided by paraprofessionals. When this happens, a key issue is how to provide the training and supervision structure so that the work of paraprofessionals is assured to be high quality.

Experience shows that paraprofessionals or aides can be extremely effective in delivering small-group intervention instruction. There are two critical conditions for success. First, they must receive extensive training. One effective approach is for aides to attend the same professional development that the teachers receive, which also makes it more likely that teachers and aides will become a team with regard to intervention instruction. They need to work together, which requires that aides get some of the same training that teachers receive. The second condition is that the aides must be supervised extremely closely. In most schools, this is accomplished through aides conferencing with teachers regularly to discuss lesson plans and the progress of students.

Small Groups Are Just as Effective as One-on-One Instruction

Research has shown that small groups can be just as effective as individual tutoring in this area. One research study where a similar treatment was provided for 11 weeks to struggling second-grade readers in three different sizes of groups found that a 3:1 student to instructor ratio is just as effective as one-on-one tutoring (Vaughn and Linan-Thompson 2003). Yet the group size can't be too large. This same study demonstrated that group sizes of 10:1 were less effective than 3:1 in improving some important skills. Some schools have to start their groups with four or five in a group. If resources are so tight that this has to happen, then the students who are most below benchmark should still be placed in small groups of three, and the students who are closer to benchmark can be in groups of five students.

While groups of five are not optimal, by January about one-third of the students who began intervention in September will have reached benchmark and can be exited from intervention. This, then, provides the opportunity to regroup so that the group size can be reduced to three if at all possible. As more students are exited out of intervention groups because they are achieving benchmark, the students whose progress monitoring scores show a decided lack of progress can be placed in groups of two, and finally even one-on-one, as the year progresses and the need is demonstrated for more intensive instruction.

> *Although whole group lessons are effective, small group lessons reach more students. Students are receiving the help that they need, and no one gets "lost" in the group. It is also easier to hold the student accountable for their knowledge.*
>
> Third-Grade Teacher

How Many Times per Week Should the Groups Meet?

The ideal intervention time for a Tier 2 group is 30 minutes, five days a week. If a compromise must be made, it is better to provide regular instruction at least four times per week, even if for a shorter period of time, than to meet only twice a week for a longer time. Students need frequent, distributed practice, and meeting more often, even if for a shorter period of time, allows for more frequent practice. Students whose skills are the lowest typically need a minimum of 20 minutes at least four times a week. Less time with less frequency is unlikely to yield noticeable progress for the students who are most at risk according to *DIBELS* scores. Students who have only one skill that is emerging and others on target can benefit from a less frequent schedule. The only reason to even consider intervention shorter than 30 minutes and for fewer than five days a week is that some schools simply cannot accomplish 30 minutes, five days a week for all students who need intervention. However, these schools have been able to serve all below-benchmark students with 15 or 20 minutes of intervention three or four times a week, and they have seen results when the instruction was appropriately focused and given by well-trained interventionists.

General Guidelines for Intervention Instruction

Several general guidelines for intervention instruction include:

- Start intervention at the lowest deficient skill.

- Make sure that students reach automaticity or mastery at each level before increasing the complexity.

- Consider increasing complexity within a skill.

- Use a scope and sequence that makes sense to teachers.

- Provide individualized practice as much as possible so students can't look on or copy each other's work and follow without thinking it through themselves.

- Move along the skills continuum as rapidly as possible.

Intervention in the *DIBELS* Next Skill Areas

This section includes a discussion about intervention instruction in each major skill area.

Letter Naming Fluency (LNF) Skill

Students need to learn to name letters accurately and fluently. As with many other skills, accuracy generally precedes fluency. A helpful activity that can be used to help students become accurate and then fluent in naming the letters is called the Alphabet Arc (see *Table 6.4*) and is offered through the *Reading Readiness Manual* by the Neuhaus Education Center (2002). All the letters are arranged in an arc shape on an 11 × 17 paper. Students place plastic letters over the correct spot on the arc while simultaneously naming them.

Many students who enter kindergarten knowing very few letters cannot work with an arc that contains all 26 letters at the same time. In order to keep from overwhelming these students with too many letters at once, an effective way to begin is to ask these students to work with cards that have five letters per card and give them only the five plastic letters that correspond with the letters shown on the cards. These cards can be called "Pre-Arc Cards." By mastering only five letters at a time before moving to the next five, students can progress in a manner that is comfortable for them.

After a student can name each letter while placing it on the appropriate place on the pre-arc card, it is possible to work with two cards and ten letters at a time.

Once the student has practiced all five of the pre-arc cards, he is ready to work with all 26 letters and the entire arc. Kindergarten students in intervention groups generally work on this arc for a number of weeks before they can confidently name and place all the letters on the arc. Then the interventionist can shift from teaching accuracy to working on fluency through asking students to alphabetize the letters on the arc in 2 minutes. Many interventionists have found that students love to chart their own progress in moving from 6 to 7 minutes down to 2 minutes after extended practice.

There are two versions of the Alphabet Arc—one has the 26 letters on the arc and the other arc has only four letters to anchor each end and the top of the arc with lines drawing in the rest of the shape of the arc. This second arc is more difficult than the first arc because it involves more skills. Students not only name the letters but also learn the sequence from A to Z. Once a student can place the letters on this arc accurately with unlimited time, then establish a goal of completing it in 2 minutes. Timing students as they complete the arc directs their attention to fluency.

Table 6.4

Progression in Letter Naming

Pre-Arc Cards	Alphabet Arc I	Alphabet Arc II
5 letters at a time	26 letters	26 letters
Accuracy matching limited number of letters on a card and naming them.	Accuracy naming letter while placing plastic letter on arc. Develop fluency after accuracy.	Accuracy naming and placing all letters along arc line with only 4 letters on arc. Fluency after accuracy.

First Sound Fluency (FSF) and Phoneme Segmentation Fluency (PSF)—Phonological Awareness Continuum

Phonological skills develop along a progression from easy to more complex. Some commonly accepted levels of phonological awareness are:

- Syllables

- Onset and rime, and identifying words that rhyme

- Phonemic awareness

Often students are exposed to rhyming at a very young age through reading nursery rhymes and other poems before they learn about syllables. The skill of rhyming is more complex than syllable identification. One red flag indicator for phonological awareness difficulties, or even a phonological processing deficit, is difficulty hearing which words rhyme or producing a word that rhymes with another word.

Phonemic awareness is the top level of phonological awareness, or the most complex. Yet within this top step, there are additional levels of complexity, as outlined in three levels from easiest to middle to hardest (see *Figure 6.4*).

Following are examples of phonemic awareness activities that fall along a progression.

Figure 6.4

95 Percent Group's Phonological Awareness Continuum

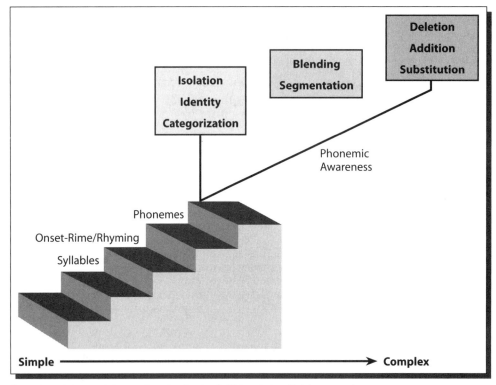

Easiest Level

- **Phoneme identity and isolation.** Find pictures that begin with a target sound. Then answer questions such as, What is the first sound in the word *man*? (/m/)

- **Phoneme identity.** What sound is the same in *kite, can,* and *king*? (/k/)

- **Phoneme categorization.** Which word doesn't belong? *Cat, car,* or *mop*? (*mop,* because it has a different beginning phoneme)

Middle Level

- **Phoneme segmentation.** What are the sounds in the word *dog*? (/d/ /ŏ/ /g/)

- **Phoneme blending.** Say the sounds /g/ /r/ /ă/ /b/. What's the word? (*grab*)

Hardest Level

- **Phoneme addition.** Say the word *eye*. Now say it again with /s/ at the beginning. (*sigh*)

- **Phoneme deletion.** Say the word *spark*. Now say it again without the /s/. (*park*)

- **Phoneme substitution.** Say the word *cat*. Now change /k/ to /h/. What's the new word? (*hat*)

These skills build upon each other. In order to identify which word doesn't belong in a set of three words, it is necessary to isolate the first sounds and then determine which one isn't the same as the two other words. Phoneme segmentation requires isolation skills. In order to delete the initial sound in a word, first the student must isolate the initial sound from the other phonemes, delete the sound from the word, and then blend the remaining sounds for a new word. The "granddaddy" phonemic awareness skill is phoneme substitution. Not only is it considered the most complex, but it also incorporates several other skills in the continuum. To substitute, a student must isolate one sound, delete it, add a different sound, and then blend the new sound with the remaining sounds to make a new word.

In *DIBELS Next*, there are two measures of phonemic awareness. First Sound Fluency (FSF), which is administered in the fall and winter of kindergarten, measures phoneme isolation at the initial sound level. This task requires the student, when given spoken words, to identify the first sound and say the sound for the assessor. The skill measured by FSF, phoneme isolation, falls into the easiest level of phonemic awareness.

Phoneme Segmentation Fluency (PSF), which is administered from the middle of kindergarten through the beginning of first grade, measures the student's ability to segment sounds in words with two to five sounds. Segmenting is a skill from the middle level of our phonemic awareness progression, and it is more complex for four- and five-sound words than for two- and three-sound words.

Nonsense Word Fluency (NWF)—Early Phonics

There is also a progression of skills in the area of alphabetic principle, phonics, and word study. Students who have developed an adequate and sufficient level of phonemic awareness and letter naming knowledge are well prepared to associate letters with sounds. Most programs develop phonemic awareness and letter knowledge concurrently to a point and then begin matching letters with sounds, which is the very beginning of phonics instruction.

Although it may be best to keep phonemic awareness and letter-sound correspondence instruction separate to a point, research shows that it is advantageous to combine them as soon as possible because one skill may reinforce the other. For a large portion of our alphabet, the sound of the letter is similar to its name. A reciprocal relationship exists whereby learning to work with sounds in words helps with letter-sound correspondence and vice versa.

However, for the student who had difficulty with phonemic awareness, instruction must focus on sounds without letters until the student demonstrates mastery in identifying at least the initial, final, and middle sounds in three-sound words. These students have not learned phonemic awareness through the core curriculum, which may have introduced letter-sound relationships too early. It is especially true that phonemic awareness needs to be taught without letters to the student who can memorize words but cannot read unfamiliar words because she doesn't understand that letters represent sounds, which is called the alphabetic principle.

> *. . . phonemic awareness needs to be taught without letters to the student who can memorize words but cannot read unfamiliar words because she doesn't understand that letters represent sounds . . .*

Students who are learning to associate sounds with letters often benefit from using cards that contain the letter and a picture for a key word. Most core reading programs contain a set of letter-sound cards that can be tacked along a corkboard strip over the blackboard in a classroom. It is helpful for students in intervention groups to be able to see these cards, especially if the cards match what the student is accustomed to using with his core program. After students become fairly proficient in naming the letter when asked the sound, or the sound when shown the letter, it may be time to move to cards with only letters and no key word pictures. The student who can name sounds for letters without pictures is ready to begin learning to blend sounds into simple words.

Phonics instruction is teaching letter-sound correspondences and the application of these correspondences to reading and writing. It is critical to be able to apply letter-sound correspondences right away within the context of reading words. This is why so many curricula teach a mixture of consonants and vowels, so that students can read words before completing the study of all 44 phonemes. Although the exact selection of letters varies, the pattern is remarkably similar in major core reading programs. The sequence typically starts with:

- four to five consonants and one short vowel;

- another four to five consonants and a different short vowel; and

- a third set of three to five consonants and a third short vowel.

This pattern continues until all the consonants and the short vowels have been taught. Typically some of the more complex phonics concepts are included toward the end of this progression. Digraphs are often taught at this point, as well as the common inflectional endings -s, -es, -ing, and -ed. Eventually, the silent-e spelling for long vowels is taught. Some of the more complex concepts, such as consonant blends and vowel team spellings for the long vowels, come later in the sequence. *Table 6.5* on the next page provides a sample sequence for a phonics intervention program.

Table 6.5

Sample Sequence for Phonics Intervention Program

Main Skill	Skill	BASIC Skill Description
1	n/a	Letter Names and Sounds NOTE: No need for lesson plans for Skill 1; the Library begins with Skill 2.
2	2.1	Short a
	2.2	Short a (Followed by Nasals)
	2.3	Short i
	2.4	Short o
	2.5	Short e
	2.6	Short u
3	3.1	Initial S-Blends
	3.2	Initial L-Blends
	3.3	Initial R-Blends
	3.4	Initial 3-Letter Blends
	3.5	Final-S Blends
	3.6	Final-L and -T Blends
	3.7	Preconsonant Nasal Blends
	3.8	Past Tense (Inflected -ed)
4	4.1	Initial Digraphs (ch/sh)
	4.2	Final Digraphs (ch/sh)
	4.3	Initial and Final Digraphs (th/wh)
	4.4	Final Digraphs (ck)
	4.5	Floss Rule
	4.6	Qu- and Final-X
5	5.1	CVCe Long a
	5.2	CVCe Long i
	5.3	CVCe Long a, e, i, o, u
	5.4	Long Vowel Open Syllable
	5.5	Phonograms (ing, ang, ong)
	5.6	Phonograms (ink, ank, onk)
	5.7	Phonograms (ild, ind)
	5.8	Phonograms (old, olt, ost)
	5.9	Phonograms (all, oll, alk)
	5.10	CVCe Long e
	5.11	CVCe Long o
	5.12	CVCe Long u

Main Skill	Skill	ADVANCED Skill Description
6	6.1	Vowel Teams (oa/igh)
	6.2	Vowel Teams (oe/ee)
	6.3	Vowel Teams (ai/ay)
	6.4	Vowel Teams (oi/oy)
	6.5	Vowel Teams (au/aw)
7	7.1	2 Sounds of ie
	7.2	2 Sounds of ow
	7.3	2 Sounds of ea
	7.4	2 Sounds of oo
	7.5	2 Sounds of ou
	7.6	2 Sounds of ew
8	8.1	Vowel-r (ar/or)
	8.2	Vowel-r (er/ir/ur)
	8.3	Words Beginning with W + ar & or
	8.4	Vowel-r Phonograms (air/are)
	8.5	Vowel-r Phonograms (oar/ore)
	8.6	Vowel-r Phonograms (ear/ere)
9	9.1	Silent Letters (kn/gn)
	9.2	Silent Letters (wr/mb)
	9.3	Complex Consonants (ck/k)
	9.4	Complex Consonants (tch/ch)
	9.5	Hard and Soft c & g
	9.6	Phonograms (ace/age/ice)
	9.7	Complex Consonants (dge/ge)
	9.8	Past Tense (Complex)

Main Skill	Skill	Multisyllable Skill Description
10	10.1	Closed: Single Syllable
	10.2	Closed: Simple Multisyllable
	10.3	Closed: Complex Multisyllable
	10.4	Closed: Schwa Multisyllable
11	11.1	Long Vowel Silent-e: Single Syllable
	11.2	Long Vowel Silent-e: Simple Multisyllable
	11.3	Long Vowel Silent-e: Complex Multisyllable
12	12.1	Open: Single Syllable
	12.2	Open: Simple Multisyllable
	12.3	Open: Complex Multisyllable
13	13.1	Vowel Team: Predictable Single Syllable
	13.2	Vowel Team: Predictable Multisyllable
	13.3	Vowel Team: Unpredictable Single Syllable
	13.4	Vowel Team: Unpredictable Multisyllable
14	14.1	Consonant-le: Single and Multisyllable
15	15.1	Vowel-r: Single Syllable
	15.2	Vowel-r: Simple Multisyllable
	15.3	Vowel-r: Complex Multisyllable

One critical component of teaching phonics is to begin using the learned letter-sound correspondences to read words as soon as possible. Often short *a* and short *i* are two of the first vowels taught. An enormous number of consonant-vowel-consonant (CVC) words can be read and spelled with ten consonants and two short vowels. This is fortunate because it is critical to ask students to read and write words as soon as possible to practice applying the letter-sound correspondences they are learning. Students can read and write sentences once they have gained proficiency with even a few simple words.

Once students have learned to read and write single-syllable CVC words, there are more complex phonics patterns to learn to be able to read more unusual words, including multisyllabic words. Study continues with exploring root words and affixes. Word origin and morphology are two additional areas of study about the English language.

Nonphonetic, high-frequency sight words are generally taught at the same time as the teaching of the letter-sound correspondences. Instruction in these common words that are spelled irregularly, many of which come from the Anglo-Saxon language, typically begins in kindergarten. Most core reading curricula teach students to begin to recognize some of the most common irregularly spelled words in kindergarten, including the words *the*, *and*, *you*, and *said*.

Vocabulary and Oral Language

As of the date of publication of this book, DMG was still researching the vocabulary measure. It is likely to be available in the future, so this skill is discussed in this chapter, and there is a vocabulary chapter in Part II of this book. Some indicators measure targeted skills, such as letter naming, phonemic awareness, and phonics at the CVC level. In word use, oral language and vocabulary skills develop over a long time in many ways. Most students develop their oral language usage, including use and understanding of vocabulary, through their lifetime of experiences in the home, school, on family trips, with peers, etc. When a student's word use is low, there can be a multitude of diverse causes. Sometimes it is because the student has grown up in an environment where there is not much discourse or in a home where they do not hear stories read aloud.

Intervention to build vocabulary and oral language skills occurs over a long time. The *DIBELS Next* indicators are not as likely to show the impact of the work on word usage as quickly. This is best understood by considering that if the words the student has learned since the last assessment period are not one of the 15 or so words on that benchmark, then the score may not show the improvement the student made. What this measure is more sensitive to is whether a student has learned to give more elaborate responses to the words. For this reason, it may not be worthwhile to progress monitor every two or three weeks using a *DIBELS Next* vocabulary indicator. A less-frequent schedule may be merited for students who are in intervention groups focused on improving word use fluency, possibly monthly.

Retell (Included in DORF)—Comprehension

Retell predicts a student's ability to comprehend what is read by asking the student to retell what they read in the DORF passage. When providing intervention to students with low Retell scores, it is important to teach not only how to retell the facts from the story but also to teach more complex comprehension skills than a simple retell. Some interventions help students articulate a set of characteristics about what they just read, including:

- stating the main idea;

- recounting the story in sequence of the events;

- describing the characters;

- developing a story web to summarize observations about the story; and

- determining the main events of the story that led to the climax.

Many teachers use graphic organizers to help students remember to think about these story characteristics as they read.

Other interventions are designed to model what comprehension looks like through think-aloud techniques. One of these techniques is called "Questioning the Author," by Isabel Beck and colleagues (Beck et al. 1997). It is an approach whereby the teacher models the types of queries that good readers ask while reading a passage for the first time.

Chapter 7

Designing Lesson Plans

> DIBELS® *pinpoints specific problem areas for students instead of just saying, "they have difficulty with reading skills." While comparing my students' scores over a period of time, I found one was not yet proficient with vowel sounds. He is now in an intervention group that is concentrating on the alphabetic principle.*
>
> First-Grade Teacher

To ensure that the assessment-instruction link is tight, it is critical to use lesson plans to guarantee that instruction is concentrated on the appropriate skill areas. These plans articulate the focus of the intervention group's instruction and ensure that the interventionist and the classroom teacher are communicating and planning the activities and strategies that will meet the needs of the group. The focus of this chapter is how to develop data-informed lesson plans for teachers who are designing their own intervention program.

Overview of Lesson Planning

Using lesson plans is critical to get the best results in intervention groups. Following a brief justification of why lesson plans are helpful, they will be described and sample lesson plans will be shown.

Why Interventionists Need Lesson Plans

There are several important reasons that developing lesson plans is encouraged and supported in this book. The process of developing lesson plans reminds teachers that instruction needs to be carefully planned in order for students to receive the maximum effectiveness. Except for all but the most highly experienced, intervention teachers acknowledge that it's extremely difficult to think of good lesson strategies on the spot. Well-designed intervention includes attention to the specific sounds and words that are used in teaching, so word lists are very helpful.

Additionally, lesson plans provide documentation of the instructional strategies that were employed with a particular group.

Key Characteristics of Lesson Plans

Lesson plans include several important things:

- Instructional focus skill

- List of materials needed for lesson

- Word list

- Instructional steps for the "I Do, We Do, You Do" modeling

- Practice activities to follow explicit instruction

- Time allocation (by noting amount of time planned for each step)

Sample lesson plans are included later in this chapter.

Why Documentation Is Critical

Intervention teachers typically teach eight to ten groups daily. It's easy to become confused about what was done with each group by the end of the day, let alone the end of the week. Keeping a record of the type of intervention that was provided to each group is critical. If a student is failing to respond to intervention instruction after a reasonable period of time, it's necessary to know what types of instruction he has received. This information helps in planning other strategies to try next in order to increase the instructional intensity for this student. Ultimately, these records will be used in making decisions about referring the student for further diagnostic testing.

One of the most compelling types of data about a struggling student can be found in progress monitoring charts that show the struggling student's intervention peers who started at the same point, but who have improved dramatically while the struggling reader has not. It's critical to know how much time was spent instructing in specific skill areas and which activities and strategies have been provided.

Sample Lesson Plans

Schools that choose not to purchase intervention program materials will need an approach for developing lesson plans. Many schools have achieved excellent results by developing their own approach for some of the instructional areas; although, it is most difficult to create your own instruction in systematic phonics. If teachers are developing their own curricula, then providing professional development and coaching is essential to assure good planning. One advantage of professional development and creation of lesson plans is that instruction is more customized to the needs of the individual group rather than merely following a set sequence of skills. Teachers who are designing intervention lessons need to be well trained to make informed decisions about which strategies to teach, how best to provide explicit instruction, and which activities can offer students the opportunity to practice after they have received the instruction. This process can build teacher buy-in because of their ownership for the program and its results.

In this chapter, sample intervention lesson plans are provided for students at different grade levels. A lesson plan format is also provided as an example to get teachers started in designing lessons, along with a weekly planning format. In my experience, teachers who are initiating intervention groups rigorously plan lessons carefully at the beginning. About a month or two after initiating the program, teachers will be able to ease off the planning and begin to use a biweekly planning approach similar to the one provided in Chapter 8, "Progress Monitoring and Record Keeping."

Lesson Plans to Address a Phonological Awareness Deficit

Kindergarten students who require intervention at the beginning of the year generally fall into one of two groups—those who are below benchmark in only FSF and those who are below in both FSF and LNF. Planning interventions to address deficits in oral language and vocabulary are typically handled separately.

For students scoring below benchmark in FSF, instruction in phonological awareness is recommended. Even though the student's low FSF score indicates that she may need instruction in initial sounds in words, this may not be the place to start her instruction. Students learn better when they begin intervention at the lowest deficient skill and work up the developmental continuum. A student who cannot isolate and identify initial sounds may not be proficient at other phonological awareness tasks, such as segmenting words into syllables or onset-rimes.

DIBELS Next® provides information about the student's ability to identify initial sounds in the FSF indicator. The PSF indicator measures phoneme segmentation skills. Yet *DIBELS Next* does not provide information about the student's phonological awareness at lower levels. The easiest way to determine which phonological awareness skills a student has acquired and is lacking is to assess him with a diagnostic phonological awareness (PA) screener. A comprehensive PA screener will, at a minimum, assess the following skills:

- **Rhyming**—Students can recognize words that rhyme and produce a rhyming word when given a word.

- **Phoneme isolation**—Students can identify the initial sound in a spoken word.

- **Phoneme identification**—Students can tell which sound spoken words begin with.

- **Phoneme categorization**—Students are able to identify which words begin with the same sound.

The objective is to move as quickly as possible up the phonological awareness continuum to phonemic awareness. The most important skills for reading are phoneme segmentation and blending. The interventionist can determine when it is time to move from working on isolating initial sounds to phoneme segmentation by analyzing progress monitoring scores from the diagnostic screener. As the student gets closer to reaching the established level of 30 initial sounds per minute on FSF, the focus of intervention instruction can change to phoneme segmentation. The benchmark goal for PSF is 40 phoneme segments per minute (pspm) by the end of kindergarten.

Imaginary Student Named "José"

Let's take an imaginary student we'll call José—a kindergartner who has demonstrated very low scores on the *DIBELS Next* phonemic awareness measures. Let's suppose that it's late January, just past the winter benchmark, and his recent assessment reveals a low FSF and low PSF score. With these scores, it's clear that José needs intervention in the area of phonological awareness. (This example also could apply to a first-grade student with a low PSF score whose student scoring booklet reveals he does not consistently identify initial sounds correctly.)

The first step is to make sure, through a quick diagnostic assessment, that José knows the lower levels of phonological awareness (syllable awareness and onset-rime awareness–rhyming). Once the teacher has confirmed that he knows how to segment words into syllables, segment the onset from the rime, and recognize rhyming words, it's clear that he is ready for phonemic awareness instruction. Because José's group is below the benchmark score of 30 in FSF, it's obvious that he is struggling at the initial sound level.

The scoring page for José's PSF winter benchmark confirms that he doesn't consistently segment any sounds in words. Many circled words on the scoring page confirm that he repeats the entire word back to the examiner. On a few words, he attempts a beginning and ending sound, yet often these are incorrect. His scores show that accuracy is an even larger problem for him than his fluency with the task. Administering a diagnostic PA screener verifies that José understands the lower levels of phonological awareness and that he can be placed in a group to begin working on isolating initial sounds in spoken words (see *Figure 7.1*).

Figure 7.1

Sample Lesson Plan for Phoneme Isolation Group

Phonological Awareness Lesson Plan			
Target Subskill:	Phoneme Awareness—Isolation at the initial sound level		
Materials List:	Move-It-and-Say-It Mat, circles and rectangles		
Word List:	fan, fish, ham, hat, lamp, lap, like, man, mom, mouse, shop, sun		
Steps	**Instruction**		**# Min.**
Review:	Onset-rime blending, segmentation, and rhyme production using onset-rime mats and colored pieces.		5 min.
Explicit Instruction:	I Do:	Teacher models moving green circle and blue rectangle to line while isolating only the initial sound.	15 min.
	We Do:	Students join teacher in saying the initial sound and then all other sounds in the word while teacher pulls blue circle and rectangle to line.	
	You Do:	Students are given mats and shapes. Teacher gives words one at a time from word list.	
Practice:	Activity Name:	Zoo Keeper (Activity #10.5)	10 min.
	Objective:	Identify the initial sound of each zoo animal.	
	Materials:	Several green plastic berry baskets (attach picture for initial sound) 10–15 picture word cards that begin with the target sound plus distractors	
	Procedure:	Ask students to say the initial sound of each animal in the zoo.	
	Word List:	Use names of zoo animals.	

Some schools use instructional routine cards to help teachers consistently teach skills using the same approach. *Figure 7.2* on the next page shows an example of a phonological routine card.

After students demonstrate mastery of initial sound isolation, the instructor can move to working on final sound isolation and also medial sound isolation. The next step after that is to move to phoneme identification and categorization. The following activities would be ideal for José's group to use for the practice portion of his lesson for initial sound categorization because these activities emphasize matching initial sounds.

- **Initial Sound Picture Card Sort (matching)**—Two picture cards of words that begin with two different sounds serve as column headers. The interventionist hands the student a picture card, and the student places the picture under the column with the word that starts with the same first sound.

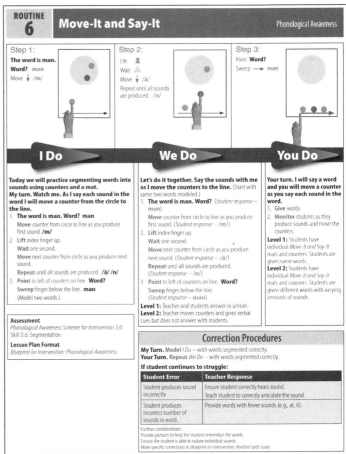

- **Initial Sound Train (matching)**—A train has five cars attached. On the engine there is a spot to place a picture card to indicate which initial sound can ride on the train. The student chooses which pictures from a small set have the matching initial sound and then places each matching picture on a car of the train.

- **Initial Sound Object Sort (matching)**—The student picks a miniature object from a brown paper bag and decides which of two piles the object belongs with, depending on the initial sound.

At the beginning, it's helpful to limit these matching activities to closed sorts, which means that all the objects or pictures fit in one of the two sounds. The rigor of the activity can be increased by using an open sort, where there is a "doesn't fit" pile or column to place the cards or objects for any sound other than the two that are designated.

Another progression from easier to harder is to consider which sounds are paired. It's easiest if the two sounds are very different. Examples of sounds that are different are stops (air flow stops) versus continuants (you can keep saying it until you run out of breath). Telling the difference between /m/ and /t/ (continuant and stop, respectively) is easier than telling the difference between /m/ and /n/ (two continuants). Not only is /m/ a continuant sound and /t/ is a stop sound, but /m/ and /n/ are both nasals (sounds made through the nose). Because both /m/ and /n/ are formed in a similar place in the mouth and they feel similar in their articulation, they are difficult for the student who is beginning to learn phonemic awareness to discriminate.

Once José's group can correctly isolate, identify, and articulate initial sounds, he is ready to begin learning to distinguish sounds in the final position in a word. Explicit instruction in this skill would mirror that provided in the lesson plan shown in *Figure 7.1* (see page 171): All the same activities that are listed for initial sounds can be changed to develop skills with the final sound. Some examples of activities to develop this skill include:

- **Thumbs Up**—Students indicate whether they hear a target sound in the final position of a word by giving a thumbs up sign.

- **Final Sound Picture Card Sort**—Students sort pictures into columns based on common ending sounds.

- **Final Sound Object Sort**—Students sort pictures into columns based on common ending sounds.

- **Final Sounds Dominos**—Students take turns placing picture dominos against a matching picture to build onto the figure on the table.

After José's group has become proficient at identifying and articulating final sounds, it's time for him to learn to identify and articulate middle vowel sounds. Middle vowel sounds are generally the last of the three to develop because vowels are more easily confused than most consonants. The same activities can be used for the middle sound as for the initial and final sounds. Later, to make things more complex, questions involving all three positions can be mixed in one activity. For example, the thumbs up game can be made more complex by mixing the questions, as follows:

- Thumbs up if you hear the sound /s/ at the beginning of *Sam*. (yes)

- Thumbs up if you hear the /m/ sound at the end of *mop*. (no)

- Thumbs up if you hear the /ĕ/ sound in the middle of *sip*. (no)

A summary of the intervention for José's group follows:

- Initial sound phoneme isolation, identification, and categorization

- Final sound phoneme isolation, identification, and categorization

- Middle sound phoneme isolation, identification, and categorization

- Mixing all the positions for phoneme isolation, identification, and categorization

After mastering isolating, identifying, and categorizing the sounds, José's group is then ready to begin segmentation and blending. Instruction begins with explicit modeling by the teacher followed by guided and independent practice using manipulatives. Once the students can successfully demonstrate their awareness during the "You Do," the lesson turns to using an activity for practice. These activities can ask students to move one object for each sound in a word so they are clearly distinguishing all the sounds in the word, not just the sound in one position. Next, José's group will be ready for activities in which they have to add, delete, and substitute a sound and blend them together to say a different word. After that, the group will be ready to move to letter-sound correspondence.

Lesson Plans to Address a Phonics Deficit

Let's explore how to create lesson plans for a first-grade student whose deficit area is a bit further along the developmental progression. For a mid-year first-grade student who has reached proficiency with phoneme segmentation, as measured by PSF, but who is low on NWF-CLS, the types of intervention activities she needs are completely different than those José's group needed.

Imaginary Student Named "Karen"

Let's call this first grade student "Karen." First, we need to make sure we know why Karen's NWF score is below benchmark. We already know that her PSF is above the benchmark of 40. Therefore, the problem is either accuracy with letter-sound correspondences or fluency in applying them. If the difficulty is accuracy, then she needs help with letter-sound correspondences. There is no point in beginning to work on fluency until she is accurate.

In order to determine which letter-sound correspondences Karen knows, we can start by examining the NWF page of her student scoring booklet. This may give us an idea of whether the issue is with consonants or short vowels. Let's assume that Karen knows all but the most uncommon consonants but is not reading the vowels accurately. Then her intervention would begin with a brief identification of which consonants she needs help with and a confirmation of whether she accurately knows any short vowels or will need instruction on all the vowels.

An informal way of assessing her letter-sound knowledge is to take a deck of plain letter cards without key word pictures. Ask Karen to name the sound for each one as quickly as she can while you flip them over. Place any sound that she doesn't know in a separate pile. Then ask her to write the letter that spells the sound while you say the sounds of the 44 speech sounds. Ask her if she knows another way to spell any sounds with alternate spellings like *k* and *c* for the /k/ sound. These two routines should only take about 5 to 10 minutes to finish, and you'll have a fairly good picture of what Karen knows and doesn't know.

Assume that Karen is struggling with all the short and long vowels. She knows a few short vowels, including *a* and *o*, but can't differentiate short *e*, short *i*, and short *u*. Make sure that she is able to spell the beginning and ending consonants of CVC words using picture cards to represent the vowel. Once you are sure that she can do this, it's time to move to instruction on the vowels. This is where intervention instruction will begin.

- **Word Chains With Short Vowel Sounds**—Using magnetic letter tiles or pocket charts with letter cards, ask Karen to spell CVC words by selecting from five or six consonants and one vowel. Give her a word chain in which one consonant changes and the vowel stays the same. After practicing with all five short vowels, ask her to choose between two vowels at a time. Select vowels that are fairly different in sound from one another, such as *i* and *o*. Then choose two other vowels. Finally, after Karen is proficient at spelling words when she can select from only two vowels, give her more choices. Eventually, she'll be able to select the appropriate vowel without any scaffolding from the interventionist. It's helpful to teach students a key word to associate with each short vowel, such as *itch* for /ĭ/, *echo* for /ĕ/, *apple* for /ă/, *octopus* for /ŏ/, and *up* for /ŭ/.

This example is one brief instructional strategy that would be included in a full phonics lesson. For an example of the steps in a lesson plan, see *Figure 7.3*, next page.

Lesson Plan for Phonics Intervention

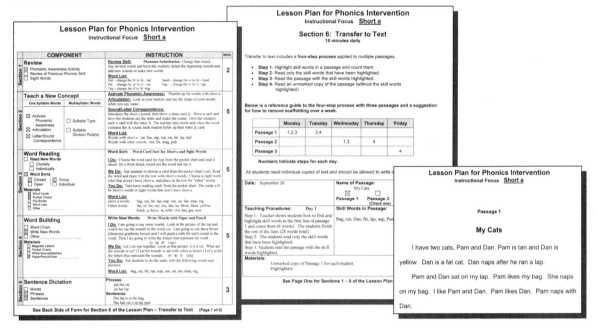

Lesson Plans for Groups

These examples of lesson plans for José's group or Karen's group demonstrate how to plan daily lessons. Skilled interventionists differentiate what they ask students to do based on the needs of each student. For example, if the students are all working on the sound train activity for phonemic awareness, the task can be changed slightly for each student. Each student has a train and is matching picture cards based on a target sound, but the target sound each student is assigned may be varied. One student who is still working on consonants in the initial sound position can be matching pictures that begin with the initial sound /m/. A second student who has mastered initial sounds and is working on sounds in the final position in a word can be asked to select pictures to add to his train if they end with the sound /p/. The third student, who is furthest along in phonemic awareness, can be matching pictures on her train based on whether they have the target sound /ă/ in the middle position of the word.

Skilled intervention instructors are able to differentiate nearly any instructional strategy as long as they know each student's instructional level in phonemic awareness, reading, spelling, or language. Creating lesson plans takes time, but it's essential for effective instruction. After the first few weeks, planning becomes easier and the same format can be used for multiple groups. The activities in Part II of this book are intended to be used as examples for practicing after explicit instruction is provided.

Chapter 8

Progress Monitoring and Record Keeping

> DIBELS® *has been a valuable tool for me to find who needs immediate attention for intervention. The progress monitoring is equally valuable for me to see at a glance who has improved or reached benchmark, and who needs more intense instruction that hadn't been at risk or progressed at too slow of a rate.*
>
> Kindergarten Teacher

Overview of Progress Monitoring

What Is Progress Monitoring?

Perhaps the most important characteristic of using a curriculum-based measure such as *DIBELS Next®* is its capacity to monitor the progress of students while they are receiving intervention instruction. Yet many times schools that are using *DIBELS* for benchmark screening three times a year are not regularly monitoring progress of the students receiving extra help. Given how much teachers value progress monitoring, this is a lost opportunity.

The U.S. Department of Education's Reading First Assessment Committee (2002) provided a definition of progress monitoring, as follows:

> *Assessments that determine if students are making adequate progress or need more intervention to achieve grade level reading outcomes.*

If the purpose of administering a screening assessment is to predict which students are at risk of later reading difficulties, then we must monitor to see how well our intervention efforts are doing in helping the student reach critical reading milestones.

When a student's *DIBELS Next* scores indicate that he is at risk of failing to learn to read, teachers are compelled to respond by planning extra help in the form of intervention instruction. Knowing exactly what type of instruction will work for each individual student is not always simple. The *DIBELS* data, along with other information about the student, help teachers decide on a focus for the intervention instruction. Additionally, data from different students is reviewed to determine which students should be placed together in a small group. The person or team that oversees the intervention instruction, whether at the classroom or school level, must determine several additional factors:

- Amount of time for intervention instruction

- Size of intervention group

- Instructional materials or programs

- Instructor

All of these factors add up to make the decision about the course for an individual student complex. As with any complex decision, it is not always possible to balance all the factors correctly every time. One of the greatest benefits of using *DIBELS* is that it is possible to repeatedly administer alternate forms of the indicators and monitor if progress is evident and make adjustments if things aren't progressing.

Separate student scoring booklets are provided for progress monitoring that contain 20 alternate forms of a single indicator for FSF, PSF, NWF, DORF and Retell, and 10 forms for Daze. Whereas a student's Benchmark Scoring Booklet provides the various indicators needed for each assessment period, the Progress Monitoring Scoring Booklet contains multiple alternate forms for one specific indicator. The chart in the Progress Monitoring Scoring Booklet appears on the outside cover and enables the examiner to record the scores each time the measure is administered to the student.

Why There Isn't an LNF Progress Monitoring Scoring Booklet

The *DIBELS* research team views letter naming as a risk indicator and not an essential skill for reading. Therefore, progress monitoring probes are not provided. Letter naming is included as an indicator because it is a predictor of reading success, and the team encourages teachers to devote their intervention instruction to teaching students the sounds and letter-sound correspondences (the skills measured by FSF, PSF, and NWF) rather than the names of the letters.

If you wish to monitor the progress of students using LNF, it is possible to create your own progress monitoring materials.

- Use current edition benchmark probes off grade level. If working with a first grade student, use the three LNF pages from a Kindergarten Benchmark Scoring Booklet for the examiner to use for scoring. Use the student materials page from the kindergarten kit to place in front of the student during the assessment.

- For schools that retained copies of earlier editions of *DIBELS*, use LNF probes from these editions for progress monitoring.

- Use rows from the bottom of the student scoring booklet that the student never reached during the minute. There are a total of 11 rows of letters in the probes. If the student scored below 40 on LNF, then she got only to the first four rows with ten letters per row. She didn't reach the last seven rows on the LNF page. You can cover the rows at the top that she read previously and use the bottom half of a page from an earlier benchmark screening.

You can create a chart to track the student's progress by using a chart from the front of another student scoring booklet and labeling it LNF.

Which Students Should Be Progress Monitored?

Progress monitoring is primarily for students who are below benchmark on *DIBELS* and are receiving intervention instruction. For all the students who are at benchmark and are reaching important milestones in reading, there is no need to monitor progress more often than the three times a year they participate in the benchmark screening. Progress monitoring is designed for the students whose scores are below benchmark; therefore, you'll be administering progress monitoring only to a portion of your class. As the year progresses, more and more students will be exited from intervention groups back to core instruction only, and, therefore, the number of students receiving progress monitoring decreases over time.

How Often Should Students Be Progress Monitored?

We recommend assessing students in intervention groups at least every three weeks. Some experts recommend that the frequency of progress monitoring assessment varies by the tier of his instruction. In some cases, students in Tier 3 are assessed weekly and those in Tier 2 are assessed biweekly. While there are circumstances that suggest assessing weekly is beneficial, my preference is for this to be the exception rather than the rule. The purpose of progress monitoring is to check on the rate of progress of each student in order to make changes in a timely fashion. Most schools don't change groups weekly as a matter of course. However, if there is an individual student who is under close observation by a problem-solving team, assessing weekly helps because the more data points available, the easier it is to feel more confident about the rate of progress. Additionally, it improves the certainty of the trend line.

My recommendation to assess with progress monitoring instruments every three weeks is based on the following observations:

- Unless you are ready to respond by changing the instruction or the group members every week, weekly progress monitoring is not necessary.

- The trend line of the rate of progress can be observed for nearly all students by assessing every three weeks, rather than weekly or biweekly.

- It is more important to spend time instructing rather than assessing.

Since most of the time, the person who is instructing the intervention group is also administering the progress monitoring assessment, it is critical to minimize any tasks that take away from time devoted to instruction. Although it only takes a little over 1 minute per student for each indicator, assessment still distracts from instruction time. Because most schools don't systematically analyze and act upon data weekly, it may be better to dedicate the time to instruction.

In order to draw a good trend line, a minimum of three data points is necessary. Assessing every three weeks generally allows the instructor to see a good trend line of progress after nine weeks. Monitoring progress every three weeks, within nine weeks of the fall benchmark, allows plotting of 3 points—the initial benchmark in which the student was flagged for intervention instruction and two progress monitoring scores.

There are some important circumstances in which weekly or biweekly progress monitoring makes sense. If a student's scores are bouncing around rather than following a line, then you may need to assess more often to understand why. Also, if a student is placed in a group that is a little bit of a stretch for her, then you'll want to monitor her progress more often to make sure that the group placement is appropriate. If you assess every three weeks, you can always increase the frequency for any student for any reason. If you opt for more frequent intervals for progress monitoring on a case-by-case basis, you will avoid wasting time unnecessarily.

A sample calendar for assessment is shown in *Table 8.1*. There are nine assessment periods planned for progress monitoring, along with the three benchmark periods.

Table 8.1

Sample Assessment Schedule*

September	December	March
Week 1	Week 1	Week 1
Week 2—Fall Benchmark	Week 2—PM #4	Week 2
Week 3	Week 3	Week 3—PM #7
Week 4	Week 4	Week 4
October	**January**	**April**
Week 1—PM #1	Week 1	Week 1
Week 2	Week 2—Winter Benchmark	Week 2—PM #8
Week 3	Week 3	Week 3
Week 4—PM #2	Week 4	Week 4
November	**February**	**May**
Week 1	Week 1—PM #5	Week 1—PM #9
Week 2	Week 2	Week 2
Week 3—PM #3	Week 3	Week 3
Week 4	Week 4—PM #6	Week 4—Spring Benchmark

* PM = Progress Monitoring

Which Indicators Are Assessed for Progress Monitoring?

Although a student may be below benchmark in several indicators, you may need to monitor progress on only one or two skills at a time. The skills to assess are the skills you are currently teaching. For example, let's explore what to assess for a student at the middle of first grade whose scores are below benchmark in NWF and DORF. If the current instructional focus for this student is on teaching accurate and fluent blending of words with short vowels, then it's necessary to progress monitor only NWF at the moment. Once the student gets closer to reaching benchmark of NWF-CLS and WWR, then you can begin assessing both NWF and DORF until eventually you'll drop NWF and monitor only DORF. Therefore, the rule of thumb is to assess only one or two indicators at a time and only those that measure the skill or skills you are explicitly teaching in your intervention group.

The *DIBELS Next* indicators that are ideal for progress monitoring are FSF, PSF, NWF, and DORF, depending on the focus of the group's instruction. For kindergarten students placed in an intervention group where the instructional focus is phonemic awareness, FSF or PSF are strong measures. However, there are many skill groups that are best monitored with an informal phonological awareness or phonics diagnostic screener. When using a diagnostic screener for regular progress monitoring, it's often recommended to assess with *DIBELS* less frequently.

As shown on *Figure 8.1*, *DIBELS* measures specific skills, yet there are many other skills on the continuums that are not measured.

***DIBELS* Skills Versus All Skills on the Continuums**

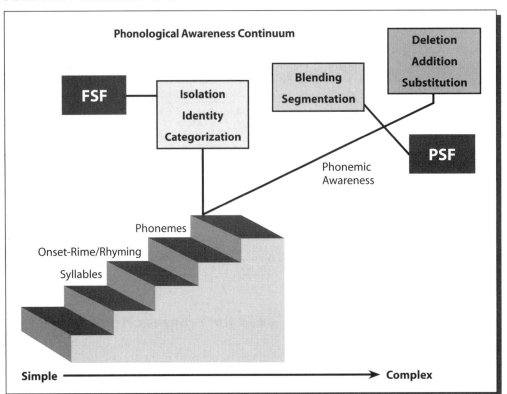

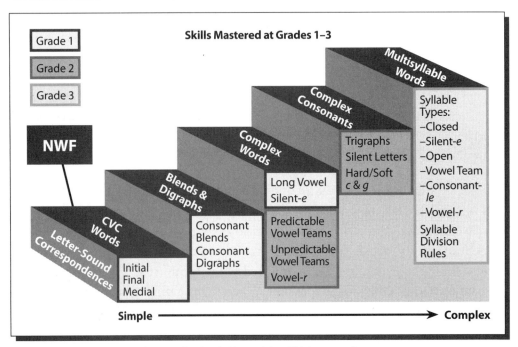

In many cases, progress monitoring regularly with a diagnostic screener gives better information than using *DIBELS*. For example, kindergarten students whose intervention begins with the earlier levels of phonological awareness of syllable and onset-rime are best progress monitored with a phonological awareness diagnostic screener. Students in second grade in a group working on all phonics concepts other than CVC words can be monitored better with alternate forms of a phonics screener. Using a phonics screener enables the teacher to assess the specific phonics skill and to see how well a student is progressing on that one skill (see example in *Figure 8.2*). When students are working in phonics groups it's impossible to see improvement on specific phonics skills by administering progress monitoring forms of DORF because any given passage may contain very few examples of the focus skill. Teachers can assess just one skill in the phonics screener, which takes less than a minute. Students exit one skill and move to another skill until they are accurate at reading words with phonics patterns. When students are in intervention groups to work on improving their fluency at reading connected text, the DORF progress monitoring passages are ideal for detecting if students are making improvements.

Figure 8.2

Example of Phonics Screener

Skill 3: Consonant Blends					
triz flug vug blet plit mond gamp					# Correct
strom stom splet sprit prant brund grut prest					5/10
Fred was *glad* to *swim* to the *raft* at *camp*.					# Target Words Correct
Brad *held* on to the *strap* so he could *jump* off the *stilts*.					10/10

Using Progress Monitoring Data

Informing Decisions for an Individual Student

When you look at the data from progress monitoring assessments for an individual student, your concern is not only whether she is making progress, but also if the rate of progress is adequate for her to catch up to benchmark in time. We want a student to reach benchmark in the skill area and also to reach the benchmark level on time. Therefore, whenever a student is in intervention instruction, our goal is to catch her up on the deficient skill as soon as possible so that she won't lag behind on the next skill as well. There is no time to waste. We should not be satisfied merely with progress; we need to relentlessly focus on catching her up as fast as possible.

Because catching a student up to benchmark is an urgent concern, one of the most important things to review on the progress monitoring chart (see *Figure 8.3*) is the slope of the line. For example, if you have three data points plotted during the first nine weeks the student received intervention instruction, extend the line out to the end of the year and observe whether the student will make it to the benchmark range at this rate of progress. Depending on how far behind the student is, achieving benchmark range by year-end may not be good enough. If she will still be behind in the next skill along the continuum, then she has to reach benchmark in both skills by year-end.

Figure 8.3

Progress Monitoring Chart

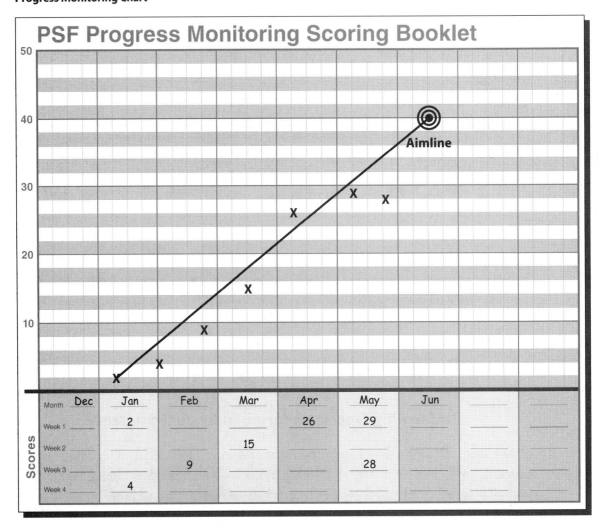

For example, if a kindergarten student is below benchmark at middle of the year in both PSF and NWF, she needs to reach benchmark in PSF as soon as possible or she will not make enough progress to also benchmark NWF. The success of intervention instruction depends on accelerating her rate of progress rather than settling for some degree of improvement.

What to Do if the Student's Rate of Progress Is Too Slow

If the rate of progress is too slow for the student to catch up to benchmark at a reasonable point, some possible adjustments are:

- Lengthen the amount of intervention time for the group. If all of the students in the 30-minute group need a more accelerated rate of growth, then change the schedule to enable the group to receive intervention instruction for 45 minutes daily until the rate of progress is better.

- Change the student to a group that meets for a longer period of time. For example, place the student in a group that meets for two 30-minute sessions daily. In the Three-Tier Reading Model, this may represent a move from a Tier 2 to a Tier 3 group.

- Change the intervention materials. Have the instructor use a more systematic and explicit instructional program. For some skill areas, this may mean changing materials. For other areas, it may be possible for the instructor to change the way he uses the materials.

- Change instructors or provide more coaching to the instructor. If the entire group's progress is not as strong as desired rather than just one individual student's progress, this may signal that the group should be reassigned to a different teacher. Alternatively, if the school has a reading coach, it may be possible for the coach to spend more time helping the instructor use techniques that increase the intensity of instruction.

Some publications suggest that students stay in Tier 2 instruction for 10 to 12 weeks. At the end of the first cycle in Tier 2, a student may enter another round of 10 to 12 weeks in Tier 2. If the student has not made enough progress at the end of the second round, he can be moved to Tier 3. Although this model is a useful framework, most schools implement a more flexible version within the first year. Students can be moved between levels of intensity on schedules that aren't tied to the 10- to 12-week cycle, and intensity within a group can be increased at any point as needed.

One way to analyze whether a student is in an appropriate group is to view the progress monitoring data on a single indicator for the three to five students in a group all on one chart. It will be apparent if they should stay together because the rate of progress will be about the same for the students (see *Figure 8.4*).

Figure 8.4

Progress Monitoring Data for an Intervention Group

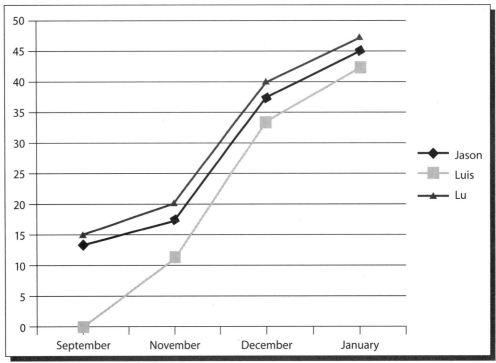

Similarly, if one student's rate of progress is much slower than the other two, it will be obvious on this chart. The student making slower progress should be considered for placement in a different group.

When to Exit a Student From Intervention Instruction

When a student's progress monitoring score reaches benchmark on three consecutive assessments, it's time for him to exit the group. He has caught up to benchmark and may need only core reading instruction at this point. One of the most interesting things to observe is that teachers have a hard time exiting students out of intervention. One possible reason is concern about whether the student's skills will continue to progress. If that is a concern, the teacher can progress monitor the student for a few weeks after he is exited from the intervention group just to be sure that he stays on track. If at any point his skills aren't continuing to make progress, he can reenter the intervention group. In my experience, very rarely does a student who is exited from the intervention group have to reenter it. Generally, with effective and early intervention, once the student catches up, he continues to make progress with core reading instruction alone.

Procedures to Analyze Data Periodically

At least during the first year of using the *DIBELS* data, most schools prefer to institute a systematic procedure for when and how data are analyzed. One of the best processes is for a team of teachers to study the data regularly at grade-level meetings. The team looks at the grouping and regrouping cycles, makes sure that all below-benchmark students at the grade level are in groups, and that all groups are moving along the continuum of skill mastery. The team is making sure that the entire process is working for the grade level and discussing any problems that need to be resolved. There is time for brief conversations about individual students, but most of the time when a student is not making progress, a discussion that may need much more time is referred to the problem-solving meeting.

Monitoring the progress of the entire grade level is the key purpose of these meetings. *Table 8.2* is an example of a table that is completed gradually across the year after each progress monitoring/regrouping cycle. This example is for a second-grade team, and the phonics skill numbers relate to the diagnostic screener the school uses.

Table 8.2

Grade-Level Team Review of Student Progress

Lincoln Elementary School		Year 2009–2010						
End of Cycle: 6								
Grade: 2								
Grade 2 Students—2009–2010 (87 Students)								
Skill		**Pre-test**	**Cycle 1**	**Cycle 2**	**Cycle 3**	**Cycle 4**	**Cycle 5**	**Cycle 6**
Phonics Groups*	Skill 1: Letter Names/Sounds	10%	1%	0%	0%	0%	0%	0%
	Skill 2: VC/CVC	10%	5%	1%	0%	0%	0%	0%
	Skill 3: Consonant Blends	5%	3%	3%	3%	1%	1%	0%
	Skill 4: Consonant Digraphs	5%	4%	2%	0%	0%	0%	0%
	Skill 5: Silent-*e*	33%	26%	18%	9%	7%	3%	2%
	Skill 6: Predictable Vowel Teams	0%	3%	6%	5%	4%	4%	5%
	Skill 7: Unpredictable Vowel Teams	3%	4%	1%	10%	4%	3%	1%
	Skill 8: Vowel-*r*	0%	1%	1%	0%	2%	1%	3%
	Skill 9: Complex Consonants	9%	28%	24%	12%	11%	12%	8%
	Skill 10: Closed Syllable							
	Skill 11: Silent-*e* Syllable							
	Skill 12: Open Syllable							
	Skill 13: Vowel Team Syllable							
	Skill 14: Consonant-*le* Syllable							
	Skill 15: Vowel-*r* Syllable							
SUBTOTAL Phonics Groups		75%	75%	56%	38%	29%	24%	19%
Fluency Groups		14%	13%	22%	32%	39%	20%	15%
Comprehension/Enrichment Groups		11%	12%	22%	30%	32%	56%	66%
TOTAL		100%	100%	100%	100%	100%	100%	100%

*Based on 95 Percent Group's Phonics Screener for Intervention (PSI).

[handwritten note:] % needing the skill support

The purpose of the grade-level team meeting is different from the problem-solving team meeting, in which the purpose is to examine the data of individual students in depth and to make decisions about moving a student to more intense intervention through increasing time or reducing group size or moving the student to a different curriculum. Ideally, teachers who are concerned about a student not making progress will sign up for a 20-minute time slot to talk about a student. If possible, the classroom teacher and the teacher instructing his intervention group would attend, along with the RTI coordinator and the principal.

A sample agenda and meeting notes from a grade-level team are shown here in *Figures 8.5* and *8.6*.

Figure 8.5

Sample Agenda for Grade-Level Team Meeting*

Data Team Meeting Date: _____

End of Cycle #: _____

Grade: _____

2010–2011

Agenda

1. Review testing and adjust students' self-stick notes on data board to reflect new cycle of needed interventions.
2. Review trends and percentages of student skill performance on completed cycle.
3. Discuss any non-progressing students and how intervention can be adapted. (Use problem-solving sheet to refer to problem-solving team, if needed.)
   - Determine if any student needs to be considered for Tier 3 intervention and fill out a referral for reading coach.
4. Share any relevant grade-level team data (if just following benchmark period).
5. Discuss use of materials/lesson plans/routines.
6. Review testing procedure and administration, as needed.
7. Address any additional instructional concerns; share ideas for activities, organizing materials, etc.; share activities for independent practice students.
8. Determine new intervention groups (if possible, keep groups to no more than five—especially for paras—and address the lowest needs at the grade level.
9. Submit new grouping lists, most recent data, and meeting notes to reading coach, RTI coordinator, and principal.
10. Confirm next meeting date and adjourn.

*Based on examples provided by Karin Lewis, West Aurora School District, Illinois.

Figure 8.6

Sample Grade-Level Team Meeting Notes*

Grade Level: *Fourth*
Date: *October 27*

In Attendance:
John Smith, Maria Llamas, Susan Torence

Student/Teacher Successes:
All students in this cycle's phonics screener (Phonics Screener for Intervention—PSI) Skill 2 and Skill 3 phonics intervention groups showed mastery.

Data Trends Observed:
Six students are repeating silent-e for the third time.
Students are seldom showing deficit in phonics PSI Skill 8, vowel-r.

Discussion/Problem Solving on Students:
Gary Colling is repeating Skill 2 for the third time and has not improved his score at all. He is also the only student in the class needing that skill. We feel these materials may not be enough for him to improve, and we have exhausted all other options to change the intervention (smaller group, different teacher). Classroom teacher will fill out form to refer him to problem-solving meeting for further discussion.

Materials/Progress Monitoring (Successes/Challenges With):
By focusing on only a paragraph in the decodable text as suggested by consultant, interventionists are better able to complete the whole lesson.

Questions/Follow-Up for Principal/Reading Specialist:
We'd like Gary Colling to be considered for Tier 3 services. He is high risk on DIBELS, two grade levels below on his reading inventory, and now going into his third cycle of PSI Skills 2 with no improvement.

---

*Based on examples provided by Karin Lewis, West Aurora School District, Illinois.

Establishing Schoolwide Goals

> *Before we placed students into groups to work with different teachers, students were categorized as "reading kids," "special ed kids," or "ELL kids." Now, they are all "our students," as many teachers work with them throughout the year.*
>
> Third-Grade Teacher

Many schools state explicit goals for their early intervention programs. The overarching goal is typically to improve student reading outcomes or to reduce the number of students who are below benchmark. Some sample school goals are:

- No more than 5% of students will be below benchmark by the end of the first year of implementation.

- All students below benchmark will receive at least 30 minutes of intervention daily in a group no larger than five students.

- All students in the lowest 10% will receive two 30-minute intervention lessons daily for as many weeks as needed in groups no larger than three students.

- Data for each student and group receiving intervention instruction will be analyzed at least every nine weeks.

- If after nine weeks a student is not making an adequate level of progress to reach benchmark by year-end, his intervention will be intensified.

- Students will remain in intervention instruction until they reach *DIBELS* benchmark on two consecutive progress monitoring assessments (or six weeks).

Another use for the progress monitoring data is to analyze how effective the school's intervention instruction is in catching up struggling readers. If you are using Cambium Learning® Sopris' VPORT, DMG's DIBELS.net, Wireless Generation, or the University of Oregon's data-management system, one of the best ways to see this is to review the Effectiveness reports. It's possible to follow the progress of the students who entered the year at benchmark and to see what percentage of them stayed at benchmark in the following period. Similarly, the effectiveness of Tier 2 and Tier 3 in moving below-benchmark students up to benchmark can also be seen. Keep in mind that there is no way to separate the effectiveness of the core instruction from the intervention instruction because the students who were below benchmark received both. However, it doesn't really matter which instruction contributed the most to catching up the students to benchmark; what is important is that the combination of services helped the students.

Record Keeping for Intervention Groups

There are several important records to keep about the time and type of intervention offered so if a student is referred for possible special education qualification later, the data are available.

Intervention Lesson Plans

Chapter 7 provided some sample lesson plan forms. If teachers are creating lesson plans for intervention groups, it's helpful to store them in a three-ring binder and keep a copy of the lesson plans filed for each group. These lesson plans provide documentation about the types of materials used in the intervention and the level of intensity the students in that group have already received. It's important to keep this information for analysis. When the reading coach or content leader meets with a teacher to decide whether the intervention should be changed for a student who didn't make adequate progress, these plans provide critical information.

Intervention Logs

In addition to the lesson plans, most intervention teachers keep some kind of log so they can make notes about students' attendance, attentiveness to the task, progress on specific skills, and any apparent difficulties. These notes also provide important information, especially when the student isn't making progress. In some schools where the intervention instructor is not the classroom teacher, a copy of this log is placed in the teacher's mailbox weekly to help keep the teacher informed about the student's intervention instruction. Sample forms are shown here in *Figure 8.7* and *Figure 8.8* (next page).

Figure 8.7

Sample One-Week Intervention Log

Group Information:

Group Type: _____   Week of: _____

School/Teacher: _____

Name of Students in Group & *DIBELS Next*® Scores:

Name	FSF	LNF	PSF	NWF	DORF	RTF	Date
1.							
2.							
3.							
4.							

Time—Intervention Provided:

Monday Tuesday Wednesday Thursday Friday

Times Met:

Total Minutes/Day.

Instructor.

Instructional Focus:

Curriculum/Materials:

Attendance and Observation Records:

Student Name: Attendance (circle if present): M T W Th F	Student Name: Attendance (circle if present): M T W Th F
Student Name: Attendance (circle if present): M T W Th F	Student Name: Attendance (circle if present): M T W Th F

*Add more boxes on back if more than 4 students.

Figure 8.8

Sample Three-Week Intervention Log

Teacher: _____

Group Focus	Focus:					Focus:					Focus:				
Dates for the Week	Dates:					Dates:					Dates:				
Record minutes of intervention for each day.	Mon	Tues	Wed	Thurs	Fri	Mon	Tues	Wed	Thurs	Fri	Mon	Tues	Wed	Thurs	Fri
Student Name:	M	T	W	Th	F	M	T	W	Th	F	M	T	W	Th	F
BM / PM / PM / PM															
Student Name:	M	T	W	Th	F	M	T	W	Th	F	M	T	W	Th	F
BM / PM / PM / PM															
Student Name:	M	T	W	Th	F	M	T	W	Th	F	M	T	W	Th	F
BM / PM / PM / PM															
Student Name:	M	T	W	Th	F	M	T	W	Th	F	M	T	W	Th	F
BM / PM / PM / PM															
Student Name:	M	T	W	Th	F	M	T	W	Th	F	M	T	W	Th	F
BM / PM / PM / PM															

Part II

Sample Intervention Activities

Chapter 9

Intervention Activities for Letter Naming Fluency (LNF)

Number	Name	Description	Skill
1	Puzzling Letter Match (page 196)	Match upper- and lowercase letters on a puzzle mat.	Reinforce and build fluency for matching and naming letters.
2	Missing Alphabet Sequence (page 197)	Place letter cards in correct alphabetic order on a sentence strip.	Reinforce and build fluency for matching and naming letters.
3	Alphabet Sequencing and Letter Identification (page 198)	Match plastic letters with correct letters in the alphabet sequence on a sentence strip.	Reinforce and build fluency for matching and naming letters.
4	Alphabet Identification (page 199)	Name all letters on a sentence strip repetitively at a faster rate.	Reinforce and build fluency for letters out of sequence.
5	Speedy Snakes (page 200)	Name all letters on different snake mats repetitively at a faster rate.	Reinforce and build fluency for letters out of sequence.
6	Snake Letter Match (page 201)	Match chips with letters on a snake mat using different snakes.	Reinforce and build fluency for letter recognition.
7	Stepping Stones (page 202)	Match chips with letters on a river mat.	Reinforce recognition of letters.
8	Swat It! (page 203)	Match letters on a mat using a fly swatter.	Reinforce recognition of letters.
9	Two-Column Sort (page 204)	Sort upper- and lowercase letters onto a two-column mat.	Reinforce recognition of upper- and lowercase letters.
10	Two-Column Match (page 205)	Match upper- and lowercase letters using a two-column mat.	Reinforce recognition of upper- and lowercase letters.

Activity 1	Puzzling Letter Match	Letter Naming Fluency
Purpose	Reinforce and build fluency for matching and naming letters.	
Materials	• Puzzle mat • Plastic letters or letter tiles	
Procedure	1. Explain to students: **This activity will help you build fluency in matching and naming letters.** 2. Hold up the puzzle mat and a letter. 3. Have the student name the letter in the first puzzle piece (work left to right). 4. Find the matching letter. Place it on the letter in the puzzle piece. 5. Repeat the letter name. 6. Continue with the next puzzle piece. **Variation** 1. Name the uppercase letter in the first puzzle piece (work left to right). 2. Find the matching lowercase letter. Place it on the uppercase letter in the puzzle piece. 3. Repeat the letter name. 4. Continue with the next puzzle piece. 5. Give students their own puzzle mat and letters. 6. Students should independently name and match letters.	
Examples	**Example** S S S r r r	**Variation Example** R r T r t

Activity 2	Missing Alphabet Sequence	Letter Naming Fluency
Purpose	Reinforce and build fluency for matching and naming letters.	

Materials	• Sentence strips with alphabet in sequence • Letter cards with two sequenced letters

Procedure	1. Explain to students: **This activity will help you build fluency in naming letters and putting them in alphabetical order.** 2. Hold up the sentence strip. 3. Name the letters in the first sequence on the sentence strip. 4. Call out the names of the first sequence of missing letters. 5. Place the letter card with the missing letters on the strip. 6. Return to the first letter on the strip and name the letters until reaching the next set of missing letters. 7. Repeat steps 3 through 6. 8. Give students their own alphabet strip and letter cards. 9. Students should independently name letters of the alphabet in sequence and place letter cards in the appropriate places. **Variation** 1. Give each pair of students an alphabet strip and letter cards. 2. Have students take turns naming the letters in sequence, naming the missing letters, and choosing the appropriate letter cards.

Example	c d g h i j m n o q r s v w z e f x y k l t u

Activity 3	Alphabet Sequencing and Letter Identification	Letter Naming Fluency
Purpose	Reinforce and build fluency for matching and naming letters.	
Materials	• Sentence strips with alphabet in sequence • Alphabet letter cards • Plastic alphabet letters (or chips)	
Procedure	1. Explain to students: **This activity will help you build fluency in naming letters in alphabetical order and identifying them on cards.** 2. Hold up the sentence strip. 3. Name all letters in the sequence on the sentence strip. 4. Show an alphabet letter card, and name the letter. 5. Place the plastic letter or chip on the matching letter on the strip. 6. Repeat steps 3 through 5 with the next letter card. 7. Give students their own strip. 8. Have all students name the alphabet in order (individually, at their own rate). 9. Show students the letter cards, but do not call out the names. 10. Students should independently name and place plastic letters or chips on the letters. 11. Periodically stop and have all students name the alphabet in order.	
Example	a b c d e f g h i j k l m n o p q r s t u v w x y z	
	a　　s　　o　　w	

Activity 4	Alphabet Identification		Letter Naming Fluency
Purpose	Reinforce and build fluency for letters out of sequence.		
Materials	• Sentence strips with targeted alphabet letters on both sides (varied with sets of letters repeated several times)		
Procedure	1. Explain to students: **This activity will help you build fluency in naming letters that you're learning.** 2. Hold up the sentence strip. 3. Name all letters. 4. Repeat at a faster rate. 5. Flip over the strip. 6. Name all letters. 7. Repeat at a faster rate. 8. Give students their own strip. 9. Have all students name the letters in the alphabet (individually, at their own rate). 10. Have students repeat steps 3 through 5 to build fluency and speed. 11. Match strips to students for targeted letter practice. 12. If students are quick, have them switch strips with other students and repeat the steps.		
Example	a m t p m a t m p t a p m a t p m s r g i y r i s y g i s y r y g s r i y		

Activity 5	Speedy Snakes	Letter Naming Fluency
Purpose	Reinforce and build fluency for letters out of sequence.	
Materials	• Snake mats	
Procedure	1. Explain to students: **This activity will help you build fluency in naming letters that you're learning.** 2. Hold up the snake mat. 3. Name all letters on the first snake mat. 4. Repeat the letter names at a faster rate. 5. Name all letters on the second snake mat. 6. Repeat the letter names at a faster rate. 7. Give each student his or her own snake mat. 8. Have all students name the letters of the alphabet on their snake mat (individually, at their own rate). 9. Have students repeat the letter names to build fluency and speed. 10. Match snake mats to students for targeted letter practice. 11. If students are quick, have them switch snake mats with other students and repeat the steps.	
Example	a m t p m a t m p s n e s e p s e	

Activity 6	Snake Letter Match	Letter Naming Fluency
Purpose	Reinforce and build fluency for letter recognition.	
Materials	• Snake mats • Letter cards • Chips • Random alphabet list	
Procedure	1. Explain to students: **This activity will help you build fluency in matching and naming letters.** 2. Hold up the snake mat, a letter card, and a chip. 3. Name all letters on the first snake mat. 4. Repeat the letter names at a faster rate. 5. Name all letters on the second snake mat. 6. Repeat the letter names at a faster rate. 7. Give students their own snake mat. 8. Show students a letter card. (Do not say the letter name.) 9. Have students identify the letter on their snake mat and cover it with a chip. 10. Continue with the next letter card. 11. When finished, have students remove all chips and name the sequence of letters on their snake mat. **Variation** 1. Give students their own snake mat and chips. Students should independently name and place chips on the letters.	
Example		

Activity 7	Stepping Stones	Letter Naming Fluency
Purpose	Reinforce recognition of letters.	
Materials	• River mats • Letter cards • Chips	
Procedure	1. Explain to students: **This activity will help you build fluency in recognizing letters.** 2. Hold up the river mat. 3. Name all letters on the river mat. 4. Show a letter card. 5. Name the letter on the letter card. 6. Place a chip on the matching letter on the river mat. 7. Repeat steps 4 through 6. 8. Give students their own river mat and chips. 9. Have all students name the letters of the alphabet on their river mat (individually, at their own rate). 10. Have students repeat the letter names to build fluency and speed. 11. Repeat steps 4 through 6. 12. Students place a chip on each letter on their river mat that matches the letter card. **Variation** 1. Give each pair of students their own river mat. 2. Have all students name letters on their river mat (individually, at their own rate). 3. Have students repeat the letter names to build fluency and speed. 4. Students should take turns choosing letter cards, naming the letters, and placing chips on the river mat.	
Example		

Activity 8	Swat It!	Letter Naming Fluency
Purpose	Reinforce recognition of letters.	
Materials	• 4 × 4 Letter grid mat • Random list of letters • Fly swatters	
Procedure	1. Explain to students: **This activity will help you build fluency in recognizing letters.** 2. Show the mat. 3. Name all letters on the mat. 4. Using the random list of letters, name the first letter. 5. Slap the fly swatter on the matching letter on the mat. 6. Repeat steps 4 and 5. 7. Give students their own mat and fly swatter. 8. Have all students name all letters on their mat (individually, at their own rate). 9. Have students repeat letter names to build fluency and speed. 10. Say the next letter on the random list of letters. 11. Have students repeat repeat the letter name and, if it is on their mat, slap it. **Variation** 1. Give students their own mat and fly swatter. 2. Pair students with a stack of shared letter cards. 3. Students should take turns flipping the letter card and naming the letter. 4. Both students swat the letter on their own mat.	
Example		

Activity 9	Two-Column Sort	Letter Naming Fluency
Purpose	Reinforce recognition of upper- and lowercase letters.	
Materials	• Two-column mat (both upper- and lowercase letters are missing, one from each column) • Plastic letters or letter tiles	
Procedure	1. Explain to students: **This activity will help you build fluency in matching uppercase and lowercase letters.** 2. Show the two-column mat. 3. Name the first letter on the mat. 4. Place the matching plastic letter or letter tile in the opposite column. 5. Repeat steps 3 and 4. 6. Give students their own mat and plastic letters or letter tiles. 7. Have students name each letter on their mat and then place the matching upper- or lowercase letter in the opposite column.	
Example		

Activity 10	Two-Column Match	Letter Naming Fluency
Purpose	Reinforce recognition of upper- and lowercase letters.	
Materials	• Two-column mat (uppercase letters are randomly listed in left column; right column is empty) • Plastic lowercase letters or letter tiles	
Procedure	1. Explain to students: **This activity will help you build fluency in matching uppercase and lowercase letters.** 2. Show the two-column mat. 3. Name the first uppercase letter on the mat. 4. Place the matching lowercase plastic letter or letter tile in the opposite column. 5. Repeat steps 3 and 4. 6. Give students their own mat and plastic letters or letter tiles. 7. Have students name each uppercase letter and then place the matching lowercase letter in the opposite column.	
Example	S s A a	

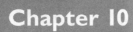

Chapter 10

Intervention Activities for First Sound Fluency (FSF)

Number	Name	Description	Skill
1	Red Light, Green Light (page 208)	Identify the initial sounds of different words using picture cards.	Practice isolating the initial sound in words.
2	Feed the Hungry-Mungries (page 209)	Name the picture cards and feed them to the Hungry-Mungry that eats the particular initial sound.	Reinforce isolating initial sounds in words.
3	Name That Sound (page 210)	Identify initial sounds in objects pulled out of the Mystery Box.	Reinforce isolating initial sounds in words.
4	Whack a Match (page 211)	Whack picture words on a grid that begin with the same initial sounds as different objects on picture cards.	Reinforce isolating initial sounds in words.
5	Zoo Keeper (page 212)	Identify the initial sound of each zoo animal using picture cards.	Reinforce isolating initial sounds in words.
6	Bad Egg (page 213)	Identify the sounds of different zoo animals using the egg cards.	Reinforce isolating initial sounds in words.
7	Mini Scramble (page 214)	Identify which objects have the same initial sounds as other words.	Reinforce isolating initial sounds in words.

Activity 1	Red Light, Green Light	First Sound Fluency
Purpose	Practice isolating the initial sound in words.	
Materials	• 30 picture cards with simple illustrations of words that students are likely to know • 5 green light cards • 2 red light cards • A large can or box	
Procedure	1. Explain to students: **This game with help you practice isolating the initial sound in words**. 2. Display the stack of picture cards and red and green light cards. 3. Shuffle the cards and place them all in the can or box. 4. Have students take turns drawing a card from the can, beginning with Player 1. 5. If the player draws a picture card and can identify the first sound in the word, the player keeps the card. 6. If the player cannot identify the first sound in the word, the card goes back in the can. 7. If the player draws a green light card, the player gets another turn and keeps the green light card. 8. If the player draws a red light card, all of the player's cards go back in the can, except the red light card. 9. Play ends when there are no more cards in the can. 10. Students count their cards to determine the winner. **Variation** 1. Modify to isolate the final sound in a word.	
Example		

Activity 2	Feed the Hungry-Mungries	First Sound Fluency
Purpose	Reinforce isolating initial sounds in words.	
Materials	• 4 "Hungry-Mungries" (glue a monster image to a small paper sack and cut out the mouth so that cards will fit through them; paper clip one picture card [solution card] to each sack—four different initial sounds in all) • 30 to 40 picture cards that begin with one of the four initial sounds	
Procedure	1. Explain to students: **This game with help you practice isolating the initial sound in words.** 2. Display the Hungry-Mungries and the picture cards. 3. Have a student take a picture card, name the picture, and feed it to the Hungry-Mungry that eats that initial sound. 4. Continue until all of the picture cards have been fed to a Hungry-Mungry. 5. Check the work against the solution card that is paper clipped to each Hungry-Mungry. **Variation** 1. Modify to isolate the final sound in a word.	
Example		

Activity 3	Name That Sound	First Sound Fluency
Purpose	Reinforce isolating initial sounds in words.	
Materials	• Box (make a hole that is big enough for a student's hand) • Enough small objects for each student to name (brush, dice, bell, etc.)	
Procedure	1. Explain to students: **This game with help you practice isolating the initial sound in words**. 2. Display the Mystery Box. 3. Have a student reach into the Mystery Box and pull out an object. 4. Have the student name the object and isolate the initial sound. 5. Allow all students to take turns completing steps 3 and 4. 6. To keep students from rummaging in the box for a long time, consider saying: **1, 2, 3, what did you find?** **Variation** 1. Place students in pairs. 2. Have Student 1 pull the object out of the box. 3. Have Student 2 name the object and isolate the initial sound. 4. Reverse roles and repeat steps 2 and 3.	
Example		

Activity 4	Whack a Match	First Sound Fluency

Purpose	Reinforce isolating initial sounds in words.

Materials	• Laminated 3 × 3 grid with picture words for each student • Picture cards face down • A mini fly swatter (or small plastic squeaky hammer) for each student to use to whack the picture

Procedure	1. Explain to students: **This game with help you practice isolating the initial sound in words.** 2. Display the 3 × 3 grid and the fly swatter. 3. Give each student a grid and a fly swatter. 4. Draw, for example, a "cake" picture card and say: **Whack a picture that begins with the same sound as cake.** 5. Have students find a picture on their grid that begins with the /k/ sound and whack it once with their fly swatter. 6. Ask: **Which picture did you whack?** **Variation** 1. Once students understand the procedure, have them take turns with a partner. 2. Have one student call out the word on the picture card while the other finds and whacks the matching picture word on the grid.

Example	

Activity 5	Zoo Keeper	First Sound Fluency
Purpose	Reinforce isolating initial sounds in words.	
Materials	• 3 to 4 green plastic berry baskets to use as animal "cages" (attach a picture of an animal to each basket, e.g., koala, bear, penguin, and monkey) • 30 to 40 picture cards placed face down (ten cards per initial sound—ten words that begin with /k/, ten with /b/, etc.)	
Procedure	1. Explain to students: **This game with help you practice isolating the initial sound in words.** 2. Display the animal cages and the picture cards. 3. Act as the "zookeeper" and have students name the animals in their zoo. 4. Have students isolate the initial sound for each animal cage. 5. Hold up a picture card and have students name the picture, isolate the initial sound, and indicate which animal cage gets the picture card. 6. Continue until all cards are used. **Variation** 1. Once students understand the procedure, have them take turns with a partner. 2. Have each student take turns being the zoo keeper who turns over the cards and the person who feeds the animals in the animal cages.	
Example		

Activity 6	Bad Egg	First Sound Fluency

Purpose	Reinforce isolating initial sounds in words.
Materials	• A large bowl or basket for the big nest • 30 to 40 egg-shaped die cuts or circles (glue a picture card on each egg) • 5 to 10 egg-shaped die cuts or circles (write the words *Bad Egg* and draw a crack on the egg) • A small bowl or basket "nest" for each student.
Procedure	1. Explain to students: **This game with help you practice isolating the initial sound in words.** 2. Display the big "nest" with the egg cards inside. 3. Give each student their own nest. 4. Show students the egg cards. Explain that there are eggs with pictures on them. If a student draws one of those, they must name the picture and say the first sound. 5. Show students a Bad Egg card. If a student draws that egg, they have to put all of their eggs back in the big nest. 6. Play continues as long as students want to play. **Variation** 1. Once students understand the procedure, have them take turns with a partner. 2. Have students take turns drawing egg cards from the big nest.
Example	

Activity 7	Mini Scramble	First Sound Fluency
Purpose	Reinforce isolating initial sounds in words.	
Materials	• Miniature objects for students to sort (provide eight to ten per student—each student should have different objects) • Laminated construction paper to use as a work mat • Tokens for keeping score	
Procedure	1. Explain to students: **This game with help you practice isolating the initial sound in words.** 2. Give each student a work mat and eight to ten miniature objects. 3. Say a word to the students. 4. Have each student repeat the word and isolate the initial sound. 5. Tell students to "scramble" to see who can be the first to find an object on their mat that has the same initial sound. 6. Give a token to the student who has the first correct answer (or to each student who finds an object that begins with the target sound). **Variation** 1. Once students understand the procedure, have them take turns with a partner. 2. Have one student call out a word and the other tries to find a miniature from their set of objects that begins with the same sound.	
Example		

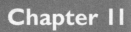

Chapter 11

Intervention Activities for Phoneme Segmentation Fluency (PSF)

Number	Name	Description	Skill
1	Build a Tower (page 216)	Identify the number of phonemes in words from different picture cards to obtain cubes to make a tower.	Practice segmenting one- to five-phoneme words.
2	Phoneme Sort (page 217)	Place picture cards in a pocket chart according to the number of phonemes in the words.	Practice sorting words by the number of phonemes.
3	Joyful Noise (page 218)	Jingle the bell every time a phoneme is identified in a word.	Practice segmenting one- to five-phoneme words.
4	Leprechaun Gold (page 219)	Count the number of phonemes on each gold coin card to determine who wins the gold coins for each round.	Practice segmenting one- to five-phoneme words.
5	Money Bags (page 220)	Segment different picture cards to collect coins based on the number of phonemes in the words.	Practice segmenting one- to five-phoneme words.
6	Under the Sea (page 221)	Move token forward based on how many phonemes are in different words.	Practice segmenting one- to five-phoneme words.
7	Graphing Phonemes (page 222)	Place an "X" on the graphing sheet in the correct column according to the number of phonemes in the words.	Practice segmenting one- to five-phoneme words.

Activity 1	Build a Tower	Phoneme Segmentation Fluency
Purpose	Practice segmenting one- to five-phoneme words.	
Materials	• Linking cubes • Deck of one- to five-phoneme picture cards or list of one- to five-phoneme words	
Procedure	1. Explain to students: **This activity will help you practice segmenting the sounds you hear in a word.** 2. Give each student a pile of unconnected linking cubes. 3. Turn over a picture card (or read a word from a list). 4. Ask students to identify the word from the picture card and raise their hand when ready. 5. Students will segment the phoneme in each word. Have students take one linking cube from their pile for each phoneme they segment. 6. Continue turning over picture cards (or reading words aloud) for the students as they segment words and take one cube for each phoneme. 7. When all picture cards have been flipped or read, have each student make a tower from their linking cubes. 8. Determine who segmented the most words by finding the tallest tower. **Variation** 1. Set the timer for 2 to 3 minutes. 2. Give each student a set of picture cards and linking cubes. 3. Have students flip cards, say the word, and segment the word. 4. Have students add 1 cube per phoneme to their tower. 5. Choose the winner by determining the tallest tower when the timer goes off.	

Activity 2	Phoneme Sort	Phoneme Segmentation Fluency
Purpose	Practice sorting words by the number of phonemes.	
Materials	• Large pocket chart • Number cards 1 through 5 • Picture cards featuring one- to five-phoneme words	
Procedure	1. Explain to students: **This activity will help you practice segmenting the sounds you hear in a word.** 2. Display the pocket chart and the deck of picture cards. 3. Place the number cards across the top of the pocket chart as column headers. 4. Tell students that you'll be using the pocket chart to sort words by the number of phonemes in them. 5. Draw the first picture card from the deck. 6. Have students name the word from the picture card and segment it. 7. Place the picture card in the pocket chart according to the number of phonemes in the word. **Variation** 1. Have students practice drawing picture cards and naming the word independently with a smaller pocket chart.	
Example		

1	**2**	**3**	**4**	**5**

Activity 3	Joyful Noise	Phoneme Segmentation Fluency
Purpose	Practice segmenting one- to five-phoneme words.	
Materials	• Little jingle bells, dog training clicker, mini tambourines, or other noisemakers • List of one- to five-phoneme words or picture cards	
Procedure	1. Explain to students: **This activity will help you practice segmenting the sounds you hear in a word.** 2. Give each student a jingle bell or other noisemaker. 3. Say a word from the word list or picture card. 4. Have students repeat the word. 5. Have students jingle the bell for each phoneme they hear in the word. **Variation** 1. Have students practice with a partner by taking turns drawing a card, naming the picture, segmenting the phonemes, and jingling the bell for each phoneme.	

Activity 4	Leprechaun Gold	Phoneme Segmentation Fluency
Purpose	Practice segmenting one- to five-phoneme words.	
Materials	• Circular gold "coin" cards with pictures on them for each team	
Procedure	*This is an adaptation of the card game called War.* 1. Explain to students: **This activity will help you practice segmenting the sounds you hear in a word.** 2. Provide teams with a deck of gold coin cards. 3. Pairs of students count, "1, 2, 3," and then each student turns over a gold coin card. 4. Have students count the number of phonemes in their word. 5. The student whose word has the most phonemes takes both cards and adds them to the bottom of his or her stack of "coins." 6. If both students' coins have the same number of phonemes, each student draws two more cards and places one card face down and then another card face up. 7. The winner of the round is the student from each team who has the highest number of phonemes in the last card he or she turned over. 8. Play continues until one student from each team is out of cards.	

Activity 5	Money Bags	Phoneme Segmentation Fluency
Purpose	Practice segmenting one- to five-phoneme words.	
Materials	• Plastic gold coins • Small bags • Deck of picture cards	
Procedure	1. Explain to students: **This activity will help you practice segmenting the sounds you hear in a word.** 2. Display the gold coins and give students their own small bag to hold their coins. 3. Have students take turns drawing a picture card and segmenting the word. 4. Students should take one gold coin for each phoneme in their word. 5. When cards run out, students stop to count their coins. 6. The winner is the student with the most coins.	

Activity 6	Under the Sea	Phoneme Segmentation Fluency
Purpose	Practice segmenting one- to five-phoneme words.	
Materials	• Board game in which students move tokens along a path "under the sea"* • Tokens • Deck of picture cards	
Procedure	1. Explain to students: **This activity will help you practice segmenting the sounds you hear in a word.** 2. Display the Under the Sea board game and allow students to select their tokens. 3. Have students place their tokens on "start." Then, have them take turns drawing a picture card, naming the picture, and segmenting the word. 4. Students move their tokens the same number of squares as the number of phonemes in the word. 5. Play continues until a student reaches the finish square. **Variation** 1. Two students can play at the same time—make two copies of the game board. 2. Set the timer and see which student gets closest to the finish at the end of 2 or 3 minutes.	

*Any board game in which students can move tokens a number of spaces on the board will do.

Activity 7	Graphing Phonemes	Phoneme Segmentation Fluency
Purpose	Practice segmenting one- to five-phoneme words.	
Materials	• Laminated graphing sheet for each student, with numbers 1 through 5 as column headers • Deck of picture cards • Dry-erase markers	
Procedure	1. Explain to students: **This activity will help you practice segmenting the sounds you hear in a word.** 2. Give each student a graphing sheet and dry-erase marker. 3. Draw a picture card from the deck. 4. Have students name the picture and segment the word. 5. Have students find the column with the number that matches the number of phonemes in the word and place an "X" in one of the cells in that column. 6. Continue with more words from the deck. 7. Compare graphs. 8. The winner is the student who matches the solution (teacher keeps track while students are completing the activity). **Variation** 1. Once students understand the process, give them a set of picture cards and their own graph. 2. Each student draws a picture card, names the picture, and segments the word. 3. Then the student places an "X" in one cell in the correct column on the graph.	
Example		

1	2	3	4	5
X	X	X		
		X		

Chapter 12

Intervention Activities for Nonsense Word Fluency (NWF)

Name	Name	Description	Skill
1	Word Flowers (page 224)	Identify real and nonsense words when a vowel is placed between two consonants.	Reinforce reading VC and CVC words.
2	Word Ladders (page 225)	Change single sounds in words to create new words using the word ladder.	Reinforce reading VC and CVC words.
3	Roll a Word (page 226)	Roll different colored cubes to form words and identify whether they are real or nonsense words.	Reinforce reading and spelling VC and CVC words.
4	Presto Change-o (page 227)	Change real words to nonsense words by altering the spelling of real words on a dry-erase board.	Reinforce reading and spelling VC and CVC words.
5	End of the Trail (page 228)	Move tokens on game board based on the number of words read correctly.	Reinforce reading VC and CVC words.
6	Spin It and Change It (page 229)	Change beginning, middle, or end sound of real words to create new real words.	Reinforce reading and spelling CVC words.
7	Go Fish (page 230)	Play Go Fish using word cards instead of playing cards.	Reinforce reading VC and CVC words.
8	Accurate Speller (page 231)	Write words on dry-erase board.	Reinforce spelling VC and CVC words.
9	CVC Bingo (page 232)	Match tokens with words when the words are called.	Reinforce reading VC and CVC words.
10	Fish Pond (page 233)	Read words on different fish as they are caught with a small pole.	Reinforce reading VC and CVC words.
11	Ears, Eyes, and Fingers (page 234)	Match a finger to different words when the words are read aloud.	Reinforce reading VC and CVC words.
12	Kaboom! (page 235)	Read word cards correctly to earn points.	Reinforce reading VC and CVC words.
13	Snap! (page 236)	Match word card with five playing cards to run out of playing cards as quickly as possible.	Reinforce reading VC and CVC words.
14	Winner Takes All (page 237)	Read word cards to determine who has the card that is first alphabetically.	Reinforce reading VC and CVC words.
15	This Is Nuts! (page 238)	Read word cards correctly to avoid taking cards from the discard stack.	Reinforce reading VC and CVC words.
16	Build Up (page 239)	Change single sounds in words to create new words, noting whether they are real or nonsense words.	Reinforce reading VC and CVC words.

Activity 1	Word Flowers*	Nonsense Word Fluency
Purpose	Reinforce reading VC and CVC words.	
Materials	• Laminated Word Flowers (see Example below) • Dry-erase markers • Writing paper/dry-erase board	
Procedure	1. Explain to students: **This activity will help you practice reading words.** 2. Display a Word Flower and the paper/dry-erase board. 3. Write a vowel letter between the two consonants.** 4. Read the word. 5. If the word is a real word, write the word on the sheet of paper. 6. Point to the word and read it after you print it. 7. Continue with each vowel letter on the Word Flower. 8. When all vowels have been written and pronounced, read down the list of words. 9. After modeling the process, provide students with their own laminated Word Flowers. 10. Have students write a vowel letter between the two consonants. 11. Depending on which variation (above) you use, have students record and then read each word. 12. Before switching to a new Word Flower, students should read their lists aloud. **Variation** 1. Make a T-chart with column headers of "Real" and "Nonsense." 2. Write a vowel letter between the two consonants on the Word Flower. 3. Read the word. 4. If the word is a real word, write it in the Real column. If the word is a nonsense word, write it in the Nonsense column. 5. Point to the word on the sheet of paper and read it after you print it. 6. Continue with each vowel letter on the Word Flower. 7. When all vowels have been written and pronounced, read down both lists of words.	
Example		

*This is adapted from the Florida Center for Reading Research (FCRR) Activity P.034 "Vowel Stars."
**May begin with VC words.

Activity 2	Word Ladders*	Nonsense Word Fluency
Purpose	Reinforce reading VC and CVC words.	
Materials	• Word Ladder student sheet (see Examples below)	

Procedure	1. Explain to students: **This activity will help you practice spelling and reading words.**
	2. Display a Word Ladder sheet.
	3. Write the word *it* at the top rung of the ladder and then read the word.
	4. Say: **I'll add /s/ at the beginning of *it* to make a new word.**
	5. Write *sit* on the second rung and then read the word.
	6. Continue using this pattern:
	   a. Underline the /ĭ/ sound as you say: **I want to change /ĭ/ to /ă/.**
	   b. Write the new word on the next rung and then read the word.
	7. Change single sounds to create new words until you get to the last rung of the ladder.
	8. Read the entire ladder when all words have been written.
	9. Give students their own Word Ladder sheet and call out a different set of words.
	
	Variation
	1. Follow the procedure above, except change the level of teacher support.
	2. Begin with the word *bag* on the top rung.
	3. Read the word and say: **I want to change *bag* to *bat* so I'll change the *g* to *t*.**
	4. Write *bat* on the second rung.
	5. Continue using this pattern:
	   a. Say: **I want to change *bat* to *bit*.**
	   b. Write the new word on the next rung and then read the word.
	6. Change single sounds to create new words until you get to the last rung of the ladder.
	7. Read the entire ladder when all words have been written.
	8. Give students their own Word Ladder sheet and call out a different set of words.

Examples

Example

it		it	
		sit	
		sat	
		sap	
		tap	
		tip	

Variation Example

bag		bag	
		bat	
		bit	
		hit	
		hat	
		hut	

* This is adapted from the Florida Center for Reading Research (FCRR) Activity "Word Steps."

Activity 3	Roll a Word	Nonsense Word Fluency
Purpose	Reinforce reading and spelling VC and CVC words.	

| **Materials** | • 3 cubes—one green, one yellow, and one red (green cube features six consonants, yellow cube has five vowels plus one repeated vowel letter, and red cube has six consonants)*
• T-chart with column headings of "Real" words and "Nonsense" words
• Dry-erase board | |

| **Procedure** | 1. Explain to students: **This activity will help you practice reading real words and nonsense words.**
2. Display the T-chart and the three letter cubes. The green cube is for the first letter sound in the word, yellow is for the medial letter sound, and red is for the final letter sound.
3. Roll the green cube. Write the consonant letter on the dry-erase board as you make the sound for the letter.
4. Roll the yellow cube. Write the italic vowel letter and make its short sound.
5. Roll the red cube. Write the initial consonant letter and make its sound.
6. Read the word.
7. Decide whether the word you rolled is a real or nonsense word. Record the word under the correct column on the T-chart.
8. After modeling the process, provide each student (or pair of students) with a set of cubes and a T-chart.
9. Have students roll the cubes and write words in the correct column.
10. When you are ready to stop the activity, have students read their real and nonsense words aloud.

Variation
1. Instead of using cubes, use letter cards placed in three stacks—initial, medial, and final sound.
2. Follow the procedure above, but use letter cards instead of cubes. | |

Examples	**Example** 	Real	Nonsense
tub	gat
gut	fup
win	wap
			Variation Example | f	i	p	

*Do not include *k, f, l, r, s,* or *z* on the red cube.

Activity 4	Presto Change-o	Nonsense Word Fluency
Purpose	Reinforce reading and spelling VC and CVC words.	
Materials	• Real word lists comprising VC and CVC words • Nonsense word list comprising VC and CVC words • Dry-erase board • Individual student dry-erase boards	
Procedure	1. Explain to students: **This activity will help you practice reading and spelling words.** 2. Write a real word on the board and then read it aloud. 3. Tell students that you want to change this real word to a nonsense word. 4. Erase any letter and substitute a different letter. 5. Read the nonsense word aloud. 6. Invite students to help you change more real words to nonsense words. 7. After modeling the process, give students individual dry-erase boards. 8. Call out a VC or a CVC word for students to write on their board. 9. Then, have each student change a letter to make a nonsense word from the real word. 10. Have students hold up their boards for other students to read the nonsense word that they made. **Variation** 1. Begin the activity with a nonsense word. 2. Follow the same steps as in the procedure above.	

Activity 5	End of the Trail	Nonsense Word Fluency
Purpose	Reinforce reading VC or CVC words.	
Materials	• Game board* • Word cards with VC or CVC word, marked with the numbers 1, 2, or 3 • Game tokens, one for each student	
Procedure	1. Explain to students: **This game will help you practice reading words.** 2. Have students take turns drawing and reading a word card. 3. If a student reads the word correctly, the student moves his/her token ahead according to the point value on the card. 4. If a student reads the word incorrectly, the student does not move his/her token. 5. The game is over when the first student reaches the end of the trail. **Variation** 1. Pairs of students may play this game as a team. 2. Students should be very accurate with their word reading in order to play this game independently.	

*Any board game in which students can move tokens a number of spaces on the board will do.

Activity 6	Spin It and Change It	Nonsense Word Fluency
Purpose	Reinforce reading and spelling CVC words.	
Materials	• Set of CVC word cards • Spinner marked *b*, *m*, *e*	
Procedure	1. Explain to students: **This activity will help you practice reading and spelling words.** 2. Demonstrate how to spin the spinner and explain that the *b* stands for <u>beginning</u> sound, *m* stands for <u>middle</u> sound, and *e* stands for <u>ending</u> sound. 3. Shuffle the stack of CVC word cards. Draw the top card and have students read the word, for example, *tap*. 4. Spin the spinner. If it lands on *b*, change the first sound in *tap* to a different beginning sound so that it makes a new real word, for example, *tap* to *nap*. 5. Do not make a nonsense word. 6. Draw another card and begin again with a new word. 7. After modeling the process, provide each pair of students with a deck of CVC word cards and a spinner. 8. Have students take turns drawing a card, reading the card, spinning the spinner, and saying a new word. **Variation** 1. Have students practice individually. 2. Provide each student with a set of CVC word cards, paper, and a spinner. 3. The student draws a card, writes the word on a sheet of paper, and then spins the spinner to determine which letter should be changed. 4. The student writes the new word below the original word on the paper.	
Example		

Activity 7	Go Fish	Nonsense Word Fluency
Purpose	Reinforce reading VC and CVC words.	
Materials	• Deck of VC and CVC word cards (15 pairs of VC and CVC words for a total of 30 cards) • Private office folder for each student (glue two manila folders together to form a three-sided box) (Have students place the "private office" in front of them on the table. Most six-year-olds are unable to hold a hand of cards. With the private office, they can place their cards on the table instead of trying to hold them in their hands. This helps students avoid seeing each other's cards.)	
Procedure	1. Explain to students: **This activity will help you practice reading words.** 2. Display the deck of cards. 3. Demonstrate how to set up the private office. 4. Explain the traditional rules of Go Fish. Deal five cards to each player and then model playing the game with your students. 5. Ask one student if they have *pat*. 6. If the student has the card, he/she gives it to you. If the student does not have the card, he/she tells you: "Go Fish." 7. If the student has given you the card, save the two cards stacked together on the table. You now have one pair. Otherwise, draw a card from the deck. 8. Next, let that same student ask you if you have a word he/she needs. 9. Play a hand with each student at the table. 8. The object of the game is to have the highest number of word pairs when the cards run out. 10. After modeling the process of playing Go Fish, have students play with a partner. 11. It is likely that students will need a bit of support to learn to play Go Fish. **Variation** 1. Play Go Fish using a deck that consists of nonsense words.	

Activity 8	Accurate Speller	Nonsense Word Fluency
Purpose	Reinforce spelling VC and CVC words.	
Materials	• List of VC and CVC words • Individual student dry-erase boards	
Procedure	1. Explain to students: **This activity will help you practice spelling words.** 2. Call out a VC or CVC word. 3. Have students repeat the word and then write it on their dry-erase board. 4. Count to ten and then have students show you their board. 5. Keep track of how many times all of the students spelled the word correctly. 6. Encourage students to try to beat their record in subsequent sessions. 7. The suggested count is to ten. As students become very accurate, you may reduce the number of seconds before having them show their board to work on fluency. **Variation** 1. Follow the procedure above, but use nonsense words. 2. If you use nonsense words, it's very important that students repeat the word back to you before they spell the word. By having students repeat the word, you'll know whether they heard you correctly.	

Activity 9	CVC Bingo	Nonsense Word Fluency
Purpose	Reinforce reading VC and CVC words.	
Materials	• Laminated blank bingo cards (3 × 3, 4 × 2, or 4 × 4 grids) • List of VC and CVC words • Dry-erase markers • Tokens to cover the words	
Procedure	1. Explain to students: **This activity will help you practice reading words.** 2. Before students play the game, write real VC and CVC words randomly on the bingo cards for students. 3. Display a bingo card. Demonstrate how to use a token to cover the words on the card. 4. Call out the words for students. If they hear one of their words called, they cover it with a token. 5. With a 4 × 2 bingo grid, play "Cover Up." If you used a 3 × 3 or a 4 × 4 grid, play straight-line or diagonal bingo. 6. This activity could be moved to a Literacy Center for student use. **Variation** 1. Follow the procedure above, but write nonsense words on the bingo card instead of real words.	

Activity 10	Fish Pond	Nonsense Word Fluency
Purpose	Reinforce reading VC and CVC words.	
Materials	• Fish cut outs with VC or CVC words written on each fish • Small pole with string and magnet attached • Paper clips (attached to the fish)	
Procedure	1. Explain to students: **This activity will help you practice reading words.** 2. Have students use the magnet on the pole to catch fish. 3. As each student catches a fish, have him/her read the word that's printed on it. 4. Continue fishing until all fish have been caught. 5. Give each student a fishing pole and a set of fish. 6. Students may work independently or take turns fishing and reading words with a partner.	
Example		

Activity 11	Ears, Eyes, and Fingers	Nonsense Word Fluency
Purpose	Reinforce reading VC and CVC words.	
Materials	• Individual student word grid • Deck of VC and CVC word cards	
Procedure	1. Explain to students: **This activity will help you practice reading words.** 2. Display the word grid each student will use. 3. Flip a card from the deck and then read the word aloud. 4. Have students repeat the word and then find the word on their grid. 5. When a student finds the word, have the student put his/her finger on it and read the word aloud. 6. Continue through the deck of word cards. **Variation** 1. Follow the procedure above, but use a deck of nonsense VC and CVC word cards.	

Activity 12	Kaboom!	Nonsense Word Fluency
Purpose	Reinforce reading VC and CVC words.	
Materials	• 40 Word cards with VC and CVC words • 10 Word cards with the word *Kaboom!*	
Procedure	1. Explain to students: **This game will help you practice reading words.** 2. Display a VC, a CVC, and a Kaboom! word card. 3. Shuffle the deck, including the Kaboom! cards. 4. Have pairs of students take turns playing this game. 5. Player 1 draws a card from the deck. 6. If the student can read the word card, he/she keeps the card. The student continues drawing cards as long as he/she can read the word. 7. If the student cannot read the word, play moves to the other student. 8. If the student draws a Kaboom! card, his/her turn is over. 9. Play ceases when all the cards are gone. The player with the most card wins. 10. Each team can play this game using one deck of word cards. **Variation** 1. Play the card game using a deck of nonsense VC and CVC word cards.	

Activity 13	Snap!	Nonsense Word Fluency
Purpose	Reinforce reading VC and CVC words.	
Materials	• 2 decks of 15 to 20 word cards (Snap! cards) with VC and CVC words printed on them in two different colors	
Procedure	1. Explain to students: **This game will help you practice reading words.** 2. Deal five Snap! cards from Deck 1 to each pair of players. Put that deck aside. 3. Have students place their five cards face up on the table. 4. Place Deck 2 face down between the two students. 5. Turn over the top card from Deck 2. 6. Have students read the word and then look at their five cards. 7. If a student has a matching word card, he/she touches the card and says "Snap!" 8. The player who says "Snap!" gets to discard his/her matching card. 9. Play continues until a student discards all of his/her cards. **Variation** 1. Use two decks of nonsense VC and CVC word cards.	

Activity 14	Winner Takes All	Nonsense Word Fluency
Purpose	Reinforce reading VC and CVC words.	
Materials	• 1 deck of VC and CVC word cards containing 20 to 30 VC and CVC words	
Procedure	1. Explain to students: **This game will help you practice reading words.** 2. Show students the deck of word cards. Explain that the winner is the player who takes all of the cards. 3. Deal all of the word cards to students. 4. Each player turns up their top card and reads the word. 5. The player whose word is first alphabetically takes both cards. 6. If both words begin with the same letter, the players turn over another card and read the new word. The player whose second word is first alphabetically takes all of the cards. 7. Play continues until one player has all of the cards. 8. Monitor students for accurate word reading—not just focusing on the first letter. **Variation** 1. Play this game with a deck made up of nonsense words.	

Activity 15	This Is Nuts!	Nonsense Word Fluency
Purpose	Reinforce reading VC and CVC words.	
Materials	• 1 deck of word cards containing 20 to 35 VC and CVC words and six This Is Nuts! cards (could put a picture of an acorn on this card)	
Procedure	1. Explain to students: **This game will help you practice reading words.** 2. Show students the deck of cards. Explain that the winner is the player who runs out of cards. 3. Deal all of the word cards to the students. 4. Have students keep their stack of cards face down in front of them. 5. The first player turns over the top card in his/her stack and reads it. 6. If the student reads the card correctly, the card is placed face up in a discard stack between the two students. 7. If the student reads the card incorrectly, he/she takes all of the cards in the discard stack and adds them to the bottom of his/her stack. 8. If a player turns over a This Is Nuts! card, he/she keeps that card and takes all of the cards in the discard stack. 9. Play continues until one player has no cards left. 10. Monitor students for accurate word reading—not just focusing on the first letter. **Variation** 1. Play this game with a deck made up of nonsense words.	

Activity 16	Build Up	Nonsense Word Fluency
Purpose	Reinforce reading VC and CVC words.	
Materials	• Stacking letter tiles or small letter cards (for each round, students will need all five vowels and six or so consonants)	
Procedure	1. Explain to students: **This activity will help you practice reading words.** 2. Display the letter tiles or cards. 3. Begin with a simple CVC word, for example, *bit*. 4. Read the word aloud, and then choose one letter tile to place on top of any of the letters in the first word. 5. Read the new word, for example, *sit*, and identify it as real or nonsense. 6. Keep the word *sit* and demonstrate adding a letter on top of the vowel and reading the new word, for example, *set*. 7. Continue to build on the initial word, for example, *set*, *fet*, *feg*, *peg*. 8. Begin again with a new word and new vowel letters. 9. Give students their own set of letter tiles or cards. 10. Give them a word to spell using the tiles/cards. 11. Have students work independently to build and read new words. 12. Monitor students for accuracy and understanding.	

Chapter 13

Intervention Activities for *DIBELS*® Oral Reading Fluency (DORF)

Number	Name	Description	Skill
1	Build a Tower (page 242)	Correctly read words aloud to earn cubes to build a tower.	Increase reading accuracy and fluency with words.
2	Tick Tock Word Reading (page 243)	Read words aloud at a rate set by a metronome.	Increase student fluency at reading words.
3	Busy Bee (page 244)	Read words from tongue depressors as quickly and accurately as possible.	Increase student fluency with words.
4	Fast and Right Words (page 245)	Read words from a word grid as accurately as possible in 1 minute.	Increase student fluency with words.
5	Gotcha! (page 246)	Read phrases from tongue depressors as quickly and accurately as possible.	Increase student fluency in simple phrases.
6	Fast and Right Phrases (page 247)	Read phrases from a phrase grid as accurately as possible in 1 minute.	Increase student fluency in simple phrases.

Activity 1	Build a Tower		DORF
Purpose	Increase reading accuracy and fluency with words.		
Materials	• Linking cubes • Deck of word cards • Timer		
Procedure	1. Explain to students: **This activity will help you practice reading words correctly and quickly.** 2. Give each student a pile of unconnected linking cubes. 3. Set the timer for 1 or 2 minutes. 4. Flip a word card at the rate of about one every 2 seconds. 5. Have students read words aloud; for each word read correctly, students take one linking cube from their pile. 6. Continue flipping word cards as students continue reading words and taking a cube for each word read correctly until time is up. 7. Have students make a tower from their linking cubes. 8. Determine who read the most words by the height of the towers. 9. Give students their own deck of word cards and linking cubes. 10. Set the timer for 1 or 2 minutes, and let pairs of students read words and build their towers. **Variation** 1. Follow the procedure above using a deck of nonsense word cards.		

Activity 2	Tick Tock Word Reading		DORF
Purpose	Increase student fluency at reading words		
Materials	• Word lists (poster and individual) • Metronome (If you don't have a metronome, try www.webmetronome.com. The metronome can be set to tick anywhere from one beat per minute up to 220 beats per minute.)		
Procedure	1. Explain to students: **This activity will help you practice reading words accurately and quickly.** 2. Introduce the metronome to students and explain that each time it ticks, it's time to read a word from the list. 3. Set the metronome at 15 or 20 beats per minute. Let students become accustomed to the rhythm. 4. Use a poster-sized word list. Point to the first word and tell students to read the word aloud when they hear the first tick of the metronome. 5. As soon as the metronome ticks and students read the first word, slide your finger to the second word, and so on, having students read through the word list. 6. After each fluency session, you may increase the number of beats per minute or continue at the same rate. 7. The goal is that students can read the words at a rate of 60 beats per minute. 8. Once students understand the process of the timed word reading, they may read from individual word lists. Student accuracy rates should stay high during these fluency drills. 9. Once students are able to read the word lists at a higher rate, discontinue the metronome and switch to 1-minute word list readings. **Variation** 1. Follow the procedure above using nonsense words. 2. Start with a lower number of beats and move the students to a faster rate.		
Examples	**Example** 	up	cat	did	if
pet	lid	pot	at
Sam	yes	on	map
etc.					**Variation Example** | ip	cug	dib	ig
ped	lud	fot	et
sim	yed	og	fop
etc.					

Activity 3	Busy Bee	DORF
Purpose	Increase student fluency with words.	
Materials	• Word lists featuring any specific word pattern • Busy Bee can (can with a picture of a bee on it) • Tongue depressors/tag board strips (Write word lists on the tongue depressors. Place tongue depressors in the can. The tongue depressors should be easy to remove from the can.) • Timer	
Procedure	1. Explain to students: **This game will help you practice reading words.** 2. Hold up the Busy Bee can. Show students that each tongue depressor has a word printed on it. 3. Set the timer for 1 minute. 4. Have students pull one tongue depressor at a time from the can and read the words. 5. Monitor student accuracy. 6. When time is up, students stop and count their words. 7. Set the timer for 1 more minute and challenge students to read more words. 8. Give students their own Busy Bee can so they can independently read the words on the tongue depressors. **Variation** 1. Follow the procedure above using nonsense words on the tongue depressors.	
Example		

Activity 4	Fast and Right Words	DORF
Purpose	Increase student fluency with words.	
Materials	• Word grids (same words, but each grid has the words in different order), one for each student • 100's paper for graphing results (optional)	
Procedure	1. Explain to students: **This activity will help you practice reading words correctly and quickly.** 2. Show and explain the word grid and a 100's paper. 3. Set the timer for 1 minute. 4. Have students read their own word grid during that minute. 5. Monitor student accuracy. 6. When time is up, students stop, put their finger on the last word they read, and wait for the teacher to count their words. 7. Optional: Have students graph their results on the 100s paper.	

Activity 5	Gotcha!	DORF
Purpose	Increase student fluency with simple phrases.	
Materials	• Phrase lists featuring VC and CVC words and preprimer sight words • Gotcha! can (can decorated with a monster, dragon, dinosaur, etc.) • Tongue depressors/tag board strips (Write phrases on the tongue depressors. Place tongue depressors in the can. The tongue depressors should be easy to remove from the can.)	
Procedure	1. Explain to students: **: This game will help you practice reading phrases.** 2. Hold up the Gotcha! can. Show students that each tongue depressor has a phrase printed on it. 3. Set the timer for 1 minute. 4. Have students pull one tongue depressor at a time from the can and read the phrases. 5. Monitor student accuracy. 6. When time is up, students stop and count their phrases. 7. Set the timer for 1 more minute and challenge students to read more phrases. 8. Give students their own Gotcha! can so they can independently read the phrases on the tongue depressors. **Variation** 1. Follow the directions in Variation 1 using nonsense words	
Example	to the top on the hat in the pot	

Activity 6	Fast and Right Phrases	DORF
Purpose	Increase student fluency with simple phrases.	
Materials	• Phrase grids (same phrases, but each grid has the phrases in different order), one for each student • 100's paper for graphing results (optional)	
Procedure	1. Explain to students: **This activity will help you practice reading phrases correctly and quickly.** 2. Show and explain the phrase grid and the 100s paper. 3. Set the timer for 1 minute. 4. Have students read their own phrase grid during that minute. 5. Monitor student accuracy. 6. When time is up, students stop, put their finger on the last phrase they read, and wait for the teacher to count their phrases. 7. Optional: Have students graph their results on the 100s paper.	

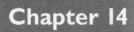
Intervention Activities for Comprehension— Retell and Daze

Number	Name	Description	Skill
1	How Do You Know? (page 250)	Choose one trait that describes a character from a text and record all the events from the text that lead to that conclusion.	Practice providing support for inferences about characters.
2	Character Counts (page 251)	Recall a character who displays a certain character trait—using textual evidence to support the claim—and record all the findings on chart paper.	Reinforce character analysis.
3	Is It Real or Is It Fantasy? (page 252)	Read the statement cards and determine whether they are elements of realistic or fantasy stories.	Practice identifying statements as real or fantasy.
4	Then What Happened? (page 253)	Read a cause statement and list potential effects.	Practice identifying the relationship between cause and effect.
5	Multiple Character Map (page 254)	Update the multiple character map throughout a story to reinforce the importance of conflict between two characters.	Reinforce student understanding of character view point.
6	Ask Me (page 255)	Ask review questions about a text by randomly pulling question words out of a bag.	Use question words to review text.
7	True or False? (page 256)	Read statement cards aloud to determine whether they are true or false.	Practice identifying statements as true or false.
8	What Do You Infer? (page 257)	Read a scenario to determine the possible inferences that could be made.	Practice making inferences.
9	Is That a Fact? (page 258)	Read statements on tongue depressors to determine if they are factual.	Review identifying statements as facts.
10	Mini Book Origami (page 259)	Update a mini book throughout a text to illustrate multiple components of a story.	Multiple-use practice opportunities.
11	Just the Facts (page 260)	Discuss several facts from a story to determine which are more important than others.	Identify important details in nonfiction text.
12	Story Element Sticks (page 261)	Read story element sticks to determine which element belongs in the correct section of a pocket chart.	Identify story elements.
13	Touch and Retell (page 262)	Read a short story, and then retell the story by identifying each story element on the Touch and Retell chart.	Practice story retelling.

Activity 1	How Do You Know?	Comprehension

Purpose	Practice providing support for inferences about characters.

Materials	• A list of character traits • Chart paper

Procedure	1. Explain to students: **This activity will help you clarify and provide proof for conclusions you make about different characters in stories we've read.** 2. Hold up a blank sheet of chart paper. 3. Brainstorm words used to describe a character (e.g., *lazy, industrious, compassionate*). 4. Choose one trait that describes a character in a text that students have read. Write that trait on the top of the chart (e.g., *industrious*). 5. Point out to students that there are many words in English that we use to describe characters. It's easy to say Karana (*Island of the Blue Dolphins*) is *industrious*, but what made us come to that conclusion? What did we read that made us know that Karana is industrious? 6. Guide students to think back to different points in the story where they remembered Karana being industrious. 7. At each point, ask: **What exactly did she do to make you know she's industrious?** 8. Record events that allowed the students to describe Karana as industrious. 9. Display the chart you created in the large group. 10. Allow pairs of students to choose a different character/character trait to analyze. **Variation** 1. Follow the procedure above, but list multiple character traits and record story events to support the inference.

Activity 2	Character Counts	Comprehension

Purpose	Reinforce character analysis.
Materials	• Chart paper

Procedure	1. Explain to students: **This is an activity that we'll come back to all through the school year as we study different characters in the texts we read. This year, we will study character traits—those you would like to have and those you wouldn't like to have.** 2. Begin with three or four traits (e.g., intelligence, loyalty, jealousy, kindness). 3. Begin this year-long activity with words that describe characters in the first anthology selection of the year. You will add characters to this chart for the rest of the year. 4. Write one character trait on each sheet of chart paper. Write a student-friendly definition for each trait. 5. Share the charts with students. 6. Begin with one chart: for example, loyalty. Ask students to recall a character from the story who is loyal. 7. Ask students to give evidence from the story that proves that the character is loyal. 8. Come to consensus on the best example of the character's loyalty and record the story title, character name, and evidence on the chart. 9. Add a character to each of the charts. 10. Add more traits as you go through the school year. 11. As a writing prompt, students may choose one of the traits and write about a time they displayed that trait **Variation** 1. Make small posters of each character trait and its definition. Stick index cards with character name, story, and evidence around the poster. 2. Add character cards throughout the year. 3. Add more character traits throughout the year.

Example	**Loyalty** *A person who sticks up for his friends and family* Charlie Bucket, <u>Charlie and the Chocolate Factory</u> Charlie takes Grandpa Joe to the factory. Toad, <u>Frog and Toad Are Friends</u> Toad always shares whatever he has with Frog.

Activity 3	Is It Real or Is It Fantasy?	Comprehension
Purpose	Practice identifying statements as real or fantasy.	
Materials	• Deck of statement cards (Write a statement that reflects a real story or a fantasy story on each card.) • Header cards: Real, Fantasy	
Procedure	1. Explain to students: **This activity will help you practice identifying a statement as real or fantasy.** 2. Show students the Real and Fantasy header cards. Stack the deck of statement cards beside them. 3. Discuss characteristics of realistic and fantasy stories. 4. Show students how to choose a card from the deck, read the statement, and decide whether the statement is real or fantasy. 5. Once the genre has been identified, place the statement card face up below the correct header card. 6. Continue through the stack of cards, identifying each correctly. 7. Provide students with their own set of header cards and statement cards to practice independently.	
Examples	Real: Bob brushed his teeth before bed. Fantasy: Jill's dog said, "I've been in the house all day. Let's go for a walk."	

Activity 4	Then What Happened?	Comprehension
Purpose	Practice identifying the relationship between cause and effect.	
Materials	• List of sentences that are the "cause" portion of a cause-and-effect set (see Examples)	
Procedure	1. Explain to students: **This activity will help you practice identifying a logical effect for a cause.** 2. Remind students that they have studied cause-and-effect relationships. 3. Read one of the cause statements from the list. 4. Ask students to give possible effect(s) of the cause. 5. Discuss the logic behind each effect. **Variation** 1. Change the activity by beginning with reading an effect. 2. Have students supply a cause statement.	
Examples	John missed the bus. I stuck my finger in the bird cage. Jill rode her bike with only one hand on the handlebars.	

Activity 5	Multiple Character Map		Comprehension
Purpose	Reinforce student understanding of character view point.		
Materials	• Multiple character map		
Procedure	1. Explain to students: **This multiple character map will help you explore contrasting character view points.** 2. Remind students that the conflict between characters is an important part of most stories. Both characters have goals, but those goals conflict. 3. Display the multiple character map and explain it to students. 4. During reading, stop frequently to update the map. 5. After reading, complete the map as a whole-group activity. 6. Once students are familiar with the multiple character map, they can use it independently during reading to help monitor comprehension.		

Example

Multiple Character Map	
Title: The Trojan War	
Main Character 1 **King Menelaus**	Main Character 2 **King Priam**
Setting **Greece and Troy**	Setting **Troy**
Problem(s) **1. Trojans charged a toll** **2. Trojans kidnapped Helen** **3. The war goes on and on**	Problem(s) **1. Greeks attacked Troy** **2. Keep the Greeks out of Troy**
Goal(s) **1. Rescue Helen** **2. Defeat Trojans** **3. No more tolls**	Goal(s) **1. Keep Helen** **2. Defeat Greeks and keep them out of Troy**
Attempts **1. Attacked Troy** **2. Made a Trojan Horse—sneak attack**	Attempts **1. Fight back** **2. Keep the gates of the city closed**
Outcome **Got into the city of Troy—surprise!**	Outcome **Defeated**
Reaction **Hooray!**	Reaction **Boo!**
Theme **Use your head to solve your problems.**	Theme **Things aren't always what they seem to be. Beware of Greeks bearing gifts.**

Activity 6	Ask Me	Comprehension
Purpose	Use question words to review text.	
Materials	• 1½-inch circles cut from card stock (print one question word on each circle) • Can or bag to hold the circles	
Procedure	1. Explain to students: **This activity will help you ask and answer important questions about the text we read.** 2. Show students the bag of circles printed with question words. 3. Tell students that they will play a game that will help them review the important ideas in the text they just read. 4. Pull one circle from the bag and read the question word on it. 5. Ask students a question that begins with that question word. 6. Students should be able to answer the question. If they can't, provide support by looking back in the text to find the answer. 7. Continue pulling circles from the bag and asking review questions. 8. Question word examples: *who, what, when, where, why, how, summarize, what caused, define.* **Variation** 1. Have a student pull a circle from the bag and ask peers a question about the text.	

Activity 7	True or False?	Comprehension
Purpose	Practice identifying statements as true or false.	
Materials	• Deck of statement cards consisting of 20 to 30 true and false statements • Header cards: True, False • Pocket chart	
Procedure	1. Explain to students: **This activity will help you practice identifying statements about _____ as true or false.** 2. Show students the deck of statement cards and place the True and False header cards into the pocket chart. 3. Tell students that they will play a game to practice identifying statements as true or false. 4. Draw the top card from the deck and read the statement aloud. 5. Ask students to identify the statement as true or false. 6. Place the card under the correct header card in the pocket chart. 7. If the statement is false, have the student say why it is false. 8. Continue until all cards are used. 9. Students may use the decks to review concepts independently. **Variation** 1. Follow the procedure above, but if a student identifies a statement as false, have him/her rephrase it to make it a true statement.	

Activity 8	What Do You Infer?	Comprehension
Purpose	Practice making inferences.	
Materials	• A set of short scenarios that support a logical inference	
Procedure	1. Explain to students: **This activity will help you practice making inferences. Good readers can use clues an author gives to understand what the author means but hasn't said.** 2. Discuss inferences with students. 3. Read a scenario to students and ask them what they infer from the scenario. 4. Discuss clues the author gave and the knowledge a student would need to make the inference. 5. Continue until all scenarios are used. 6. More advanced students can write their own short scenarios to share with classmates.	
Examples	Jan walks to the bus. She looks up at the sky. Suddenly, Jan runs back to her house to grab a rain coat. Bill walks to the end of the board. He looks at the cool blue water. He takes a deep breath and thinks, "I hope the judges like this one." He jumps twice and sails up into the air.	

Activity 9	Is That a Fact?	Comprehension
Purpose	Review identifying statements as facts.	
Materials	• Set of 20 to 30 tongue depressors (write a fact on half of the tongue depressors and an opinion on the other half) • Is That a Fact? can (to hold tongue depressors; write the words *Is that a fact?* on the can)	
Procedure	1. Explain to students: **This game will help you practice identifying factual statements.** 2. Display the can that holds the tongue depressors. 3. Discuss with students the definition of a fact. 4. Have the first student draw a tongue depressor from the can, read the statement, and decide whether it is a fact. 5. If the student decides correctly, he/she keeps the tongue depressor. If the student decides incorrectly, the tongue depressor is taken out of play. 6. Students take turns until all of the tongue depressors have been drawn. 7. The winner is the student who has accumulated the most tongue depressors. 8. Students should be able to play independently once they've learned the game. **Variation** 1. Follow the procedure above, but have students decide whether the tongue depressor they chose is an opinion.	

Activity 10	Mini Book Origami	Comprehension
Purpose	Multiple-use practice opportunities.	
Materials	• 1 sheet of 8½ × 11 paper folded into a miniature book	

Procedure	1. Explain to students: **We will use this mini-book to practice _____.**
	2. Use the mini book to:
	   a. Summarize and illustrate a story.
	   b. Create a mini dictionary of terms for a unit of study.
	   c. Create a Latin-Greek root reference.
	   d. Summarize and illustrate a nonfiction text.
	   e. Create a mini reference for cause and effect, synonyms, antonyms, homographs, homophones, parts of speech, prefixes and their meanings, or as a book report.	

Activity 11	Just the Facts		Comprehension
Purpose	Identify important details in nonfiction text.		
Materials	• A "Just the Facts" template for each student • Markers or crayons • Nonfiction text		
Procedure	1. Explain to students: **This activity will help you identify the most important details in the text we read.** 2. Display a blank Just the Facts template. 3. Remind students that good readers identify and remember important details as they read. 4. Attach the Just the Facts template to the board. 5. Discuss the text students recently read. Elicit several facts and lead a discussion to combine those facts into the most important ones. 6. With the students' help, model completing the template. 7. Once students have seen the template modeled, they may work with it independently after reading nonfiction text. They can use the Just the Facts template to study for tests. **Variation** 1. Have students complete the template—except for the Topic box. 2. Have students share their completed Just the Facts template with classmates. 3. Classmates should infer the topic of the Just the Facts template.		
Example	Topic — Detail 1 — Detail 2 — Detail 3 — Diagram/Illustration		

Activity 12	Story Element Sticks		Comprehension

Purpose	Identify story elements.
Materials	• Tongue depressors (write one story element on each stick: characters, title, setting, character goals, problem, solution, lesson learned/theme) • Can for the sticks • Pocket chart with story element header cards
Procedure	1. Explain to students: **This activity will help you review the story we just read by identifying the different story elements. Story elements are characters, setting, character goals, character problems, solution, and lesson learned.** 2. Display the can filled with story element sticks and the cover of the book from the read aloud. 3. Tell students that you'll play a game to see whether they can remember the important story elements from the book you just read aloud. 4. Draw one stick from the can and read the story element printed on it. 5. Ask students to recall the story element from the book. Place the story element stick in the pocket chart. 6. Continue drawing sticks until all elements in the book are reviewed. 7. Review story elements by discussing each element posted in the pocket chart. **Variation 1** 1. Have students play Story Element Sticks with a partner. **Variation 2** 1. Make multiple sets of the story element sticks and give each student three or four sticks. 2. As you read a story aloud, ask students to hold up the stick that matches the part of the story you are reading. For example, if you read, "they lived in a tiny house in the deep dark woods," students should hold up the "setting" stick. 3. Stop and ask students how they knew that was the correct story element.

Activity 13	Touch and Retell	Comprehension

Purpose	Practice story retelling.
Materials	• Touch and Retell chart • Read-aloud book
Procedure	1. Explain to students: **This activity will help you identify different story elements. Story elements are: title, setting, characters, character goals, problems, solution, and lesson learned.** 2. Display the Touch and Retell chart. 3. Tell students that if they look carefully, the pictures on the Touch and Retell Chart tell a story. 4. Touch, explain, and discuss each story element on the chart. 5. Read a short book aloud and then retell the story with students. 6. Touch the book icon and ask students to tell you the title. 7. Touch the house icon and ask for the setting. 8. Continue through the rest of the Touch and Retell Chart. 9. Even younger students can infer the lesson of a story. You may use the Touch and Retell Chart as a rubric if you assess students' ability to retell a story. **Variation 1** 1. After reading or hearing a story, give each pair of students a Touch and Retell chart. 2. Have students touch the icons and retell the story to their partner. **Variation 2** 1. You may use the Touch and Retell chart as a template for written retellings. 2. For a simple retelling, students should write one sentence for each story element, in paragraph form.
Example	**Touch and Retell** |	Title
	Setting
	Characters
	Character Goals
	Problem
	Solution
	Lesson Learned	

Chapter 15

Intervention Activities for Vocabulary

Number	Name	Description	Skill
1	Hot Seat (page 264)	Guess the vocabulary term on the whiteboard within 1 minute to earn points.	Reinforce vocabulary.
2	Survivor (page 265)	Record vocabulary words that fit within a chosen topic until students can no longer think of any.	Reinforce content area vocabulary.
3	Shout Out (page 266)	Guess the terms on the opposing team's topic list within 1 minute to earn points.	Reinforce vocabulary.
4	Hold the Bus! (page 267)	Think of words that fit into different categories based on the starting letter of the word.	Reinforce vocabulary.
5	Make a Match (page 268)	Match pairs of word cards with one another to create pairs.	Reinforce vocabulary.
6	Make a Match Card Game (page 269)	Match pairs of word cards with one another to create pairs.	Reinforce vocabulary.
7	Semantic Feature Analysis (page 270)	Complete the Semantic Features Chart based on the word at the beginning of the row.	Reinforce content area vocabulary and concepts.
8	Triplets (page 271)	Match one yellow tongue depressor with two green tongue depressors to create two definitions for a word.	Reinforce vocabulary.
9	Synonym Sticks (page 272)	Match two tongue depressors to create synonym pairs.	Reinforce vocabulary.
10	Categories (page 273)	Record and place words that correspond with different categories in a pocket chart.	Reinforce vocabulary.
11	Tired Old Words (page 274)	Record and place alternative definitions of generic words in a pocket chart.	Reinforce vocabulary.
12	Shades of Meaning (page 275)	Reorganize words based on their degree of meaning—from most generic to most specific.	Reinforce shades of meaning.

Activity 1	Hot Seat	Vocabulary
Purpose	Reinforce vocabulary.	
Materials	• Vocabulary list for any current content area • Timer	
Procedure	1. Explain to students: **This activity will help you review terms we've learned in _____.** 2. Divide the group into two teams. 3. Place two chairs facing each other in front of the whiteboard. 4. Two students from the same team play at the same time. 5. Student 1 sits facing the whiteboard so that they can see the vocabulary term. 6. Student 2 sits in the Hot Seat facing away from the whiteboard so that the vocabulary term will not be visible. 7. Write the vocabulary term on the whiteboard. 8. Set the timer for 1 minute. 9. Student 1 reads the word to himself/herself and then gives meaning clues to Student 2. 10. Student 1 can use any word as a clue <u>except</u> the word written on the board. 11. If Student 2 names the word within 1 minute, the team scores a point. 12. Alternate teams on the Hot Seat. 13. Scoring variation: Record the number of seconds it took for the student to name the vocabulary term; the lowest team score wins. **Variation** 1. Write the word on the board for everyone to see while Student 2 shuts his/her eyes. 2. Erase the word and start the timer for 2 minutes. 3. Student 1 draws a picture to help Student 2 name the vocabulary word. 4. If Student 2 names the word within 2 minutes, the team scores a point.	

Activity 2	Survivor	Vocabulary
Purpose	Reinforce content area vocabulary.	
Materials	• Different content vocabulary topics	
Procedure	1. Explain to students: **This activity will help you review vocabulary words that come from our study of _____.** 2. Have students stand in a circle. 3. Tell the class what topic their words should fit (e.g., tornadoes). 4. While the first student thinks of a word that goes with the category, the rest of the class quietly and slowly does a "clap, clap, snap" beat three times. 5. When the beat stops, the student must give a word that fits the topic. 6. If the student's word fits the category, record it on the board. The student should remain standing. 7. If the student cannot give a word that fits the topic, he/she sits down. 8. Continue to the next student. 9. Students may not give a word that does not fit the topic or that another student used. 10. The "survivor" is the last student standing. 11. A student may be the recorder and write the topic words on the board that other students give during the game.	

Activity 3	Shout Out	Vocabulary
Purpose	Reinforce vocabulary.	
Materials	• A topic from any current content area • Paper and pencils • Timer	
Procedure	1. Explain to students: **This activity will help you review terms we've studied in relation to _____.** 2. Divide students into two teams and assign captains. 3. Assign each team a topic based on current studies (e.g., Team A has photosynthesis and Team B has parasites). 4. Do not let the teams know each other's topic. 5. Give each team 5 minutes to discuss their topic and write a list of ten terms relating to it. 6. Set the timer for 1 minute, and tell Team A what Team B's topic is. 7. Team A has 1 minute to shout out terms that might be on Team B's list. 8. The captain of Team B checks off the terms as Team A gets them correct. 9. Team A scores 1 point for each word they get correct. 10. Reverse play and have Team B shout out terms on Team A's list. 11. Play more rounds with different topics. 12. Monitor students' choice of terms for clear connections to the topic. **Variation** 1. Instead of students shouting out the other team's terms, tell each team the other team's topic. 2. Give each team 3 minutes to write down the ten terms they think are most likely on the other team's list. 3. Write Team A's original topic on the board and have a student from each team write his/her team's terms below the topic. Cross out duplicates. 4. Team A's points are equal to the number of terms that are not crossed out. 5. Reverse play with Team B's topic. 6. The team with the most number of unique words wins.	

Activity 4	Hold the Bus!	Vocabulary
Purpose	Reinforce vocabulary.	

Materials	• 5 categories that relate to current content areas • Paper and pencils

Procedure	1. Explain to students: **This game will help you review and categorize terms you've learned in _____.** 2. Divide the group into teams of four to five students and assign captains. 3. On the board, write five categories that relate to your current topic of study (e.g., after a study of the Civil War, the topics could be food, soldiers, places, people, and transportation). 4. Have the captain of each team write the topics across the top of a sheet of paper. 5. Select a letter of the alphabet and write it on the board. 6. Teams work together to think of a word for each category that begins with the letter you selected. 7. The first team that has a word that fits each category shouts, "Hold the Bus!" 8. The other teams stop working and the captain of the team that finished first writes his/her team's words below the categories on the board. 9. The class then checks and discusses each word that the team wrote under each category. 10. If all of the words fit the categories, the team receives 1 point and play resumes with another letter or set of categories. 11. Students can produce an ABC book for the current topic, where they define and illustrate a page for every letter of the alphabet. **Variation** 1. For a longer-term assignment, students can work on one category (e.g., the category is Civil War soldiers). 2. Provide each team with a grid that has all of the letters of the alphabet (x, y, and z can go in one box). 3. The team's mission is to find a term that fits the category using every letter of the alphabet. 4. Use of textbooks is optional.

Activity 5	Make a Match	Vocabulary
Purpose	Reinforce vocabulary.	
Materials	• A set of 6 to 15 pairs of word cards, depending on the age of students (to save time, print the words/definitions on business cards) ▪ Vocabulary list (pairs of word and definition) ▪ Synonym word list (pairs of synonyms) ▪ Homophone word list (pairs of homophones) ▪ Antonym word list (pairs of antonyms) ▪ Greek root word list (pairs of root and definition) ▪ Prefix word list (pairs of prefix and definition) ▪ Suffix word list (pairs of suffix and definition)	
Procedure	1. Explain to students: **This activity will help you review _____.** 2. Provide a deck of word cards to each student or pair of students. 3. Place all cards face down in the middle of the table in a pattern of rows and columns. 4. Have a student turn over two cards. 5. If the cards match, the student reads the words and keeps the cards. 6. If the two cards do not match, the student turns both cards over. 7. Play continues until the student has collected all of the pairs. 8. You may want to include a self-check sheet for each card set. **Variation** 1. Students may play as a pair. 2. The game follows the procedure above, except students take turns turning cards. 3. If a student makes a match, he/she keeps those cards and takes another turn. 4. If a student turns two cards that do not match, his/her turn is over. 5. Play continues until all of the cards are matched.	

Activity 6	Make a Match Card Game	Vocabulary

Purpose	Reinforce vocabulary.

Materials	• A deck of 6 to 15 pairs of word cards depending on the age of students (to save time, print the words/definitions on business cards)
	  ▪ Vocabulary list (pairs of word and definition)
	  ▪ Synonym word list (pairs of synonyms)
	  ▪ Homophone word list (pairs of homophones)
	  ▪ Antonym word list (pairs of antonyms)
	  ▪ Greek root word list (pairs of root and definition)
	  ▪ Prefix word list (pairs of prefix and definition)
	  ▪ Suffix word list (pairs of suffix and definition)

Procedure	1. Explain to students: **This game will help you review _____.** 2. Provide a deck of cards to each pair of students. 3. Deal five to seven cards to each player depending on the age of the players. Place remaining cards face down in a stack between the two players. 4. Students should first check to see if they have any matching pairs of cards. 5. Students should place each matching pair on the table face up in front of them. 6. The first player asks the second player for a specific card. 7. If the second player has that card, he/she gives it to the first player. The first player reads the two cards and places that pair on the table and takes another turn. 8. If the second player does not have that card, he/she says, "Take a card, please." The first player then takes a card from the stack in the middle of the table. 9. The second player then takes a turn. 10. Play continues until all cards are matched. 11. The winner has the most pairs collected.

Activity 7	Semantic Feature Analysis		Vocabulary

Purpose	Reinforce content area vocabulary and concepts.
Materials	• Semantic Features Chart (varies in size depending on age of students and complexity of material being studied; write the category down the left column; features are written across each column—see Example below)
Procedure	1. Explain to students: **This activity will help you review vocabulary and concepts that we learned in _____.** 2. Guide students through the Semantic Features Chart. 3. As you move across the chart, ask students if the word at the beginning of the row has the features listed in each column. For example, the chart below is a study of frogs and toads, so students should decide whether a frog has dry skin. Because frogs don't have dry skin, put a minus sign in the cell. Next, students recall if toads have dry skin. Because dry skin is a characteristic of toads, put a plus sign in the cell. 4. Continue across the chart. 5. Since this is a review activity, students should have already been exposed to the information in the chart.

Example		Has Dry Skin	Lays Eggs	Has Bulging Eyes	Has Long Webbed Hind Feet	Lives in All Continents Except Antarctica	Has Poison Glands	Likes a Wet Climate
	Frog	–	+	+	+	+	–	+
	Toad	+	+	–	–	–	+	–

Activity 8	Triplets	Vocabulary

Purpose	Reinforce vocabulary.
Materials	• Triplet sticks made from two colors of tongue depressors or tag board (e.g., green and yellow) (write single words on the yellow tongue depressors and definitions [two per word] on two green tongue depressors—this makes a triplet containing a word and two definitions for it) • Word list of homographs • A can to hold the tongue depressors (tongue depressors should be easy to remove from the can)
Procedure	1. Explain to students: **This activity will help you practice recognizing homographs.** 2. Hold up the can that holds the Triplet sticks. Show students that the green tongue depressors have a definition written on them and that the yellow tongue depressors have a single word written on them. 3. The object is to match two yellow definitions to the correct green homograph. 4. Each player draws five tongue depressors. Players can draw any colors they choose. 5. Players should arrange any triplets that they drew. A triplet is one green homograph paired with two yellow definitions for the homograph. 6. If they have no triplets, they should place their tongue depressors on the table. 7. Students take turns drawing one tongue depressor out of the can at a time. If a player completes a triplet, he/she takes another turn. 8. Play ends when there are no more tongue depressors in the can. 9. The winner has the most completed triplets.
Examples	a lid cap a hat rubber on a car's wheel fire

Activity 9	Synonym Sticks	Vocabulary
Purpose	Reinforce vocabulary.	

Materials	• Tongue depressors or tag board (write a synonym on each tongue depressor; there should be pairs of synonyms) • Word list of synonyms • A can to hold the tongue depressors (tongue depressors should be easy to remove from the can)

Procedure	1. Explain to students: **This activity will help you practice recognizing synonyms.** 2. Hold up the can that holds the synonym sticks. Show students that the tongue depressors have a synonym written on them. 3. The object of the activity is to match pairs of synonyms. 4. Each player draws five tongue depressors and arranges the sticks face up on the table. 5. Players should put together synonym pairs that they drew. 6. Students take turns drawing one tongue depressor out of the can at a time. If a player completes a pair, he/she takes one more turn. 7. Play ends when there are no more tongue depressors in the can. 8. The winner has the most completed synonym pairs. **Variation** 1. Play again with antonym sticks. 2. Play again with homophone sticks. 3. Play again with Greek roots and their definitions.

Examples	child hat kid cap

Activity 10	Categories	Vocabulary

Purpose	Reinforce vocabulary.
Materials	• Vocabulary list for any current content area • Index cards • Large pocket chart
Procedure	1. Explain to students: **This activity will help you review terms we learned in _____.** 2. Put four or five content-related terms in the large pocket chart (e.g., weather events such as *tornado, hurricane, thunderstorm, blizzard,* and *dust storm*). 3. Have students read aloud the categories displayed in the pocket chart. 4. Have blank index cards available to record words that relate to each term in the chart. 5. Ask students to think of words that relate to each term in the chart. 6. As students suggest words, ask them to elaborate on their word choice. 7. Keep the card set, and allow students to recreate the chart on their own with the cards created earlier. **Variation** 1. Before doing this as a group, give students a chart that has only the heading terms to fill out on their own or with a partner. 2. Create the chart as a whole group.

Example					
	tornado	**hurricane**	**thunderstorm**	**blizzard**	**dust storm**
	Fujita scale	Saffir-Simpson Scale	hail	snow	dry
	destruction	tide surge	turbulence	wind chill	dust devils
	hook echo	erosion	spawn	wind	lightning
	wind		lightning		

Activity 11	Tired Old Words		Vocabulary

Purpose	Reinforce vocabulary.
Materials	• List of words that are overused in student writing • Index cards • Large pocket chart
Procedure	1. Explain to students: **This activity will help you find some alternative words to use in your writing.** 2. Place four or five words that students use too frequently in their writing at the top of the pocket chart (e.g., *happy*, *sad*, *said*, *pretty*, and *like*.) 3. Remind students that good writers try to use a variety of words to describe their ideas. 4. Say: **The words in the chart are some examples of tired old words—words that are overused.** 5. Tell students that the purpose of this activity is to think of many alternatives to the tired old words that are in the pocket chart. 6. Have students read aloud the tired old words. 7. Give students 3 minutes to discuss alternative words with a partner. 8. Ask students to suggest alternative words for the tired ones. 9. Record student suggestions on the index cards and place them in the chart. 10. Post the chart for students' future reference. 11. You may have students go back to a writing piece and edit for tired words. They should insert fresh, more varied words in their writing. **Variation** 1. Instead of having students discuss words with a partner, give each pair of students a thesaurus. 2. Have students use the thesaurus to look up alternative words. 3. Caution students that a pair may not suggest a word they haven't heard before or can't pronounce.
Example	<table><tr><th>happy</th><th>sad</th><th>said</th><th>pretty</th><th>like</th></tr><tr><td>glad</td><td>morose</td><td>replied</td><td>beautiful</td><td>adore</td></tr><tr><td>ecstatic</td><td>bereft</td><td>shouted</td><td>stunning</td><td>love</td></tr><tr><td>euphoric</td><td>gloomy</td><td>murmured</td><td>good looking</td><td>crave</td></tr><tr><td></td><td>depressed</td><td></td><td></td><td></td></tr><tr><td></td><td></td><td></td><td></td><td></td></tr></table>

Activity 12	Shades of Meaning	Vocabulary

Purpose	Reinforce shades of meaning.
Materials	• 5 large paint chip samples or colored squares that range from light to dark of the same color • List of overused words and synonyms that reflect different degrees of the overused word • Large pocket chart
Procedure	1. Explain to students: **This activity will help you think about the strength, or shades or meaning, that a group of words has.** 2. Place the five colored squares from lightest to darkest across the top of the pocket chart. 3. Remind students that many words in English describe the same action or idea. However, the degree, or shade, of meaning might be different. 4. Write the first five words on the board in random order and have students read them aloud. 5. Write the overused word on the lightest square. 6. Have students discuss which word is a little stronger than, for example, *said*. Write that word on the second colored square, and so on. 7. Post the Shades of Meaning squares for future reference. 8. Students may edit writing to identify places where they could use a stronger word. **Variation** 1. Provide student pairs with a thesaurus and a set of colored cards. 2. Give students a tired word to work through the shades of meaning. 3. Caution students that a pair may not use a word they haven't heard before or can't pronounce.
Examples	said replied snapped snarled shouted like fond of favor love adore

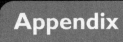

Resources for RTI

PROFESSIONAL DEVELOPMENT

Cambium Learning® Solutions	Online professional development; see http://www.bettereducator.com
Implementing Response to Intervention: A Principal's Guide	Hall, S., Corwin, 2008
Jumpstart RTI: Using RTI in Your Elementary School Right Now	Hall, S., Corwin, 2011
Language Essentials for Teachers of Reading and Spelling (LETRS®)	Flexible professional development in person, in print, or online; see http://www.letrs.com
Logistics of Literacy Intervention	Allain, J., Cambium Learning® Sopris, 2008
Raising Reading Achievement in an RtI World: A Principal's Primer	Montgomery, P., Ilk, M., Moats, L., Cambium Learning® Sopris, 2012
Response to Intervention: Policy Considerations and Implementation	Batsche, G. J., Elliott, J. L., Graden, J., et al., National Association of State Directors of Special Education, 2006
RTI Toolkit: A Practical Guide for Schools	Wright, J., Dude Publishing, 2007
Teaching Reading Essentials: Video Demonstrations of Small-Group Interventions	Moats, L., Farrell, L., Cambium Learning® Sopris, 2005
The Reading Coach: A How-to Manual for Success	Hasbrouck, J., & Denton, C., Cambium Learning® Sopris, 2005
The Reading Coach 2	Hasbrouck, J., & Denton, C., Cambium Learning® Sopris, 2010

INSTRUCTIONAL MATERIALS

50 Nifty Activities for 5 Components and 3 Tiers of Reading Instruction	Dodson, J., Cambium Learning® Sopris, 2008
50 Nifty Speaking and Listening Activities Promoting Oral Language and Comprehension	Dodson, J., Cambium Learning® Sopris, 2011
eSolution: Fluency, Vocabulary, and Comprehension	Adams, G., Van Zant, S., Cambium Learning® Sopris, 2013
ExploreLearning	Interactive online simulations math and science; see http://www.explorelearning.com

Continued next page

INSTRUCTIONAL MATERIALS (Continued)

The New Herman Method	Sekel, P., & Herman, R., Cambium Learning® Sopris, 2010
Voyager Passport™	Print and online strategic intervention; see http://www.voyagerlearning.com
Power Readers	Ebbers, S. M., Cambium Learning® Sopris, 2007
RAVE-O®	Wolf, M., Cambium Learning® Sopris, 2011
Reading A–Z	Online reading resources; see http://www.readinga–z.com
Read Well®	Language arts curriculum; see http://www.voyagerlearning.com
REWARDS: Multisyllabic Word Reading Strategies	Archer, A. L., Gleason, M. M., Vachon, V., Cambium Learning® Sopris, 2005 – 2006 • REWARDS: Multisyllabic Word Reading Strategies (Intermediate and Secondary levels) • REWARDS Plus: Reading Strategies Applied to Science Passages • REWARDS Plus: Reading Strategies Applied to Social Studies Passages
Supercharged Readers	Ebbers, S. M., Cambium Learning® Sopris, 2010

ASSESSMENT TOOLS

DIBELS Next® Survey	Powell-Smith, K. A., Good, R. H., Kaminski, R., Wallin, J., Cambium Learning® Sopris, 2012
Literacy Intervention Toolkit	Dodson, J., Cambium Learning® Sopris, 2011
LETRS® Second Edition—Module 8 Assessment for Prevention and Early Intervention	Moats, L. C., Hancock C., Cambium Learning® Sopris, 2012

WEB SITES AND BLOGS

DIBELS® from Cambium Learning® Sopris	http://www.soprislearning.com/dibels
EdView360	http://soprislearning.wordpress.com
National Center on RTI	http://www.rti4success.org
Reality 101: CEC's Blog for New Teachers	http://cecblog.typepad.com
RTI Action Network	The National Center for Learning Disabilities, Inc.; see http://www.rtinetwork.org See the seven-part series "Create Your Implementation Blueprint" by Susan Hall at http://www.rtinetwork.org/getstarted/develop/create-your-implementation-blueprint
RTI Source	95 Percent Group Inc.; see http://www.rtisource.com
RTI Source Blog	Susan L. Hall.; see http://www.95percentgroup.com/rtiblog

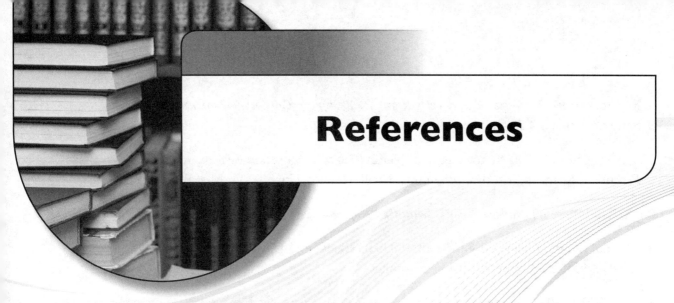

References

95 Percent Group Inc. 2007. *Blueprint for Intervention: Phonics*. Lincolnshire, IL: Author.

——— 2009. *Blueprint for Intervention: Phonological Awareness*. Lincolnshire, IL: Author.

——— 2010. *Blueprint for Intervention: Phonological Awareness Routine Cards*. Lincolnshire, IL: Author.

——— 2011. *Phonics Lesson Library*. Lincolnshire, IL: Author.

——— 2011. *Phonics Screener for Intervention*. Lincolnshire, IL: Author.

——— 2011. *Phonological Awareness Screener for Intervention*. Lincolnshire, IL: Author.

Allen, Kay, and Marilyn Beckwith. 1999. "Alphabet Knowledge: Letter Recognition, Naming, and Sequencing." In *Multisensory Teaching of Basic Language Skills*, edited by Judith R. Birsh, 85–117. Baltimore: Paul H. Brookes.

American Federation of Teachers, editors. 2004. *Preventing Early Reading Failure*. Washington, DC: Author.

Armbruster, Bonnie, Fran Lehr, and Jean Osborn. 2001. *Put Reading First: The Research Building Blocks for Teaching Children to Read*. Washington, DC: Partnership for Reading.

Baumann, J. F., Edward J. Kame'enui, and G. Ash. 2003. "Research on Vocabulary Instruction: Voltaire Redux." In *Handbook of Research on Teaching the English Language Arts*, 2nd ed., edited by James Flood, Diane Lapp, James R. Squire, and Julie M. Jensen, 752–758. Mahwah, NJ: Lawrence Erlbaum.

Beck, Isabel L., Margaret G. McKeown, R. Hamilton, and Linda Kucan. 1997. *Questioning the Author: An Approach for Enhancing Student Engagement with Text*. Newark, DE: International Reading Association.

Beck, Isabel L., Margaret G. McKeown, and Linda Kucan. 2002. *Bringing Words to Life: Robust Vocabulary Instruction*. New York: Guilford Press.

Bell, Nanci. 1991. *Visualizing and Verbalizing for Language Comprehension and Thinking*. San Luis Obispo, CA: Gander Educational Publishing.

Biemiller, Andrew. 1999. "Language and Reading Success." In *From Reading Research to Practice: A Series for Teachers*, edited by J. Chall. Newton Upper Falls, MA: Brookline Books.

Birsh, Judith R. 1999. *Multisensory Teaching of Basic Language Skills*. Baltimore: Paul H. Brookes.

Blachman, Benita, Eileen Whynne Ball, Rochella Black, and Darlene M. Tangel. 2000. *Road to the Code*. Baltimore: Paul H. Brookes.

Blevins, Wiley. 1997. *Phonemic Awareness Activities for Early Reading Success*. New York: Scholastic.

Blevins, Wiley. 1998. *Phonics from A to Z*. New York: Scholastic.

Carlisle, Joanne, and Melinda Rice. 2002. *Improving Reading Comprehension: Research-Based Principles and Practices*. Baltimore: York Press.

Catts, Hugh, and Tina Olsen. 1993. *Sounds Abound: Listening Rhyming and Reading*. East Moline, IL: Linguisystems.

Daane, Mary C., Jay R. Campbell, Wendy S. Grigg, Madeline J. Goodman, and Andreas Oranje. 2005. *Fourth-Grade Students Reading Aloud: NAEP 2002 Special Study of Oral Reading*. Washington, DC: National Center for Education Statistics

Davidson, Marcia, and J. Towner. 2001. "The Reliability, Validity, and Applications of Oral Reading Fluency Measures." Paper presented at the Society for the Scientific Study of Reading, Boulder, CO.

Deno, Stanley L. 1985. "Curriculum-Based Measurement: The Emerging Alternative." *Exceptional Children*, 52(3): 219–232.

Deno, Stanley L., and Lynn S. Fuchs. 1987. "Developing Curriculum-Based Measurement Systems for Data-Based Education Problem Solving." *Focus on Exceptional Children*, 19(8): 1–16.

Deno, Stanley L., and Phyllis K. Mirkin. 1977. *Data-Based Program Modification: A Manual*. Reston, VA: Council for Exceptional Children.

Denton, Carolyn, and Patricia Mathes. 2003. "Intervention for Struggling Readers: Possibilities and Challenges." In *Preventing and Remediating Reading Difficulties: Bringing Science to Scale*, edited by Barbara K. Foorman. Baltimore: York Press.

Dynamic Measurement Group. 2010a. "A New Measure of Reading Comprehension: *DIBELS* Daze." From the *DIBELS Next Newsletter*, Volume 3, No. 1. July 2010. Page 1. Eugene, OR: Author.

——— 2008. *DIBELS 6th Edition Adequacy Information, Technical Report 6*. Eugene, OR: Author. Available at http://dibels.org/pubs.html.

——— 2009. "*DIBELS* ORF Readability Study." From the *DIBELS Next Newsletter*, Volume 2, No. 2. July 2009. Pages 2-3. Eugene, OR: Author.

——— 2010c. "New *DIBELS Next* Measure: First Sound Fluency." From the *DIBELS Next Newsletter*, Volume 3, No. 1. July 2010. Page 2. Eugene, OR: Author.

——— 2010d. "New for *DIBELS Next*: NWF Whole Words Read." From the *DIBELS Next Newsletter*, Volume 3, No. 2. October 2010. Page 2. Eugene, OR: Author.

——— 2011a. *DIBELS Next Assessment Manual*. Longmont, CO: Cambium Learning® Sopris.

——— 2010b. "*DIBELS Next* Benchmark Goals." Eugene, OR: Author.

——— 2010e. "*DIBELS Next* Composite Score." From the *DIBELS Next Newsletter*, Volume 3, No. 2. October 2010. Page 1. Eugene, OR: Author.

——— 2011c. *DIBELS Next Technical Manual*. Eugene, OR: Author.

——— 2011b. *Frequently Asked Questions about* DIBELS Next. http://www.dibels.org/faqsNext/html. Retrieved June 14, 2011. Eugene, OR: Author.

——— 2011d. "Initial Instructional Grouping Suggestions." Eugene, OR: Author.

——— 2011e. "Why is Retell a Required Part of DORF in *DIBELS Next?*" May 3, 2011. Eugene, OR: Author.

Ehri, Linnea, and L. S. Wilce. 1979. "The Mnemonic Value of Orthography among Beginning Readers." *Journal of Educational Psychology* 71: 26–40.

Felton, Rebecca. 1993. "Effects of Instruction on the Decoding Skills of Children With Phonological-Processing Problems." *Journal of Learning Disabilities* 26: 583–589.

Francis, David J., Sally Shaywitz, K. K. Stuebing, Bennett Shaywitz, and Jack Fletcher. 1996. "Developmental Lag Versus Deficit Models of Reading Disability: A Longitudinal Individual Growth Curves Analysis." *Journal of Educational Psychology* 88: 3–17.

Gillon, Gail. 2003. *Phonological Awareness: From Research to Practice*. New York: Guilford Publications.

Good, Roland H., J. Gruba, and Ruth A. Kaminski. 2001. "Best Practices in Using *Dynamic Indicators of Basic Early Literacy Skills (DIBELS)* in an Outcomes-Driven Model." *Best Practices in School Psychology* IV: 679–700.

Good, Roland H., Edward J. Kame'enui, Deborah C. Simmons, and David Chard. 2002. "Focus and Nature of Primary, Secondary, and Tertiary Prevention: The Circuits Model." *Technical Report 1*. College of Education, Institute for the Development of Educational Achievement. Eugene, OR: University of Oregon.

Good, Roland H., Ruth A. Kaminski, M. Shinn, J. Bratten, and L. Laimon. 2003. "Technical Adequacy and Decision Making Utility of *DIBELS*." *Technical Report 7*. Eugene, OR: University of Oregon.

Good, Roland H., Ruth A. Kaminski, S. Smith, Deborah C. Simmons, Edward J. Kame'enui, and J. Wallin. 2003. "Reviewing Outcomes: Using *DIBELS* to Evaluate Kindergarten Curricula and Interventions." In *Reading in the Classroom: Systems for the Observation of Teaching and Learning*, edited by Sharon Vaughn and Kerri L. Briggs, 221–259. Baltimore: Paul H. Brookes.

Good, Roland H., Joshua U. Wallin, Deborah C. Simmons, Edward J. Kame'enui, and Ruth A. Kaminski. 2002. "System-wide Percentile Ranks for *DIBELS* Benchmark Assessment." *Technical Report 9*. Eugene, OR: University of Oregon. Available at dibels.uoregon.edu/techreports/DIBELS_Percentiles.pdf (accessed September 26, 2011).

Hall, Susan L. 2004. "Embedding Practices through Professional Development: Establishing an Early Intervention Program to Prevent Reading Difficulties." Ed.D. dissertation. National-Louis University, Evanston, IL.

Hall, Susan L. 2008. *Implementing Response to Intervention: A Principal's Guide*. Thousand Oaks, CA: Corwin.

Hart, B., and T. Risley. 1995. *Meaningful Differences in the Everyday Experience of Young American Children*. Baltimore: Paul H. Brookes.

Hintze, John M., Amanda L. Ryan, and Gary Stoner. 2003. "Concurrent Validity and Diagnostic Accuracy of the Dynamic Indicators of Basic Early Literacy Skills and the Comprehensive Test of Phonological Processing." *School Psychology Review* 32(4): 541–557.

Jordano, Kimberley, and Trisha Callella. 1998. *Phonemic Awareness Songs and Rhymes*. Cypress, CA: Creative Teaching Press.

Juel, Connie. 1988. "Learning to Read and Write: A Longitudinal Study of 54 Children from First through Fourth Grades." *Journal of Educational Psychology* 80: 437–447.

Klingner, Janette K., Sharon Vaughn, Joseph A. Dimino, J. Schumm, and D. Bryant. 2001. *Collaborative Strategic Reading: Strategies for Improving Comprehension*. Longmont, CO: Sopris West.

Lenchner, Orna, and Blanche Podhajski. 1998. *The Sounds Abound Program*. East Moline, IL: LinguiSystems.

Lyon, G. Reid, and Jack Fletcher. 2001. "Early Warning System." *Education Matters* 2001 (Summer): 23–29.

Moats, Louisa C., and Susan L. Hall. 2009. *Language Essentials for Teachers of Reading and Spelling (LETRS®), Module 7*. 2nd Edition. Longmont, CO: Sopris West.

National Assessment of Educational Progress. 1992. *National Association of Educational Progress Report*. Washington, DC: National Center for Education Statistics.

National Reading Panel. 2000. *National Reading Panel Report*. Washington, DC: National Center for Literacy.

Neuhaus Education Center. 2000. *Language Enrichment*. Houston: Author.

——— 2000. *Practices for Developing Accuracy and Fluency*. Houston: Author.

——— 2000. *The Colors and Shapes of Language*. Houston: Author.

——— 2002. *Reading Readiness Manual*. Houston: Author.

Powell-Smith, K. A., R. H. Good, and T. Atkins. 2010. *DIBELS Next Oral Reading Fluency Readability Study, Technical Report 7*. Eugene, OR: Dynamic Measurement Group.

RAND Reading Study Group. 2002. "Reading for Understanding: Toward a Research and Development Program in Reading Comprehension." Available at www.rand.org/pubs/monograph_reports/2005/MR1465.pdf (accessed September 26, 2011).

Reading First Academy Assessment Committee. 2002. *The Reading Leadership Academy Guidebook*. Washington, DC: U.S. Department of Education.

Reading First Leadership Academy. 2002. *The Reading Leadership Academy Guidebook*. Washington, DC: U.S. Department of Education.

Scott, Judith, and William E. Nagy. 2004. "Developing Word Consciousness." In *Vocabulary Instruction: Research to Practice*, edited by J. Baumann and Edward Kame'enui, 201–217. New York: Guilford Press.

Shaw, D., and R. Shaw. 2002. "*DIBELS* Oral Reading Fluency-Based Indicators of Third Grade Reading Skills for Colorado State Assessment Program (CSAP)." *Technical Report*. Eugene, OR: University of Oregon.

Shaywitz, Sally E. 1996. "Dyslexia." *Scientific American* Vol. 275, No. 5 (November): 98–104.

Shinn, Mark R. 1989. *Curriculum-Based Measurement: Assessing Special Children.* New York: Guilford.

Simmons, Deborah C., and Ed Kame'enui. 2003. *Scott Foresman Early Reading Intervention.* Lebanon, IN: Scott Foresman.

Texas Education Agency. 2003–2004. *Intervention Activities Guide.* Austin: Author.

Torgesen, Joseph K. 2004. "Avoiding the Devastating Downward Spiral: The Evidence That Early Intervention Prevents Reading Failure." *American Educator* Vol. 28, No. 3 (Fall): 6–19.

Torgesen, Joseph, and Brian Bryant. 2004. *Phonological Awareness Training for Reading.* Austin: ProEd.

Torgesen, Joseph K., Patricia M. Mathes, and M. L. Grek. 2002. "Effectiveness of an Early Intervention Curriculum That is Closely Coordinated with the Regular Classroom Reading Curriculum." Paper presented at the Pacific Coast Research Conference, San Diego, CA, February.

Torgesen, Joseph K., Richard K. Wagner, Carol A. Rashotte, and J. Herron. (Manuscript in preparation). "A Comparison of Two Computer Assisted Approaches to the Prevention of Reading Disabilities in Young Children." Unpublished paper. Tallahassee, FL: Florida State University.

Torgesen, Joseph K., Richard K. Wagner, Carol A. Rashotte, E. Rose., Pat Lindamood, T. Conway, and C. Garvin. 1999. "Preventing Reading Failure in Young Children with Phonological Processing Disabilities: Group and Individual Responses to Instruction." *Journal of Educational Psychology* 91: 579–594.

United States Department of Education. 2002. *The Reading Leadership Academy Guidebook.* Washington, DC: Author.

University of Texas and Texas Education Agency. 2002. *First Grade Teacher Reading Academy, Vocabulary.* Austin: Author.

University of Texas Center for Reading and Language Arts. 2003. *Three-Tier Reading Model: Reducing Reading Difficulties for Kindergarten through Third Grade Students.* Austin: Author.

University of Virginia, Curry School of Education. PALS Web site.

Vaughn, Sharon, and Sylvia Linan-Thompson. 2003. "Group Size and Time Allotted to Intervention: Effects for Students with Reading Difficulties." In *Preventing and Remediating Reading Difficulties: Bringing Science to Scale*, edited by Barbara K. Foorman. Baltimore: York Press.

Vellutino, Frank R., D. M. Scanlon, and G. Reid Lyon. 2000. "Differentiating between Difficult-to-Remediate and Readily Remediated Poor Readers: More Evidence Against the IQ-Achievement Discrepancy Definition for Reading Disability." *Journal of Learning Disabilities* 33: 223–238.

Vellutino, Frank R., D. M. Scanlon, E. R. Sipay, S.G. Small, A. Pratt, R. Chen, and N. B. Denckla. 1996. "Cognitive Profiles of Difficult-to-Remediate and Readily Remediated Poor Readers: Early Intervention as a Vehicle for Distinguishing between Cognitive and Experiential Deficits as Basic Causes of Specific Reading Disability." *Journal of Educational Psychology* 88: 601–638.

World's Best Teachers. 2001. *Colleague in the Classroom*. Boise: Wide Eye Productions.